THE
50 GREATEST PLAYERS
IN
DALLAS COWBOYS
HISTORY

ROBERT W. COHEN

LONE STAR BOOKS

GUILFORD, CONNECTICUT
HELENA, MONTANA

LONE STAR BOOKS

An imprint of Globe Pequot

Distributed by NATIONAL BOOK NETWORK

British Library Cataloguing in Publication Information Available

Library of Congress Cataloging-in-Publication Data available

ISBN 978-1-63076-313-8 (hardcover)
ISBN 978-1-63076-314-5 (e-book)

♾™ The paper used in this publication meets the minimum requirements of American National Standard for Information Sciences—Permanence of Paper for Printed Library Materials, ANSI/NISO Z39.48-1992.

Printed in the United States of America

CONTENTS

ACKNOWLEDGMENTS   v

INTRODUCTION   vii
   The Cowboy Legacy   vii
   Factors Used to Determine Rankings   xii

THE RANKINGS

1	Roger Staubach	1
2	Bob Lilly	12
3	Emmitt Smith	19
4	Randy White	30
5	Michael Irvin	37
6	Larry Allen	47
7	Mel Renfro	54
8	Troy Aikman	62
9	Tony Dorsett	71
10	Jason Witten	80
11	Drew Pearson	88
12	Rayfield Wright	96
13	DeMarcus Ware	102
14	Chuck Howley	109
15	Ralph Neely	116
16	Harvey Martin	121
17	Ed "Too Tall" Jones	128
18	Darren Woodson	133
19	Lee Roy Jordan	140
20	Bob Hayes	146

21	Everson Walls	156
22	John Niland	162
23	Tony Hill	167
24	Cliff Harris	173
25	Tony Romo	180
26	Cornell Green	191
27	Dez Bryant	197
28	Erik Williams	204
29	Deion Sanders	210
30	Don Perkins	219
31	Nate Newton	226
32	George Andrie	232
33	Mark Stepnoski	239
34	Jim Jeffcoat	245
35	Jethro Pugh	250
36	Charlie Waters	257
37	Jay Novacek	264
38	Eugene Lockhart	271
39	Calvin Hill	277
40	Don Meredith	284
41	Dexter Coakley	292
42	Larry Cole	297
43	DeMarco Murray	303
44	Charles Haley	310
45	Herschel Walker	318
46	Danny White	327
47	Billy Joe DuPree	335
48	Bill Bates	340
49	Frank Clarke	347
50	Tyron Smith	353

SUMMARY	358
HONORABLE MENTIONS (THE NEXT 50)	359
GLOSSARY	408
SELECTED BIBLIOGRAPHY	409

ACKNOWLEDGMENTS

I wish to thank the Dallas Cowboys, Steve Liskey of RetroCards.net, Troy Kinunen of MEARSonlineauctions.com, Kate of RMYauctions.com, Pristineauction.com, ICollector.com, Mainlineautographs.com, Its AlreadySigned4u.com, AutographsForSale.com, AmericanMemorabilia.com, George A. Kitrinos, Keith Allison, and Bruce Adler, each of whom generously contributed to the photographic content of this work.

INTRODUCTION

THE COWBOY LEGACY

The first expansion team to join the NFL since the league absorbed the Cleveland Browns, Baltimore Colts, and San Francisco 49ers from the disbanded All-America Football Conference 10 years earlier, the Dallas Cowboys came into being in 1960, when the National Football League awarded a franchise in Texas to a group of local investors headed by oilman Clint Murchison Jr., who earlier tried unsuccessfully to purchase the Washington Redskins from George Preston Marshall. After assigning the moniker "Dallas Cowboys" to his new team on March 19, 1960, Murchison and his older brother, John D., displayed a considerable amount of foresight by hiring Tex Schramm to serve as general manager, while also naming Gil Brandt player personnel director and Tom Landry head coach.

Spending their first 11 seasons playing their home games a few miles east of downtown Dallas at the Cotton Bowl, the Cowboys shared that stadium with the newly formed American Football League's Dallas Texans until Lamar Hunt moved his AFL franchise to Kansas City in 1963 and renamed it the "Chiefs." Yet, even though the presence of the Cowboys eventually forced the Texans to relocate to the Midwest, Dallas experienced very little success its first few years in the NFL. After compiling a record of 0-11-1 in their inaugural season of 1960 as a member of the 13-team league's Western Division, the Cowboys posted an overall mark of just 18-35-3 from 1961 to 1964 while taking up residence in the Eastern Division, which they shared with the New York Giants, Cleveland Browns, Washington Redskins, Philadelphia Eagles, Pittsburgh Steelers, and St. Louis Cardinals. However, the Cowboys' fortunes began to change in 1965, when they finished 7-7, thereby avoiding a losing record for the first time in their existence. They joined the NFL's elite the following year, when they posted a mark of 10-3-1, en route to earning a berth in the NFL champion-ship game, which they lost to Vince Lombardi's Green Bay Packers 34–27. Facing Green Bay for the championship once again in 1967, Dallas suffered another heartbreaking defeat, losing to the Packers in the final seconds by a score of 21–17 in a legendary contest that came to be known as the "Ice Bowl" for its frigid temperatures and unbearable playing conditions.

Tex Schramm and Gil Brandt served as key figures in the Cowboys' rise to prominence, with both men making huge contributions to the success of the team with their astute player evaluation and clever use of the college football draft. Extremely innovative and intelligent, Schramm and Brandt helped turn the Cowboys into an NFL powerhouse by instituting the now widespread practice of employing computers when scouting players. Mean-while, Coach Landry's brilliant defensive mind and complicated offensive schemes often put the Cowboys one step ahead of the opposition, enabling them to compile a winning mark an NFL-record 20 straight times between 1966 and 1985, as they gradually shifted from the NFL's Eastern Division to the NFC's Capitol Division and, finally, to the NFC East after the two leagues merged and each conference adopted a new three-division setup. Advancing to the playoffs in 18 of those 20 seasons, the Cowboys won 13 division titles, five conference championships, and two Super Bowls along the way.

Yet, in spite of the extraordinary level of success the Cowboys experi-enced throughout the period, they developed a reputation during the late 1960s as being a team that lacked the ability to win the big game, earning in the process the nickname "Next Year's Champions." After losing the NFL championship game to the Packers in back-to-back years, the Cowboys came up short against the Cleveland Browns in the playoffs in both 1968 and 1969, before losing to the Baltimore Colts on a last-second field goal in Super Bowl V. The Cowboys suffered these devastating defeats in spite of the fact that they arguably possessed more talent than any other team in the NFL. Dallas's powerful and dominating defense, which became known as the "Doomsday Defense," featured perennial Pro Bowlers Bob Lilly and George Andrie up front, standouts Lee Roy Jordan and Chuck Howley at linebacker, and superb cover men Mel Renfro and Cornell Green in the secondary. The Cowboys also possessed one of the league's most dynamic offenses, with the quarterback / wide receiver tandem of Don Meredith and Bob Hayes striking fear into the hearts of opposing defenses. Meanwhile, Pro Bowl offensive linemen Rayfield Wright, Ralph Neely, and John Niland opened up huge holes for running backs Don Perkins and Calvin Hill.

The Cowboys finally achieved their ultimate goal of winning the world championship when they defeated the Miami Dolphins 24–3 in Super Bowl VI, accomplishing the feat the same season they began playing their home games in brand new Texas Stadium, which opened its doors to the public on October 24, 1971. Situated just outside Dallas, in suburban Irving, Texas, 65,024-seat Texas Stadium remained home to the Cowboys for the next 38 years, during which time it served as the backdrop for countless memorable games and extraordinary feats. Posting a winning record in each of the next 15 seasons, the Cowboys performed particularly well from 1971 to 1983, advancing to the playoffs in all but one of those years, capturing seven division titles, appearing in nine NFC championship games, and winning four conference championships and two Super Bowls. After defeating Miami in Super Bowl VI, the Cowboys next appeared in the big game four years later, losing to the Pittsburgh Steelers 21–17 in Super Bowl X. They then handily defeated Denver in Super Bowl XII, rolling over the Broncos 27–10, before once again losing to Pittsburgh in Super Bowl XIII, this time by a score of 35–31. After being eliminated in the first round of the postseason tournament by the Los Angeles Rams in 1979, the Cowboys made three straight appearances in the NFC title game, losing to Philadelphia 20–7 in 1980, before being outscored 28–27 by San Francisco in 1981 and 31–17 by Washington in 1982. Several outstanding players graced the Cowboys' roster during this period, with linemen Randy White, Harvey Martin, and Ed "Too Tall" Jones and safeties Cliff Harris and Charlie Waters excelling on defense. Meanwhile, wide receivers Drew Pearson and Tony Hill, running back Tony Dorsett, and quarterback Roger Staubach starred on offense.

The Cowboys ended up winning more games (105) during the 1970s than any other team in the NFL, contributing greatly to the growing popularity they enjoyed as the decade progressed. They also attracted many new fans with their exciting style of play and innovative practices of broadcasting games in Spanish, employing a modern cheerleading squad that performed sophisticated choreographed routines, and scheduling an annual Thanksgiving Day game that the entire nation had an opportunity to view. As a result, even though the Pittsburgh Steelers' four Super Bowl championships during the 1970s earned them the nickname "Team of the 70s," the Cowboys emerged as the decade's most glamorous franchise, prompting many to begin referring to them as "America's Team."

Unfortunately, all good things must come to an end, as the Cowboys discovered in 1986, when they experienced their first losing season in more than two decades, compiling a record of just 7-9. Four more losing seasons followed, with the Cowboys reaching their nadir in 1989, when they finished just 1-15. However, the situation in Dallas changed dramatically shortly after H. R. "Bum" Bright, who had purchased the Cowboys from Clint Murchison in 1984, sold the team to billionaire businessman Jerry Jones in February 1989. After unceremoniously firing longtime head coach Tom Landry, whom he replaced with former University of Miami coach Jimmy Johnson, Jones relieved general manager Tex Schramm of his duties and assumed complete control over football matters, taking on the roles of team president and general manager. Coach Landry, who had been with the Cowboys since their inception in 1960, left the organization with a career record of 250-162-6 in regular-season play, along with a playoff record of 20-16, with his total of 270 victories placing him third all-time among NFL coaches, behind only Don Shula and George Halas.

The abrupt firing of their team's legendary head coach left most Cowboys fans feeling resentful of Jones, who seemed to care little for sentimentality. Their anger continued to grow when Dallas posted just one victory in Jimmy Johnson's first year at the helm. However, after selecting Michael Irvin, Troy Aikman, and Emmitt Smith in successive drafts, the Cowboys began to turn things around, compiling a record of 7-9 in 1990, before posting an overall mark of 70-26 over the course of the next six seasons, en route to winning five more division titles, three NFC championships, and three Super Bowls. Following a successful 1991 campaign in which they went 11-5 before eventually losing to the Detroit Lions in the second round of the playoffs, the Cowboys easily defeated the Buffalo Bills in each of the next two Super Bowls, posting a lopsided 52–17 victory over their AFC counterparts in Super Bowl XXVII, before outscoring them 30–13 in Super Bowl XXVIII. After a clash of egos between Jerry Jones and Jimmy Johnson forced the latter out of Dallas following the conclusion of the 1993 campaign, the Cowboys won their third straight NFC East title in 1994 under new head coach Barry Switzer, who earlier had coached the University of Oklahoma to three National Championships. However, after thumping the Green Bay Packers 35–9 in their divisional playoff matchup, the Cowboys suffered a 38–28 defeat at the hands of the San Francisco 49ers in the NFC championship game. Once again establishing themselves as the class of the NFC in 1995, the Cowboys rolled over Philadelphia and Green Bay in the playoffs, before recording a 27–17 victory over the Pittsburgh Steelers in Super Bowl XXX, thereby becoming the first team of the Super Bowl era to win three world championships over a four-year period. Although Aikman, Smith, and Irvin served as the driving forces behind Dallas's successful championship run, they received ample support from the team's exceptional offensive line, which featured perennial Pro Bowlers Larry Allen, Erik Williams, Mark Stepnoski, and Nate Newton. The Cowboys also had a considerable amount of talent on defense, with end Charles Haley, cornerback Deion Sanders, and safety Darren Woodson starring on that side of the ball.

Switzer remained head coach in Dallas two more years, leading the Cowboys to their fifth consecutive division title in 1996, before injuries, age, and attrition ushered in another period of mediocrity. Although the Cowboys advanced to the playoffs in both 1998 and 1999, they exited the postseason tournament quickly both times, losing the wild card game to the Arizona Cardinals in the first of those campaigns, before experiencing a similar fate against the Minnesota Vikings the following year. Meanwhile, as control of the team passed from Switzer to Chan Gailey, and, then, to Dave Campo, Dallas posted a winning record just once between 1997 and 2002, compiling an overall mark during that time of just 39-57.

The Cowboys experienced a brief resurgence under new head coach Bill Parcells in 2003, advancing to the playoffs for the first time in four years by finishing the season with a record of 10-6. However, they once again lost the wild card game, this time suffering a 29–10 defeat at the hands of the Carolina Panthers. Parcells led the Cowboys into the playoffs as a wild card once more over the course of the next three seasons, before Jerry Jones's meddlesome ways prompted him to announce his retirement. Before he left Dallas, though, Parcells turned over the starting quarterback duties to Tony Romo, who, despite going undrafted by all 32 NFL teams, later emerged as one of the league's better quarterbacks. Linebacker / defensive end DeMarcus Ware also established himself as one of the NFL's top pass-rushers under Parcells.

Following Parcells's departure, Wade Phillips began a successful three-year stint as Dallas head coach, during which time the Cowboys christened Cowboys Stadium as their new home. Officially opened to the public on May 27, 2009, Cowboys Stadium, which has since been renamed AT&T Stadium, is the largest domed stadium in the world, featuring a retractable roof and a seating capacity of 80,000, with an ability to be expanded to 100,000 seats. Although the Cowboys responded well to their new surroundings, capturing their second NFC East title in three years in 2009 behind the passing of Romo and the receiving of Miles Austin and future Hall of Fame tight end Jason Witten, they continued to falter in the postseason, extending their string of consecutive playoff losses to seven. Phillips remained in Dallas until midway through the 2010 campaign, when Jerry Jones replaced him with offensive coordinator Jason Garrett after the

Cowboys got off to a 1-7 start. After finishing the year with five victories in their last eight games, the Cowboys went 8-8 in each of the next three seasons under Garrett, before compiling a record of 12-4 in 2014 that tied them with Green Bay and Seattle for the best mark in the conference. However, even though they posted their first playoff victory in 18 years by defeating Detroit in the opening round of the postseason tournament, the Cowboys once again fell short of their ultimate goal, losing to the Green Bay Packers 26–21 in the divisional round.

Unable to overcome an early season-ending injury to Tony Romo, the Cowboys stumbled to a record of just 4-12 in 2015. But, led by the brilliant rookie tandem of quarterback Dak Prescott and running back Ezekiel Elliott, Dallas compiled an NFC-best 13-3 record during the 2016 regular season, before losing to Green Bay in the divisional round of the playoffs 34–31 on a last-second field goal.

Although it has now been more than two decades since the Cowboys won their last NFC title, their future appears to be bright heading into the 2017 campaign. With Prescott, Elliott, and the league's best offensive line leading the way, the Cowboys seem poised to re-establish themselves as perennial championship contenders. Their next Super Bowl appearance will be their ninth, with their eight conference championships representing the highest total of any NFC team. The Cowboys have also won 23 division titles and five Super Bowls, tying them with the San Francisco 49ers and the New England Patriots for the second-most Super Bowl victories of any NFL team. (The Pittsburgh Steelers have won six.) The only NFL team to record 20 consecutive winning seasons, the Cowboys have finished .500 or better in 40 of their 57 seasons, advancing to the playoffs a total of 32 times. Featuring a plethora of exceptional performers through the years, the Cowboys have inducted 19 players into their Ring of Honor. Meanwhile, 12 members of the Pro Football Hall of Fame spent a significant amount of time playing for the Cowboys.

FACTORS USED TO DETERMINE RANKINGS

It should come as no surprise that selecting the 50 greatest players ever to perform for a team with the rich history of the Cowboys presented quite a challenge. Even after narrowing the field down to a mere 50 men, I still needed to devise a method of ranking the elite players that remained. Certainly, the names of Roger Staubach, Bob Lilly, Randy White, Emmitt Smith, Troy Aikman, and Michael Irvin would appear at, or near, the top of virtually everyone's list, although the order might vary somewhat from one person to the next. Several other outstanding performers have gained general recognition through the years as being among the greatest players ever to wear a Cowboys uniform. Mel Renfro, Chuck Howley, Tony Dorsett, and Jason Witten head the list of other Cowboy icons. But, how does one compare players who lined up on opposite sides of the ball with any degree of certainty? Furthermore, how does one differentiate between the pass-rushing and run-stopping skills of players such as Bob Lilly, Randy White, and DeMarcus Ware and the ball-hawking and punt return abilities of a Mel Renfro or Deion Sanders? And, on the offensive end, how can a direct correlation be made between the contributions made by Hall of Fame lineman Larry Allen and skill position players such as Roger Staubach and Drew Pearson? After initially deciding whom to include on my list, I then needed to determine what criteria I should use to formulate my final rankings.

The first thing I decided to examine was the level of dominance a player attained during his time with the Cowboys. How often did he lead the NFL in a major statistical category? Did he ever capture league MVP honors? How many times did he earn a trip to the Pro Bowl or a spot on the All-Pro Team?

I also chose to assess the level of statistical compilation a player achieved while wearing a Cowboys uniform. I reviewed where he ranks among the team's all-time leaders in those statistical categories most pertinent to his position. Of course, even the method of using statistics as a measuring stick has its inherent flaws. Although the level of success a team experiences rushing and passing the ball is impacted greatly by the performance of its offensive line, there really is no way to quantifiably measure the level of play reached by each individual offensive lineman. Conversely, the play of the offensive line affects tremendously the statistics compiled by a team's quarterback and running backs. Furthermore, the NFL did not keep an official record of defensive numbers such as tackles and quarterback sacks until the 1980s (although the Cowboys kept their own records prior to that). In addition, when examining the statistics compiled by offensive players, the era during which a quarterback, running back, or wide receiver competed must be factored into the equation.

To illustrate my last point, rules changes instituted by the league office have opened up the game considerably over the course of the last two decades. Quarterbacks are accorded far more protection than ever before, and officials have also been instructed to limit the amount of contact defensive backs are allowed to make with wide receivers. As a result, the game has experienced an offensive explosion, with quarterbacks and receivers posting numbers players from prior generations rarely even approached. That being the case, one must place the numbers Tony Romo has compiled during his career in their proper context when comparing him to other top Cowboy quarterbacks such as Roger Staubach and Don Meredith. Similarly, Dez Bryant's huge receiving totals must be viewed in moderation when comparing him to previous Cowboy wideouts Bob Hayes and Drew Pearson.

Other important factors I needed to consider were the overall contributions a player made to the success of the team, the degree to which he improved the fortunes of the club during his time in Dallas, the manner in which he impacted the team, both on and off the field, and the degree to which he added to the Cowboy legacy of winning. While the number of championships and division titles the Cowboys won during a particular player's years with the team certainly entered into the equation, I chose not to deny a top performer his rightful place on the list if his years in Dallas happened to coincide with a lack of overall success by the club. As a result, the names of players such as Herschel Walker and Eugene Lockhart will appear in these rankings.

One other thing I should mention is that I only considered a player's performance while playing for the Cowboys when formulating my rankings. That being the case, the names of truly exceptional players such as Deion Sanders and Charles Haley, both of whom had many of their best years while playing for other teams, may appear lower on this list than one might expect. Meanwhile, the names of other standout performers such as Drew Bledsoe and Terry Glenn are nowhere to be found.

Having established the guidelines to be used throughout this book, we are ready to take a look at the 50 greatest players in Cowboys history, starting with number 1 and working our way down to number 50.

ROGER STAUBACH

In spite of the greatness of Randy White, Michael Irvin, and Larry Allen, the top three contenders for the number one spot in these rankings ended up being Bob Lilly, Roger Staubach, and Emmitt Smith. A legitimate argument could certainly be waged on behalf of Smith, who rushed for more yards and touchdowns than anyone else in NFL history. Meanwhile, Lilly, who is generally considered to be one of the handful of greatest defensive linemen ever to play the game, earned more Pro Bowl selections and All-Pro nominations than any other Cowboys player. Yet, even though Staubach's list of accomplishments may fall just a bit short of both Smith's and Lilly's, as the first great quarterback in franchise history, he made the greatest overall impact on the Cowboys over the course of his 11 seasons in Dallas. Leading the Cowboys to six division titles, four NFC championships, and two Super Bowl victories, Staubach accomplished everything he did with style and grace, conducting himself with dignity and class during a period in which the Cowboys established themselves as "America's Team." Playing in an era long before the rules governing the game caused offensive numbers to soar, Staubach posted relatively modest numbers by today's standards, never throwing for more than 3,586 yards or completing more than 27 touchdown passes in any single season. Staubach found himself further hampered by Coach Tom Landry's rather unique handling of his quarterbacks, his team's heavy reliance on the running game his first several years in the league, and the fact that he spent four years serving in the Navy before entering the NFL. Nevertheless, the man who earned the nickname "Captain Comeback" with his ability to lead his team back from seemingly insurmountable odds retired from football as the second-highest-rated passer of all time, compiled a regular-season winning percentage of .750 as a starter over the course of his career, earned NFL Player of the Year honors once, made six Pro Bowls, and earned one All-Pro selection and five All-Conference nominations. And, after leaving the game, Staubach received the additional distinctions of being named to the Pro Football Hall

Roger Staubach led the Cowboys to six division titles, four NFC championships, and their first two Super Bowl wins.
Courtesy of RMYAuctions.com

of Fame All-1970s First Team and being inducted into both the Cowboys Ring of Honor and the Pro Football Hall of Fame. Factoring everything into the equation, Roger Staubach clearly deserves to be ranked as the greatest player in Dallas Cowboys history.

Born in Cincinnati, Ohio, on February 5, 1942, Roger Thomas Staubach grew up in the northeast suburb of Silverton and attended nearby Purcell High School. After spending one year at New Mexico Military Institute in Roswell following his graduation from Purcell High in 1960, Staubach entered the US Naval Academy, where he spent the next three years starring at quarterback for the Midshipmen, earning Heisman Trophy and Maxwell Award honors as a junior in 1963 by leading Navy to a 9-1 record during the regular season and an overall ranking of number 2 in the nation.

Yet, even though Staubach is generally considered to be one of the greatest college football players ever, earning a number 9 ranking from ESPN on that network's 2007 list of the Top 25 Players in College Football History, the Cowboys ended up acquiring his rights with a lowly 10th-round "futures" pick in the 1964 NFL Draft when teams throughout the league learned of his desire to fulfill his mandatory four-year military obligation once he graduated in 1965. Working out a unique arrangement with Tom Landry and Dallas president/GM Tex Schramm, Staubach agreed to practice with the team during his leaves from the Navy, with the additional stipulation that he would join the Cowboys once he resigned his commission in 1969.

Although Staubach had the option of requesting an assignment in the States, he chose to volunteer for a one-year tour of duty in Vietnam, where he served as a Supply Corps officer for the Navy at the Chu Lai air base, commanding a total of 41 enlisted men. After returning from Vietnam in September 1967, Staubach spent the rest of his naval career playing on various service teams as he began preparing for his days as an NFL quarterback.

Finally arriving in Dallas at 27 years of age in 1969, Staubach served primarily as Craig Morton's backup his first two seasons with the Cowboys, appearing in a total of 14 games and making just four starts. However, Staubach began to see more action in 1971, gradually assuming the starting role, after spending the first several weeks of the campaign sharing playing time with Morton. In fact, Coach Landry alternated his two quarterbacks on every play in one particular contest, before finally settling on Staubach as his starter in Week 8. From that point on, the Cowboys proved to be practically unbeatable, winning their final seven games of the regular season, before posting three more wins in the postseason, including a 24–3 victory over the Miami Dolphins in Super Bowl VI that gave them their first NFL championship. Staubach, who ended up being named the league's Most Valuable Player by the NFL Players Association and the winner of the Bert Bell Award as NFL Player of the Year, also received Super Bowl MVP honors after posting a quarterback rating of 115.9 by completing 12 of 19 passes, for 119 yards and two touchdowns.

Staubach suffered a major setback the following year when he separated his shoulder during the preseason, forcing him to miss most of the campaign. However, he returned to the Cowboys in time to lead them to a memorable comeback win over San Francisco in the divisional round of the postseason tournament by tossing two late touchdown passes after replacing an ineffective Craig Morton behind center. Staubach never again surrendered his starting quarterback duties for the remainder of his career.

Staubach subsequently emerged as arguably the NFL's best quarterback in 1973, when he ranked among the league leaders with 2,428 yards passing and a completion percentage of 62.6, while also topping the circuit with 23 touchdown passes and a quarterback rating of 94.6. He followed that up with a subpar performance in 1974, completing just 52.8 percent of his passes, posting a quarterback rating of only 68.4, and tossing 15 interceptions and just 11 TD passes for a Cowboys team that finished out of the playoffs for the first time in nearly a decade. Returning to top form in 1975, Staubach earned Pro Bowl honors for the second time by completing 56.9 percent of his passes, finishing third in the league with 2,666 yards passing, and leading all NFL quarterbacks with four game-winning drives.

Although Staubach went on to capture four NFL passing titles, he became better known during the early stages of his career for his scrambling ability, which earned him the nickname "Roger the Dodger." An elusive runner with good speed and superb instincts, the 6'3", 200-pound Staubach often frustrated opposing defenses with his ability to maneuver his way out of trouble, rushing for 2,264 yards and 20 touchdowns over 11 NFL seasons, en route to compiling a franchise-best 5.52 yards-per-carry rushing average. But, with Coach Landry constantly stressing to him the importance of avoiding hits so that he might remain healthy, Staubach strayed from the pocket less frequently as his career progressed, although he never lost his ability to extend plays by using his legs.

By 1976, Staubach had also begun to develop a reputation for his unwillingness to accept defeat, a quality that enabled him to lead the Cowboys to several unlikely comebacks over the course of his career. Staubach led the Cowboys to a total of 23 fourth-quarter come-from-behind victories during the regular season and playoffs, including 14 in the final two minutes or overtime, with the most famous of those coming in the 1975 playoffs, when his desperation "Hail Mary" pass to Drew Pearson in the closing moments of the game resulted in a touchdown that gave the Cowboys a 17–14 victory over Minnesota. Commenting on the tremendous determination Staubach displayed through the years, Tom Landry said in 1983, "You could never defeat Roger mentally or physically. He was like that in a game, in practice, or in the business world."

Staubach earned the nickname "Captain Comeback" with his ability to lead the Cowboys back from adversity.
Courtesy of MearsOnlineAuctions.com

Expressing his admiration for his former rival, Green Bay Packers Hall of Fame quarterback Bart Starr stated, "He is one of the finest to ever play the game. I think if I had some of that Staubach competitiveness, I'd have been much better."

In discussing the confidence he had in himself to lead his team back from adversity, Staubach revealed, "Every time I stepped on the field, I believed my team was going to walk off the winner, somehow, someway. . . . Life is so short, and there are only so many chances to be in pressure situations. There are only a certain number of opportunities to take your talent and ability and get things accomplished."

After earning Pro Bowl and First-Team All-NFC honors in 1976 by throwing for 2,715 yards and completing 56.4 percent of his passes, Staubach led the eventual Super Bowl champion Cowboys to a 12-2 record during the 1977 regular season by ranking among the league leaders with 2,620 yards passing, 18 touchdown passes, a pass-completion percentage of 58.2, and a quarterback rating of 87.0, earning in the process his third straight trip to the Pro Bowl and his second consecutive First-Team All-NFC selection. He also performed extremely well in that year's Super Bowl, leading the Cowboys to a decisive 27–10 victory over the Denver Broncos by completing 17 of 25 passes, for 183 yards and one touchdown.

Staubach spent two more years with the Cowboys, leading them back to the Super Bowl once and passing for more than 3,000 yards twice after the NFL implemented rules designed to help open up the passing game. Particularly outstanding in 1979, Staubach earned his fifth consecutive Pro Bowl nomination and fifth First-Team All-NFC selection by completing 57.9 percent of his passes, establishing career-high marks in passing yardage (3,586) and touchdown passes (27), and leading the league with a quarterback rating of 92.3. Yet, in spite of his excellent play, the 37-year-old Staubach, who suffered 20 concussions over the course of his playing career, elected to announce his retirement at season's end to protect his long-term health. He left the game having completed a total of 1,685 passes, for 22,700 yards and 153 touchdowns. Staubach also threw 109 interceptions, completed 57 percent of his passes, and compiled a quarterback rating of 83.4, which placed him second in NFL history, behind only Cleveland's Otto Graham (86.6), at the time of his retirement.

Admired and respected by his teammates, opponents, and coaches, Staubach received high praise from Tom Landry, who said of his longtime quarterback, "Roger Staubach might be the best combination of a passer, an athlete, and a leader ever to play in the NFL."

Following his playing days, Staubach entered into a career in business he actually began in 1977 while still a member of the Cowboys. Serving as chairman and CEO of The Staubach Company for the next 30 years, Staubach made a fortune in the commercial real estate business, before relinquishing his title as CEO on June 20, 2007. He currently serves as a minority owner of Hall of Fame Racing, a NASCAR Nextel Cup team, which he owns jointly with fellow Cowboys Hall of Fame quarterback Troy Aikman.

Inducted into the Pro Football Hall of Fame in 1985, Staubach later received the additional honor of being ranked 29th on the *Sporting News*'s 1999 list of the 100 Greatest Players in NFL History. Although that placed him 19 notches behind Bob Lilly, who received the highest ranking of any Cowboys player, a 2010 fan poll conducted by the *Dallas Morning News* named Staubach the number 1 Dallas Cowboy of all time.

CAREER HIGHLIGHTS

Best Season

Staubach never performed more efficiently than he did in 1971, when he completed 59.7 percent of his passes, threw just four interceptions, and posted a career-best quarterback rating of 104.8, en route to earning NFL Player of the Year honors and his lone All-Pro nomination. However, he started only 10 games, finally establishing himself as the Cowboys' starting quarterback midway through the campaign after spending the first several weeks sharing playing time with Craig Morton. As a result, Staubach completed just 126 passes, for only 1,882 yards and 15 touchdowns. Posting far more impressive overall numbers in 1973, Staubach completed 179 passes for 2,428 yards, compiled a career-high 62.6 completion percentage, and led the NFL with 23 touchdown passes and a quarterback rating of 94.6. Yet, in spite of his outstanding performance, Staubach failed to receive either Pro Bowl or All-Pro recognition at season's end. On the other hand, "Captain Comeback" earned Pro Bowl and First-Team All-NFC honors in 1979, when he completed 57.9 percent of his passes, led the league with a quarterback rating of 92.3, and established career-high marks in pass completions (267), passing yardage (3,586), and touchdown passes (27), finishing third in the league in the last category. Furthermore, Staubach led the Cowboys to four fourth-quarter comebacks over the course of the campaign, making his final NFL season the best of his career.

Memorable Moments / Greatest Performances

Making his first pro start in the 1969 regular-season opener, Staubach led the Cowboys to a 24–3 win over the St. Louis Cardinals by passing for

220 yards and one touchdown, with the highlight of the contest being his 75-yard TD pass to Lance Rentzel in the first quarter.

Staubach led the Cowboys to the second of their 10 consecutive victories to close out the 1971 campaign on November 14, when he passed for 176 yards and rushed for a career-high 90 yards during a 20–7 win over the Philadelphia Eagles.

Staubach recorded the first 300-yard passing game of his career on September 28, 1975, when he completed 23 of 34 passes for 307 yards and three touchdowns during a 37–31 overtime victory over the St. Louis Cardinals that ended with a 3-yard scoring strike to tight end Billy Joe DuPree.

Staubach again topped the 300-yard mark four weeks later, when he helped the Cowboys overcome a seven-point, fourth-quarter deficit to Philadelphia by passing for 314 yards and one touchdown during a 20–17 win over the Eagles. After tying the game a few minutes earlier with a 21-yard TD pass to Drew Pearson, Staubach led the Cowboys on a game-winning drive that culminated with a 42-yard field goal by Toni Fritsch.

Staubach continued his outstanding play during the 1975 postseason, when, just one week after giving the Cowboys a miraculous win over Minnesota in the opening round of the postseason tournament with a last-second Hail Mary touchdown pass to Drew Pearson, he passed for 220 yards and four touchdowns during a lopsided 37–7 victory over the Los Angeles Rams in the NFC championship game. Staubach also rushed for 54 yards during the contest.

Staubach turned in his finest performance of the 1976 campaign on September 26, when he led the Cowboys to a hard-fought 30–27 win over the Baltimore Colts by completing 22 of 28 passes for 339 yards and two touchdowns.

Staubach gave the Cowboys a 16–10 overtime win over the Minnesota Vikings in the 1977 regular-season opener by scoring himself from 4 yards out.

Staubach displayed his versatility later in the year, rushing for one score and passing for 220 yards and three touchdowns during a 42–35 victory over the San Francisco 49ers on December 12, 1977.

Staubach directed the Dallas offense to a 38–0 dismantling of the Baltimore Colts in the 1978 regular-season opener, passing for 280 yards and four touchdowns during the Monday night blowout, which featured a 91-yard TD catch-and-run by Tony Dorsett.

Staubach tossed three touchdown passes in one game on multiple occasions in 1979, doing so for the first time on September 16, when he hooked up twice with Tony Hill and once with Billy Joe DuPree during a 24–20 win over the Chicago Bears. Staubach accomplished the feat again during a lopsided 30–6 victory over the Rams on October 14, collaborating with Tony Hill, Tony Dorsett, and Jay Saldi on scoring plays that covered 18, 3, and 23 yards, respectively. Although the Cowboys lost their November 12 meeting with the Philadelphia Eagles 31–21, Staubach had a big day, passing for 308 yards and three touchdowns, with two of his TD passes being lengthy connections of 48 and 75 yards with Tony Hill.

Nevertheless, Staubach became best known during his time in Dallas for leading the Cowboys to a number of miracle comebacks, with the first of those coming in the divisional round of the 1972 playoffs, when, after missing most of the season with a shoulder injury, he replaced an ineffective Craig Morton late in the third quarter with the Cowboys trailing San Francisco 28–13. Staubach led the Cowboys on three scoring drives that resulted in a 30–28 victory over the 49ers. Particularly effective in the game's closing moments, Staubach brought the Cowboys to within one score of San Francisco by delivering a 20-yard touchdown pass to Billy Parks with less than two minutes remaining in regulation. After Mel Renfro subsequently recovered an onside kick, Staubach drove the Cowboys down to the San Francisco 10 yard line, where, with just 52 ticks left on the clock, he put his team ahead to stay with a TD pass to Ron Sellers.

Staubach experienced arguably the most memorable moment of his career against Minnesota three years later in the divisional round of the 1975 postseason tournament, when he gave new meaning to the term "Hail Mary." With the Cowboys trailing the Vikings 14–10 late in the fourth quarter, Staubach directed his team from its own 15 yard line to near midfield. Lining up in the shotgun formation with only 32 seconds left on the clock, Staubach took the snap from center, pump-faked to his left, and then threw deep down the right side to Drew Pearson, who warded off a challenge from Minnesota cornerback Nate Wright at the 5 yard line to haul in the desperation pass and then tiptoe into the end zone for the touchdown that gave the Cowboys an improbable 17–14 victory. In describing the play afterwards, Staubach said that he "closed his eyes and said a Hail Mary," thereby creating a new football expression.

Staubach led the Cowboys to another miraculous comeback win in the final regular-season game of his career, when he twice overcame deficits of at least 13 points to put his team in the playoffs with a 35–34 victory over the Washington Redskins. After leading the Cowboys on three scoring drives that turned an early 17–0 deficit to Washington into a 21–17 Dallas lead by the end of the third quarter, Staubach once again found himself in a deep hole when the Redskins scored 17 unanswered points in the final period. However, with less than five minutes remaining in the game and the Cowboys trailing 34–21, Staubach directed the Dallas offense on a pair of scoring drives, the second of which culminated with an 8-yard touchdown pass to Tony Hill with only seconds left on the clock. Staubach's final completion, which gave the Cowboys a 35–34 win and the NFC East title, punctuated an extraordinary performance in which he passed for 336 yards and three touchdowns.

NOTABLE ACHIEVEMENTS

- Passed for more than 3,000 yards twice, topping 3,500 yards once (3,586 in 1979).
- Threw more than 20 touchdown passes three times, topping 25 TD passes twice.
- Completed more than 60 percent of his passes once (62.6 in 1973).
- Posted touchdown-to-interception ratio of better than 2–1 three times.
- Posted quarterback rating above 90.0 three times, finishing with mark higher than 100.0 once (104.8 in 1971).
- Rushed for more than 300 yards three times.
- Averaged more than 5 yards per carry five times, topping 8 yards per rush twice.
- Led NFL quarterbacks in: touchdown passes once; passer rating four times; interception percentage three times; and game-winning drives twice.
- Finished second in NFL in: touchdown passes once; passer rating once; pass completion percentage once; and fourth-quarter comebacks twice.
- Holds Cowboys career record for highest rushing average (5.52 yards per carry).
- Ranks among Cowboys career leaders in: passing yardage (3rd); pass completions (4th); touchdown passes (4th); completion percentage (4th); quarterback rating (2nd); and pass attempts (3rd).
- Five-time NFC champion (1970, 1971, 1975, 1977, and 1978).
- Two-time Super Bowl champion (VI and XII).
- MVP of Super Bowl VI.
- 1971 NFL Players Association Most Valuable Player.
- 1971 Bert Bell Award winner as NFL Player of the Year.
- 1975 Vince Lombardi Sportsman of the Year Award winner.
- 1979 Byron "Whizzer" White Award winner.

- 1983 Walter Camp Man of the Year Award winner.
- Six-time Pro Bowl selection (1971, 1975, 1976, 1977, 1978, and 1979).
- 1971 Second-Team All-Pro selection.
- Five-time First-Team All-NFC selection (1971, 1976, 1977, 1978, and 1979).
- Pro Football Hall of Fame All-1970s First Team.
- Pro Football Reference All-1970s First Team.
- Number 29 on the *Sporting News*'s 1999 list of 100 Greatest Players in NFL History.
- Named to Cowboys' 25th Anniversary Team in 1984.
- Named to Cowboys' 50th Anniversary Team in 2009.
- Inducted into Cowboys Ring of Honor in 1983.
- Elected to Pro Football Hall of Fame in 1985.

2

BOB LILLY

Having fallen just short of earning the top spot on this list, Bob Lilly lays claim to the number 2 position, barely edging out Emmitt Smith for that distinction. Generally considered to be one of the two or three greatest defensive linemen in NFL history, Lilly earned nine All-Pro selections, nine All-Conference nominations, and 11 trips to the Pro Bowl over the course of his 14-year career, en route to becoming one of the few players ever to be named to the NFL's All-Decade Team for two distinct 10-year periods. The first player ever selected by the Cowboys in the NFL Draft, Lilly also later became the first player to be inducted into the team's Ring of Honor and the first Cowboy to be elected to the Pro Football Hall of Fame. Lilly's brilliant play also earned him spots on the NFL's 75th Anniversary Team in 1994 and the *Sporting News* All-Century Team in 1999, as well as a number 10 ranking in that same publication's 1999 list of the 100 Greatest Players in NFL History.

Born in Olney, Texas, on July 26, 1939, Robert Lewis Lilly grew up some 35 miles southwest of his place of origin, in the town of Throckmorton, where he resided until his senior year of high school, when the severe 1950s Texas drought forced his farming family to relocate to Pendleton, Oregon. After being named All-District in football and basketball at Throckmorton High School, Lilly continued to excel in both sports as a senior at Pendleton High School, earning All-State honors in football and Second-Team All-State honors in basketball, while also winning the state javelin championship in track and field. Lilly returned to his home state to attend Texas Christian University on a football scholarship. While at TCU, Lilly twice earned All–Southwest Conference honors and also was a consensus All-America selection as a senior in 1960.

With the Cowboys officially joining the fraternity of NFL teams too late in 1960 to participate in that year's annual draft of college players, they set their sights on making Lilly the first selection in franchise history the following year. However, they first had to put themselves in a position to

Bob Lilly earned more Pro Bowl selections (11) and All-Pro nominations (9) than any other player in Cowboys history.
Courtesy of RMYAuctions.com

do so, since they had earlier traded away the first overall pick in the 1961 NFL Draft to acquire quarterback Eddie LeBaron from the Washington Redskins. The Cowboys sent offensive tackle Paul Dickson and a future first-round draft pick to the Browns for Cleveland's first-round draft choice (number 13 overall), which they subsequently used to select Lilly.

Inserted at starting left defensive end upon his arrival in Dallas, Lilly performed extremely well his first year in the league, starting every game for the Cowboys for the first of 14 consecutive seasons, en route to earning 1961 NFL Defensive Rookie of the Year honors. After making his first Pro Bowl appearance the following year, Lilly moved to right tackle midway through the 1963 campaign—a position he manned for the remainder of his career. Excelling at his new post, Lilly earned his first of 10 consecutive Pro Bowl selections, his first of five straight First-Team All–Eastern Conference nominations, and First-Team All-Pro honors for the first of six consecutive times.

Serving as the central figure in Dallas's vaunted Doomsday Defense, Lilly proved to be virtually unblockable, with former teammate and long-time NFL head coach Dan Reeves recalling, "Nobody could beat him off the ball. Centers would try to choke-block him and a guard would pull, and they couldn't reach him—he'd be in the backfield and he'd cause so much havoc."

Equally effective against the run and pass, the 6'5", 260-pound Lilly used his quickness, strength, agility, and instincts to pressure opposing quarterbacks and contain the opponent's running game. Employing a distinct four-point stance in which he placed both hands on the field, Lilly generated tremendous straight-ahead power even though he didn't start lifting weights until his sixth year in the league. In discussing Lilly's physical strength, Dan Reeves noted, "He had no muscle definition. He didn't have Popeye muscles. He was just an ordinary looking person. You really didn't think when you looked at him that this guy was a football player, and, yet, he was the strongest guy on the team. You combine that strength with the quickness he had, and it was just impossible for people to block him one-on-one."

Double- or triple-teamed on virtually every play, Lilly still managed to spend a significant amount of time in the opponent's backfield, that is, when he wasn't pursuing plays from sideline to sideline. Referred to as "the unblockable, unstoppable force of The Doomsday Defense" in an NFL Films feature dedicated to him, Lilly established himself as arguably the most dominant defensive player in the league without even attempting to gain an advantage over his opponents by employing the "head slap"—a legal maneuver at the time.

In discussing the mental attitude he brought with him to the playing field, Lilly revealed, "The competition is what I love, that makes me a lot more intense. Personalities don't enter into it at all. My objective is to get the man with the ball. Nobody better get in my way."

Lilly then added, "A man has to figure out what has to be done and how to do it. You have to be able to spin out of a block, recognize a play

Nicknamed "Mr. Cowboy," Lilly served as the focal point of Dallas's vaunted
Doomsday Defense.
Courtesy of RMYAuctions.com

immediately, and then react accordingly. I figure I'm as strong as anyone
else; so getting the job done becomes a matter of pride and determination."

After failing to earn First-Team All-Pro honors for the first time in
seven years in 1970, Lilly earned that distinction for the final time in his
career the following year, when he continued his string of 196 consecutive
regular-season games played, en route to helping the Cowboys capture their
first world championship. Extremely durable, Lilly missed just one game
his entire career, sitting out the 1973 NFC championship game loss to the
Minnesota Vikings with an injured hamstring.

A Second-Team All-Pro selection in 1972, Lilly also received First-Team
All-NFC honors that year, before being named Second-Team All-NFC in
1973. Lilly played one more season, before announcing his retirement after
the Cowboys failed to make the playoffs for the first time in nearly a decade

in 1974. He retired having compiled an unofficial total of 94½ quarterback sacks—a figure that ties him for seventh place all-time in team annals. He also is tied for the second most fumble recoveries in franchise history (18). Meanwhile, more than 40 years after he played his last game for the Cowboys, Lilly's 11 Pro Bowl selections remain a club record.

The Cowboys inducted Lilly, whose greatness as a player and many contributions to the team through the years earned him the nickname "Mr. Cowboy," into their Ring of Honor in 1975, appropriately making him the first player to be so honored. The Pro Football Hall of Fame followed suit five years later, opening its doors to him in 1980, the first time his name appeared on the ballot. The *Sporting News* also chose to pay tribute to Lilly in 1999, when it named him a member of its All-Century NFL Team and "the greatest defensive tackle in NFL history." That same publication placed him 10th on its list of the 100 Greatest Football Players of all time, with only linebackers Dick Butkus and Lawrence Taylor receiving a higher ranking among defensive players.

Following his retirement, Lilly moved to Waco, Texas, where he successfully operated a beer distribution business until 1982, when, after witnessing a traffic accident caused by drunken driving, he decided to sell his company and launch a career in photography, which remained a passion of his throughout his playing career. After living in Las Cruces, New Mexico, from 1984 to 1989, Lilly returned to Texas, settling in the city of Graham, where he currently resides.

Expressing his admiration for Lilly in the 1972 *Street and Smith's Pro Football Yearbook*, Tom Landry stated, "A man like that comes along once in a lifetime. He is something a little bit more than great. Nobody is better than Bob Lilly."

CAREER HIGHLIGHTS

Best Season

Performing particularly well for the Cowboys from 1966 to 1969, Lilly helped anchor a defense that led the NFL in fewest rushing yards allowed in each of those four seasons, earning in the process consensus First-Team All-Pro honors each year. Although any of those campaigns would have made a good choice, I ultimately elected to go with 1969 since, in addition to leading the Cowboys to an exceptional 11-2-1 record, Lilly recovered two fumbles, one of which he returned for one of his four career touchdowns.

Memorable Moments / Greatest Performances

Lilly recorded the first of those touchdowns against the St. Louis Cardinals in the 1963 regular-season finale, when he recovered a fumble late in the first half and returned it 42 yards for a TD in a game the Cowboys went on to win 28–24.

Lilly made the only interception of his career a memorable one, picking off a George Mira pass and returning it 17 yards for a touchdown during a 39–31 victory over the San Francisco 49ers on November 7, 1965.

Lilly scored his next touchdown nearly four years later, recovering a fumble and returning it 9 yards for a TD during a 49–14 pasting of the Philadelphia Eagles on October 19, 1969.

Lilly scored the final touchdown of his career against Philadelphia as well, rumbling 7 yards for a score after recovering a fumble during a lop-sided 42–7 victory over the Eagles on September 26, 1971.

Lilly's dominance of opposing offensive linemen helped the Dallas defense turn in a number of extraordinary efforts, with one such performance taking place on November 20, 1966, when the Cowboys sacked Pittsburgh quarterbacks a franchise-record 12 times during a 20–7 win over the Steelers.

Lilly again let his presence be felt during a 21–14 victory over the Browns in the 1967 regular-season opener, leading a Dallas defense that limited Cleveland runners to just 11 yards on the ground, with the great Leroy Kelly gaining those 11 yards on 8 rushing attempts.

Lilly had another big day against the Browns in that year's playoffs, helping to lead the Cowboys to a 52–14 thumping of Cleveland in the opening round of the postseason tournament by sacking Browns quarterback Frank Ryan twice.

However, the signature moment of Lilly's career took place during the Cowboys' 24–3 victory over the Dolphins in Super Bowl VI, when he sacked Miami quarterback Bob Griese for a 29-yard loss. The sack, which resulted in the longest negative play in Super Bowl history, occurred during the relatively early stages of the contest, with the Cowboys holding a 3–0 lead over their AFC counterparts. Facing a third down and 9 yards to go situation, Griese took the snap from center and briefly scrambled around the pocket before being flushed out by Larry Cole. With Griese in retreat, Lilly doggedly pursued him all over the field until he finally brought him down 29 yards behind the original line of scrimmage. Taking note of his teammate's exceptional play throughout the contest, Dan Reeves later commented, "Bob Lilly just dominated the game. The sacking of Bob Griese was one of the big plays."

NOTABLE ACHIEVEMENTS

- Led NFL with 42 fumble-return yards in 1963.
- Scored four career touchdowns (three fumble returns and one interception return).
- Led Cowboys in sacks three straight seasons (1961, 1962, and 1963).
- Missed only one game entire career, setting Cowboys record (since broken) by playing in 196 consecutive games.
- Ranks among Cowboys career leaders with: 94½ unofficial sacks (tied-7th); 18 fumbles recovered on defense (tied-2nd); 14 seasons played (tied-4th); and 196 games started (2nd).
- Two-time NFL Eastern Conference champion (1966 and 1967).
- Two-time NFC champion (1970 and 1971).
- Super Bowl VI champion.
- 11-time Pro Bowl selection (1962 and 1964–1973).
- Seven-time First-Team All-Pro selection (1964, 1965, 1966, 1967, 1968, 1969, and 1971).
- Two-time Second-Team All-Pro selection (1970 and 1972).
- Two-time First-Team All-NFC selection (1971 and 1972).
- Two-time Second-Team All-NFC selection (1970 and 1973).
- 1961 NFL Defensive Rookie of the Year.
- NFL 1960s All-Decade Team.
- NFL 1970s All-Decade Team.
- Pro Football Hall of Fame All-1960s First Team.
- Pro Football Hall of Fame All-1970s First Team.
- Pro Football Reference All-1960s Second Team.
- Named to Cowboys' 25th Anniversary Team in 1984.
- Named to Cowboys' 50th Anniversary Team in 2009.
- Named to AFL-NFL 25-Year Anniversary Team in 1984.
- Named to NFL's 75th Anniversary Team in 1994.
- Named to *Sporting News* All-Century Team in 1999.
- Number 10 on the *Sporting News*'s 1999 list of 100 Greatest Players in NFL History.
- First player inducted into Cowboys Ring of Honor (1975).
- Elected to Pro Football Hall of Fame in 1980.

3
EMMITT SMITH

The NFL's all-time leading rusher, Emmitt Smith perhaps contributed more to the success the Cowboys experienced during the 1990s than any other player. En route to leading the league in rushing four times, Smith gained more than 1,000 yards on the ground 11 straight times, surpassing 1,500 yards on three separate occasions. A veritable touchdown-scoring machine, Smith also scored more touchdowns than any other player in the league three times, twice crossing the opponent's goal line more than 20 times in a season. A solid pass receiver as well, Smith made more than 50 receptions four times, enabling him to surpass 2,000 yards from scrimmage twice. Meanwhile, Smith's grit and determination helped give the Cowboys much of the mental and physical toughness they needed to win six division titles, three NFC championships, and three Super Bowls. Smith's stellar play over the course of his 13 seasons in Dallas earned him eight trips to the Pro Bowl, five All-Pro selections, six All-Conference nominations, one league MVP award, and a spot on the NFL 1990s All-Decade Team. And, following the conclusion of his playing career, Smith received the additional honors of being inducted into the Cowboys Ring of Honor and the Pro Football Hall of Fame.

Born in Pensacola, Florida, on May 15, 1969, Emmitt James Smith III attended local Escambia High School, where he ran track and starred on the gridiron, finishing his high school career with 106 touchdowns and 8,804 yards rushing, the second highest total in American high school football history at the time. After being named 1986 High School Player of the Year by both *USA Today* and *Parade* magazine following a senior year in which he surpassed 2,000 yards rushing for the second time, Smith still found his ability being questioned by some college recruiters, who considered him to be too small and too slow to succeed in major college football. After Smith accepted a scholarship offer to attend the University of Florida, recruiting expert Max Enfinger offered his opinion on the signing, stating, "Emmitt

Emmitt Smith rushed for more yards and touchdowns than any other player in NFL history.
Courtesy of George A. Kitrinos

Smith is a lugger, not a runner. He's not fast. He can't get around the corner. When he falls flat on his face, remember where you heard it first."

Smith ended up proving his critics wrong, setting numerous school rushing records over the course of the next three seasons, en route to earning First-Team SEC honors all three years and being named SEC Player of the Year and a unanimous First-Team All-American as a junior in 1989. However, after Florida hired Steve Spurrier to coach the Gators on January 1, 1990, Smith's concerns over his potential role in Spurrier's pass-happy offense prompted him to announce his intention to forgo his senior year of college eligibility and enter the NFL Draft, which, for the first time in history, welcomed juniors.

Still considered by some to be too small and slow to succeed at the professional level, the 5'9", 220-pound Smith slipped to the middle of the first round of the 1990 NFL Draft, where the Cowboys selected him with the 17th overall pick after moving up four spots by initiating a trade with the Pittsburgh Steelers. Smith subsequently began his pro career in questionable fashion, sitting out the entire preseason while holding out for more money. However, he joined the Cowboys in time for the start of the regular season, after which he went on to win NFL Offensive Rookie of the Year honors by rushing for 937 yards and 11 touchdowns for a Dallas team that improved its record from 1-15 to 7-9. Smith followed that up in 1991 by beginning an extraordinary five-year run during which he established himself as arguably the best running back in the game. Here are the numbers he posted over the course of those five seasons:

SEASON	RUSHING YARDS	RECEIVING YARDS	YARDS FROM SCRIMMAGE	TOUCHDOWNS
1991	**1,563***	258	1,821	13
1992	**1,713**	335	2,048	**19**
1993	**1,486**	414	**1,900**	10
1994	1,484	341	1,825	**22**
1995	**1,773**	375	**2,148**	**25**

* Please note that any numbers printed in bold throughout this book indicate that the player led the NFL in that particular statistical category that year.

In addition to leading the NFL in rushing in four of those five years, Smith scored more touchdowns than any other player in the league three times, with his 25 rushing TDs in 1995 establishing a new NFL record. He also led the league in rushing attempts three times, rushing average once, and yards from scrimmage twice, topping the 2,000-yard mark in both 1992 and 1995. Smith appeared in the Pro Bowl all five years, earned First-Team All-Pro honors in each of the last four seasons, and helped lead the Cowboys to the NFL championship in three of those five seasons, becoming in 1993 the only running back ever to win the NFL rushing title, the league MVP Award, a Super Bowl championship, and the Super Bowl MVP Award in the same season.

Although Smith lacked outstanding size and speed, he had superb balance, tremendous leg strength, excellent vision, and great desire, with Daryl Johnston, who spent most of his career blocking for Smith from his fullback position, saying of his longtime teammate, "I was amazed at what he could do from a vision standpoint and a balance standpoint. Whether it's a hand or something that gets down and props him back up, or sometimes he doesn't even get his hand down, but he could contort his body in a way where he could regain his balance and was up and running. . . . And I don't think he ever got enough credit for his toughness. He was a tough runner. He didn't run out of bounds."

In describing Smith's running style in the *Philadelphia Inquirer*, Jere Longman wrote, "He darts, feints, shifts back and forth like a typewriter carriage. He stops in the hole—comes to a complete stop—looks unhurriedly for a seam and skates across the field like a hot dog wrapper."

Meanwhile, Rick Telander wrote in a 2008 article that appeared in *Sports Illustrated*, "Smith darted, slithered, followed his blockers, and squeezed yard after yard out of plays that didn't have any yards in them. He didn't look especially fast or powerful or blindingly deceptive, yet he couldn't be stopped."

In discussing the qualities that made him such an outstanding runner, Smith offered, "As a runner, I could do a lot of things. I could run you over. I could shake you down. I could run around you. I could go through you if I had to."

A reliable receiver as well who did an outstanding job in pass protection, Smith had no real weaknesses, with perhaps the most overlooked aspect of his game being his physical and mental toughness. Missing a total of only seven games in his 13 seasons with the Cowboys, Smith drew praise from Hall of Fame running back Gale Sayers, who said, "Some guys have a bad ankle or a charley horse and they say they can't play. But Emmitt is a team player and he realizes that him on one leg is better than the second guy on three legs."

Although the Cowboys failed to win another Super Bowl during Smith's time in Dallas, he continued to perform exceptionally well the

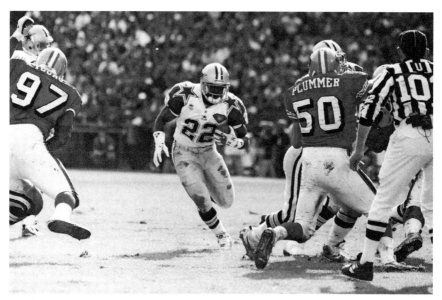

Smith gained more than 1,000 yards on the ground 11 straight times for the Cowboys.
Courtesy of George A. Kitrinos

next several seasons, rushing for more than 1,000 yards six more times from 1996 to 2001. Performing particularly well in 1998 and 1999, Smith earned his last two Pro Bowl nominations by rushing for 1,332 yards and scoring 15 touchdowns in the first of those campaigns, before gaining 1,397 yards on the ground and scoring 13 touchdowns the following year. Over the course of those two seasons, Smith also surpassed Tony Dorsett as the Cowboys' all-time leading rusher and Marcus Allen as the NFL's all-time rushing touchdowns leader.

Despite seeing his string of consecutive 1,000-yard rushing seasons come to an end in 2002, Smith eclipsed Walter Payton's career rushing record of 16,726 yards, with his 975 yards gained on the ground giving him a total of 17,162 for his career. However, with Bill Parcells taking over as head coach following the conclusion of the campaign, the Cowboys decided to release the 33-year-old running back on February 26, 2003. In addition to rushing for 17,162 yards during his time in Dallas, Smith scored 164 touchdowns, with 153 of those coming on the ground. He also amassed 20,174 yards from scrimmage, averaged 4.2 yards per carry, and accumulated a total of 3,012 yards on 486 pass receptions.

After being released by the Cowboys, Smith signed as a free agent with the Arizona Cardinals, spending his final two seasons in Arizona, during which time he lost his thirst for the game. Recalling how he felt after leaving Dallas and joining the Cardinals, Smith revealed, "The most painful moment was probably coming back here to Texas Stadium to play against the Dallas Cowboys and getting dressed in the visitor's locker room. That broke my heart because that's when I realized how much I loved the Dallas Cowboys and how much that love for that organization meant to me as a football player and made me do the things on the football field that I wanted to do. I think that day was the day that my soul for the game left."

Appearing in only 10 games for the Cardinals in 2003 after suffering a broken left shoulder blade during a 24–7 loss to the Cowboys, Smith rushed for a career-low 256 yards over the course of the campaign. However, he rebounded nicely the following year, rushing for 937 yards and nine touchdowns, before once again becoming a free agent and announcing his retirement after signing a one-day contract for one dollar with the Cowboys. Smith ended his career with more rushing attempts (4,409), rushing yards (18,355), and rushing touchdowns (164) than anyone else in NFL history. He also ranks second all-time with 175 total touchdowns and 21,579 yards from scrimmage, trailing only Jerry Rice in both categories.

Following his playing days, Smith spent four years serving as a studio analyst on various programs on the NFL Network and ESPN, before entering into an extremely successful career as a real estate developer. Yet, even in retirement, Smith continues to draw praise for his on-field performance, with fellow Hall of Fame running back Marcus Allen commenting, "He would be the first to say he's a product of the people in front of him, but they can only gain you so many yards. He did the rest."

Meanwhile, Daryl Johnston said, "You talk about great players making everyone around them better. That couldn't be more true of anybody than Emmitt Smith." Johnston then added, "We were like brothers. It was such an honor and a privilege to block for him."

COWBOYS CAREER HIGHLIGHTS

Best Season

Smith played his best ball for the Cowboys from 1991 to 1995, performing particularly well in 1992, 1993, and 1995. En route to earning First-Team All-Pro honors for the first of four straight times in 1992, Smith averaged

4.6 yards per carry, finished second in the NFL with 2,048 yards from scrimmage, and led the league with 1,713 yards rushing, 18 rushing touchdowns, and 19 total touchdowns, prompting the Newspaper Enterprise Association to name him league MVP. He followed that up in 1993 by averaging a career-high and league-leading 5.3 yards per carry, scoring 10 touchdowns, and topping the circuit with 1,486 yards rushing and 1,900 yards from scrimmage, earning in the process "official" recognition as the NFL Player of the Year and league MVP. Nevertheless, the 1995 campaign would have to be considered the finest all-around season of Smith's career. In addition to scoring an NFL-record 25 touchdowns on the ground, Smith averaged 4.7 yards per carry and led the league with 1,773 yards rushing, 2,148 yards from scrimmage, and 150 points scored, breaking in the process Tony Dorsett's single-season franchise record for most rushing yards. Smith continued to hold that mark until 2014, when DeMarco Murray rushed for 1,845 yards.

Memorable Moments / Greatest Performances

Although the Cowboys lost their September 23, 1990, meeting with the Redskins 19–15, Smith scored the first touchdown of his career during the contest, bringing his team to within six points of Washington with a 2-yard TD run in the fourth quarter.

Smith topped 100 yards rushing for the first time as a pro two weeks later, carrying the ball 23 times for 121 yards and one touchdown during a 14–10 win over the Tampa Bay Buccaneers on October 7, 1990, with his 14-yard TD run in the fourth quarter providing the margin of victory.

Smith led the Cowboys to a 27–17 win over the Washington Redskins on November 22, 1990, by carrying the ball 23 times for 132 yards and two touchdowns, with his 48-yard, fourth-quarter TD run sealing the victory for Dallas.

Smith led an assault on the Phoenix defense on December 16, 1990, rushing for 103 yards and four touchdowns during a lopsided 41–10 victory over the Cardinals.

Even though Washington defeated the Cowboys 33–31 on September 9, 1991, Smith recorded the longest run of his career during the contest, scoring from 75 yards out late in the first quarter. He finished the game with 112 yards rushing, another 42 yards on eight pass receptions, and two touchdowns.

Smith ran for a season-high 182 yards during a 17–9 victory over the Cardinals on September 22, 1991, scoring both Dallas touchdowns in the first quarter, once from 60 yards out and once from 12 yards out.

Smith claimed his first rushing title in the final game of the 1991 regular season, gaining 160 yards on the ground and scoring twice during a 31–27 win over the Atlanta Falcons that clinched a playoff berth for the Cowboys.

Smith helped lead the Cowboys to a 28–13 victory over the Los Angeles Raiders on October 25, 1992, by rushing for 152 yards and three touchdowns.

Smith followed that up by gaining 163 yards on the ground during a 20–10 win over Philadelphia one week later.

However, Smith saved his finest performance of the season for Atlanta, rushing for 174 yards and a pair of 29-yard touchdowns during a 41–17 mauling of the Falcons on December 21, 1992.

Smith had the biggest rushing day of his career on October 31, 1993, when he led the Cowboys to a 23–10 victory over Philadelphia by carrying the ball 30 times for 237 yards and one touchdown, with his 62-yard TD run in the fourth quarter representing his longest run of the season.

Smith had another big day against the Philadelphia defense five weeks later, gaining 172 yards on the ground during a 23–17 win over the Eagles on December 6, 1993.

Smith continued his outstanding play in that year's postseason, earning Super Bowl XXVIII MVP honors by rushing for 132 yards and two touchdowns during the Cowboys' 30–13 victory over Buffalo.

Picking up right where he left off the previous year, Smith led the Cowboys to a 26–9 win over Pittsburgh in the 1994 regular-season opener by rushing for 171 yards and one touchdown.

Smith helped pace the Cowboys to a convincing 38–10 victory over the Giants on November 7, 1994, by rushing for 163 yards and two touchdowns.

Smith turned in an exceptional all-around performance on Thanksgiving Day 1994, rushing for 133 yards, amassing another 95 yards on six pass receptions, and scoring a pair of touchdowns during a 42–31 win over the Green Bay Packers.

Smith proved to be a one-man wrecking crew against the Giants in the 1995 regular-season opener, leading the Cowboys to a 35–0 win over their NFC East rivals by rushing for 163 yards and four touchdowns. Smith set the tone for the game on the Cowboys' third play from scrimmage, bursting straight up the middle and going untouched for a 60-yard TD run.

Smith again came up big for the Cowboys two weeks later, rushing for 150 yards and two touchdowns during a 23–17 overtime victory over the Minnesota Vikings on September 17, with his 31-yard TD run on the Cowboys' first possession of overtime putting a sudden end to the contest.

Smith led the Cowboys to a 28–13 win over the Atlanta Falcons on October 29, 1995, by rushing for 167 yards and one touchdown, while gaining another 30 yards on five pass receptions.

Smith followed that up with another strong performance one week later, rushing for 158 yards and two touchdowns during a 34–12 win over the Philadelphia Eagles on November 6.

Smith proved to be the difference in a 38–27 victory over Green Bay in the 1995 NFC championship game, rushing for 150 yards and three touchdowns, with his two fourth-quarter scores enabling the Cowboys to overcome a 27–24 deficit.

Making a habit out of performing well on Thanksgiving, Smith gained 155 yards on the ground and scored three touchdowns during a 21–10 win over Washington on November 28, 1996.

Smith topped the 100-yard mark for the last time as a member of the Cowboys on Thanksgiving Day 2002, rushing for 144 yards during a 27–20 victory over the Redskins.

Still, Smith turned in the most memorable performance of his career in the final game of the 1993 regular season, when, despite playing most of the game with a separated right shoulder, he led the Cowboys to a 16–13 overtime victory over the New York Giants that clinched the NFC East title and a first-round bye in the playoffs for Dallas. With the Cowboys and Giants vying for the division title and home-field advantage throughout the playoffs, the two teams squared off at Giants Stadium on January 2, 1994. After suffering a first-degree shoulder separation in the second quarter, Smith returned to the fray to gain 168 yards on the ground and another 61 yards through the air, with 41 of his rushing yards coming during the game-winning drive in overtime. Smith's heroic effort, which the NFL Network later called his "gutsiest game," so inspired John Madden that the Hall of Fame coach-turned-broadcaster visited him in the locker room following the contest to express his admiration. Meanwhile, Dallas offensive coordinator Norv Turner marveled, "In my time at USC with Ricky Bell and Marcus Allen, and at the Rams with Eric Dickerson, I've coached some guys who are as physically talented as he [Smith] is. But I've never been around someone who is as good a runner—vision, break tackles, power, moves, catch the ball like he did today. And he did it with an arm tied behind his back."

NOTABLE ACHIEVEMENTS

- Rushed for more than 1,000 yards 11 straight times, topping 1,500 yards three times.
- Surpassed 1,500 yards from scrimmage seven times, topping 2,000 yards twice.
- Scored at least 10 touchdowns nine times, surpassing 15 TDs five times and 20 TDs twice.
- Scored more than 100 points three times, reaching 150-point mark once (1995).
- Averaged more than 4.5 yards per carry three times, topping 5 yards per carry once (5.3 in 1993).
- Caught more than 50 passes four times.
- Led NFL in: rushing yardage four times; rushing touchdowns three times; touchdowns scored three times; points scored once; rushing average once; rushing attempts three times; and yards from scrimmage twice.
- Finished second in NFL in: rushing touchdowns once; points scored once; yards from scrimmage once; and all-purpose yards three times.
- Led Cowboys in rushing yardage 13 straight times.
- Holds Cowboys single-season records for most: rushing touchdowns (25 in 1995); total touchdowns scored (25 in 1995); and points scored (150 in 1995).
- Holds Cowboys career records for most: rushing yardage (17,162); rushing touchdowns (153); touchdowns scored (164); points scored (986); and rushing attempts (4,052).
- Ranks fifth all-time on Cowboys with 486 pass receptions.
- Missed only seven games in 13 seasons with Cowboys.
- Holds NFL single-season record for most rushing touchdowns (25 in 1995).
- Holds NFL career records for most: rushing yardage (18,355); rushing touchdowns (164); 100-yard rushing games (78); and rushing attempts (4,409).
- Ranks among NFL's all-time leaders in: career touchdowns (2nd); yards from scrimmage (2nd); and all-purpose yards (4th).
- Holds NFL career postseason records for most: rushing yardage (1,586); rushing touchdowns (19); and 100-yard rushing games (7).
- Three-time NFC champion (1992, 1993, and 1995).
- Three-time Super Bowl champion (XXVII, XXVIII, and XXX).

- Ten-time NFC Offensive Player of the Week.
- 1990 Associated Press NFL Offensive Rookie of the Year.
- 1993 Associated Press NFL MVP.
- 1993 Bert Bell (NFL Player of the Year) Award winner.
- MVP of Super Bowl XVIII.
- Eight-time Pro Bowl selection (1990, 1991, 1992, 1993, 1994, 1995, 1998, and 1999).
- Four-time First-Team All-Pro selection (1992, 1993, 1994, and 1995).
- 1991 Second-Team All-Pro selection.
- Five-time First-Team All-NFC selection (1991, 1992, 1993, 1994, and 1995).
- 1996 Second-Team All-NFC selection.
- NFL 1990s All-Decade Team.
- Pro Football Hall of Fame All-1990s First Team.
- Pro Football Reference All-1990s First Team.
- Number 68 on the *Sporting News*'s 1999 list of 100 Greatest Players in NFL History.
- Named to Cowboys' 50th Anniversary Team in 2009.
- Inducted into Cowboys Ring of Honor in 2005.
- Elected to Pro Football Hall of Fame in 2010.

4

RANDY WHITE

ivaling Bob Lilly as the most dominant defensive player in Cowboys history, Randy White spent most of his 14-year career manning the same position as "Mr. Cowboy." Moved to his more natural position of defensive tackle in 1977 after struggling somewhat his first two seasons at linebacker, White served as the anchor of the Dallas defense for the next 12 years, helping to lead the Cowboys to six division titles, three conference championships, and one Super Bowl victory. Along the way, White earned nine Pro Bowl selections, eight All-Pro nominations, nine All-Conference selections, and recognition as the 1978 NFC Defensive Player of the Year and the 1982 NFL Defensive Lineman of the Year, making him one of the most decorated players in franchise history. Ranking among the Cowboys' all-time leaders in both tackles and sacks, White also earned spots on the NFL 1980s All-Decade Team and the Cowboys' 25th and 50th Anniversary Teams. Meanwhile, the *Sporting News* placed White 51st on its list of the 100 Greatest Players in NFL History in 1999, five years after the Pro Football Hall of Fame opened its doors to him.

Born in Pittsburgh, Pennsylvania, on January 15, 1953, Randall Lee White attended Thomas McKean High School in Wilmington, Delaware, where he starred in football as a defensive end and linebacker. After enrolling at the University of Maryland following his graduation from Thomas McKean High in 1971, White spent one year playing fullback for the Terps, before being moved to defensive end by new head coach Jerry Claiborne, who suggested that the physically gifted sophomore had the skill to be "one of the best five linemen in the U.S." Proving his coach to be an excellent judge of talent, White won numerous awards as a senior, including the Outland Trophy, the Lombardi Award, and the Atlantic Coast Conference Player of the Year, with Claiborne later proclaiming him to be "as fast as some of the offensive backs I had coached."

Supporting Claiborne's contention, former Maryland teammate John Zernhelt stated years later, "I remember when the pros came out to time

Randy White helped lead the Cowboys to six division titles, three conference championships, and one Super Bowl victory.
Courtesy of George A. Kitrinos

him in the 40-yard dash, and Randy ran with the wide receivers. He ran a 4.6. I knew on that day that 20 years down the road someone would be calling and asking me about Randy White."

However, it was against Tennessee in the 1974 Liberty Bowl that Dallas personnel director Gil Brandt first became impressed with White, with Tom Landry later commenting, "Gil was raving how he was making tackles all over the field, lining up on the left, and knocking people over to the right. Rarely did he get so excited."

With the Cowboys having acquired the second overall pick of the 1975 NFL Draft in an earlier trade with the Giants that sent quarterback Craig Morton to New York, they wasted little time in using that pick to select White, who they subsequently moved to the unfamiliar position of middle linebacker. Spending his first two years in Dallas backing up Lee Roy Jordan and playing mostly on special teams, White found himself unable to maximize his enormous potential, with former Cowboys teammate Harvey Martin stating, "The first two years, they tried to turn him into a [Dick] Butkus, but we didn't have a Butkus-like defense. Randy wanted to whip the son of a gun immediately."

Looking back at the early stages of his career, White noted, "Coming out of college, a lot was expected of me. But I never did feel comfortable playing linebacker. Those first two years I was fighting for my life out there. Then they switched me to defensive tackle, where I was a lot more comfortable, and from there my career took off."

White's career did indeed take off after Tom Landry wisely moved him to right defensive tackle, the same position formerly occupied by Cowboys legend Bob Lilly from 1961 to 1974. Assuming that post full-time in 1977, White had a breakout year, earning Pro Bowl honors for the first of nine straight times by recording 13 sacks and 118 tackles. He topped that performance the following year, though, concluding the 1978 campaign with a career-high and team-leading 16 sacks and 123 tackles, en route to earning First-Team All-Pro and NFC Defensive Player of the Year honors.

White continued to excel the next several seasons, earning All-Pro, All-NFC, and Pro Bowl honors each year from 1979 to 1985, as he developed into the league's most disruptive force on defense. Particularly dominant in 1980 and 1982, White gained recognition as the *Football Digest* NFL Defensive Lineman of the Year in the first of those campaigns, before being honored as NFL Defensive Lineman of the Year two seasons later.

With Coach Landry taking advantage of White's tremendous speed and quickness by putting him 2 or 3 yards off the line of scrimmage in the Cowboys' "Flex" Defense, the 6'4", 257-pound tackle had the ability to see, run, and hit at almost the same time. Generating an enormous amount of pressure despite being double- or triple-teamed on virtually every play, White forced opposing teams to devise new blocking schemes, with New York Giants offensive line coach Tom Bresnahan revealing that he issued a standing order that obligated any free blockers on his line "to look for Randy White."

Meanwhile, White's aggressiveness made him a favorite of Cowboys' longtime defensive coordinator Ernie Stautner, who earlier played his way into the Pro Football Hall of Fame as an extremely intense 235-pound defensive tackle with the Pittsburgh Steelers during the 1950s. Perhaps seeing a bit of himself in White, Stautner claimed that even the great Bob Lilly could not match White's relentless pace, stating, "I don't say either one was better, but, by comparison, Lilly was more up and down." When asked for clarification, he answered, "Lilly was human."

Weighing in on the Lilly vs. White debate, Charlie Waters, who played with both men, suggested in 1984, "Bob Lilly was the best in his day. Today, Randy White is simply the best football player in America. He has been for a few years."

White also drew praise from opposing players, with New York Giants guard Billy Ard stating, "White never gives you a play off, and if you're not up for every one, he'll knock you on your ass."

San Francisco 49ers guard John Ayers said that White "has no weaknesses," while Washington Redskins halfback Joe Washington admitted that the only way he could block White effectively was to "hold, tackle, and grab" him.

In discussing White, former Eagles head coach Dick Vermeil commented, "He created a war on every snap. He was mean, boy, he was tough. . . . For me, coaching against him twice a year for seven years, he might be the finest defensive player I ever had to coach against."

Tom Landry added, "His performances range anywhere from spectacular to spectacular. He could outmatch anybody's intensity from game to game."

White's combination of speed, athleticism, strength, and intensity, which made him the heart-and-soul of the Dallas defense, prompted others to nickname him "Manster," referring to his qualities as half-man, half-monster. Almost impervious to pain, White missed just one game his entire career, playing virtually the entire 1979 campaign with a broken bone in his right foot. Meanwhile, his willingness to work hard both on the field and at practice served as motivation to his teammates, who strove to maintain the same level of dedication.

White earned 1978 NFC Defensive Player of the Year honors by recording 16 sacks and 123 tackles.
Courtesy of Dallas Cowboys

White continued to anchor the Dallas defensive line until 1988, when he announced his retirement following a 14-year career during which he played in a total of 209 games. Over the course of those 14 seasons, White amassed 1,104 tackles (701 solo) and 111 sacks, placing him among the franchise's all-time leaders in both categories.

Following his playing days, White became the spokesperson for Smokey Mountain chew, a tobacco- and nicotine-free smokeless tobacco alternative. He also opened and operated his own authentic BBQ restaurant in Texas, Randy White's Hall of Fame BBQ. Totally unaffected by his celebrity status, White has retained his down-to-earth persona through the years, with Charlie Waters revealing, "I once went to his parents' farm, and Randy taught me how to grow mushrooms. That was exciting for him. He has always been humble. Reporters used to try to get these great Manster quotes about Randy's next matchup, and he would say, 'I'm going to do the best that I can and see what happens.' He's a simple person with simple pleasures."

White displayed his humility when the Cowboys inducted him into their Ring of Honor in 1994, telling those in attendance, "Any honor I receive is a reflection on the great teammates and coaches I had in my career. There's a real special group of guys with the Cowboys, and to be a part of that was a great honor."

CAREER HIGHLIGHTS

Best Season

White had a tremendous year for the Cowboys in 1977, earning the first of his nine consecutive trips to the Pro Bowl by recording 13 sacks, 118 tackles, and two fumble recoveries. He also performed extremely well from 1982 to 1984, earning NFL Defensive Lineman of the Year honors in the first of those campaigns, before sacking opposing quarterbacks 12½ times in each of the next two seasons, while also recording 100 and 108 tackles, respectively. Nevertheless, White turned in his most dominant performance in 1978, when he earned NFC Defensive Player of the Year honors by establishing career-high marks in sacks (16) and tackles (123).

Memorable Moments / Greatest Performances

Although the Cowboys ended up losing Super Bowl X to the Steelers 21–17, White proved to be a disruptive force throughout the contest, sacking Pittsburgh quarterback Terry Bradshaw twice.

Even more of a factor during the Cowboys' 27–10 victory over the Broncos in Super Bowl XII, White earned game co-MVP honors by recording a sack and applying constant pressure up the middle to Denver quarterbacks Craig Morton and Norris Weese, helping to limit them to just eight completions, 61 yards passing, and four interceptions.

White recorded two safeties during his career, with one of those coming during the regular season and the other coming during the playoffs. White lit the scoreboard for the first time on October 2, 1978, when he tackled Washington quarterback Joe Theismann in the end zone during a 9–5 loss to the Redskins. He recorded his other safety the following year, when he brought down Los Angeles quarterback Vince Ferragamo in the end zone during the Cowboys' 21–19 loss to the Rams in the divisional round of the 1979 postseason tournament.

White recorded the first of his two career interceptions during the Cowboys' heartbreaking 28–27 loss to San Francisco in the 1981 NFC championship game.

White recorded his only regular-season interception when he picked off a tipped Phil Simms pass during a 33–24 victory over the Giants on November 2, 1987.

White recorded a career-high 3½ sacks during a lopsided 35–10 victory over the Seattle Seahawks on December 4, 1983.

White enjoyed his November 22, 1984, Thanksgiving Day feast after helping the Cowboys defeat New England 20–17 by recording three of their 10 sacks of Patriots quarterback Tony Eason.

NOTABLE ACHIEVEMENTS

- Finished in double digits in sacks seven times, recording career-high 16 unofficial sacks in 1978.
- Led Cowboys in sacks three times.
- Missed just one game entire career.
- Ranks third in Cowboys history in career: tackles (1,104); solo tackles (701); and sacks (111—52 official).
- Ranks among Cowboys career leaders with 14 seasons played (tied-4th) and 209 games played (3rd).
- Three-time NFC champion (1975, 1977, and 1978).
- Super Bowl XII champion.
- Co-MVP of Super Bowl XII.
- Two-time NFC Defensive Player of the Week.
- 1978 NFC Defensive Player of the Year.
- 1980 *Football Digest* NFL Defensive Lineman of the Year.
- 1982 NFL Defensive Lineman of the Year.
- Nine-time Pro Bowl selection (1977, 1978, 1979, 1980, 1981, 1982, 1983, 1984, and 1985).
- Seven-time First-Team All-Pro selection (1978, 1979, 1981, 1982, 1983, 1984, and 1985).
- 1980 Second-Team All-Pro selection.
- Nine-time First-Team All-NFC selection (1977, 1978, 1979, 1980, 1981, 1982, 1983, 1984, and 1985).
- NFL 1980s All-Decade Team.
- Pro Football Hall of Fame All-1980s First Team.
- Pro Football Reference All-1980s First Team.
- Named to Cowboys' 25th Anniversary Team in 1984.
- Named to Cowboys' 50th Anniversary Team in 2009.
- Number 51 on the *Sporting News*'s 1999 list of 100 Greatest Players in NFL History.
- Inducted into Cowboys Ring of Honor in 1994.
- Elected to Pro Football Hall of Fame in 1994.

5
MICHAEL IRVIN

The vocal and emotional leader of Cowboy teams that won six division titles, three NFC championships, and three Super Bowls, Michael Irvin came to represent the Dallas squads of the 1990s perhaps more than any other player, with his brash, cocky, and arrogant behavior making him an extension of team owner Jerry Jones and head coach Jimmy Johnson. Irvin irritated and antagonized his opponents with his trash-talking and theatrical on-field demeanor, while often conducting himself in a lascivious manner off the gridiron. Yet, in spite of all the baggage he brought with him, Irvin earned the respect and admiration of his teammates with his strong work ethic and exceptional play, establishing himself during his time in Dallas as the greatest wide receiver in franchise history. A five-time Pro Bowler and three-time All-Pro selection, Irvin led the Cowboys in pass receptions and receiving yards eight straight seasons, topping 70 receptions and 1,000 yards seven times each. The holder of numerous Cowboy receiving records, Irvin holds franchise marks for most catches (111) and receiving yards (1,603) in a season, as well as most career receiving yards (11,904) and 100-yard receiving games (47). He also ranks among the team's all-time leaders in pass receptions, touchdown catches, and touchdowns scored. A tremendous big-game player, Irvin also ranks among the NFL's all-time leaders in career postseason receptions (87) and receiving yards (1,315), with his outstanding on-field performance earning him a spot on the NFL 1990s All-Decade Team and induction into the Cowboys Ring of Honor and the Pro Football Hall of Fame following his retirement.

Born in Fort Lauderdale, Florida, on March 5, 1966, Michael Jerome Irvin grew up in a crowded home with his 16 other siblings. After transferring from Piper High School to St. Thomas Aquinas High School, Irvin performed so well on the football field that be became one of the state's most heavily recruited athletes. Choosing to attend the University of Miami, Irvin spent three years starring at wide receiver for the Hurricanes under head coach Jimmy Johnson, setting school records for career receptions (143), touchdown catches (26), and receiving yards (2,423—later broken by Santana Moss). After helping Miami capture the National Championship in 1987, Irvin elected to forgo his final year of college eligibility and turn pro.

Selected by the Cowboys with the 11th overall pick of the 1988 NFL Draft, Irvin ended up being the last first-round draft pick ever made by the brain-trust of longtime general manager Tex Schramm, player personnel director Gil Brandt, and head coach Tom Landry. Despite missing two games due to injury and starting only 10 contests in 1988, Irvin performed relatively well as a rookie, recording 32 receptions, 654 receiving yards, and five touchdowns for a Dallas team that finished the season with a disappointing 3-13 record. Irvin subsequently took a step backward after suffering a torn anterior cruciate ligament in his right knee during a Week 6 loss to San Francisco in 1989 that limited him to just 18 games, 46 receptions, 791 receiving yards, and seven touchdowns over the course of the next two seasons for Cowboy teams that posted a composite record of 8-24 under new head coach Jimmy Johnson.

Fully healthy for the first time in three years by the start of the 1991 campaign, Irvin finally reached his enormous potential, beginning a string of five straight seasons in which he compiled more than 70 receptions and 1,000 receiving yards. Here are the numbers he posted over the course of those five seasons:

SEASON	RECEPTIONS	YARDS	TOUCHDOWNS
1991	93	**1,523**	8
1992	78	1,396	7
1993	88	1,330	7
1994	79	1,241	6
1995	111	1,603	10

After leading the NFL with 1,523 receiving yards in 1991, Irvin finished second in the league in that category in each of the next two seasons. He also placed in the league's top five in pass receptions three times, with his 111 catches and 1,603 receiving yards in 1995 both establishing single-season franchise records. Irvin appeared in the Pro Bowl each year and earned All-Pro honors in three of the five seasons. Meanwhile, the Cowboys made the playoffs all five years and won the Super Bowl at the end of the 1992, 1993, and 1995 campaigns.

Michael Irvin amassed more than 1,000 receiving yards seven times for the Cowboys.
Courtesy of George A. Kitrinos

Gradually emerging as Troy Aikman's "go-to guy" on third- and fourth-down situations, Irvin acquired the nickname "The Playmaker" due to his penchant for making big plays in big games. Revealing the confidence he had in his ability to come through in the clutch, Irvin proclaimed, "Most train to be part of the game. The greatest train to be the game: I am the game. Third-and-9, two minutes left, that's what I train for. I train for the moments everyone runs from. I run for them."

Although Irvin did not possess exceptional running speed, he had excellent hands, ran precise routes, and had outstanding size and strength, with his 6'2" 207-pound frame allowing him to manhandle opposing cornerbacks and frequently catch balls with defenders draped all over him. Commenting on Irvin's physical style of play, Troy Aikman suggested, "Michael was not the fastest guy in a race, so he had to be great in other areas. He was a big, physical guy and he used that. . . . There are a lot of guys that don't really want to take the big hit. Michael would get hit by a truck."

Supremely self-confident, Irvin also helped give the Cowboys much of the swagger they exhibited during the 1990s. In addressing his longtime teammate's colorful persona, Aikman stated, "Michael's one of those guys, you love him when he's on your team, you hate him when he's playing for somebody else. . . . As flamboyant as Michael was, I think that there were probably a lot of people who misunderstood that for selfishness. Did Michael want to do well for himself? Yes, absolutely, but Michael, more importantly, wanted to do well for the team."

Aikman continued, "Michael could get in front of the entire group and everybody knew that it wasn't self-serving—it was because this guy really wanted to win. . . . Michael Irvin was arguably the hardest-working guy that I've ever been around as an athlete. He was a guy who wanted to be great."

Daryl Johnston also considered Irvin to be a consummate teammate, saying long after he retired, "Michael was the hardest working guy on our team. . . . He was a guy who made some wrong decisions, but he never took anything public, and he never spoke out against anyone on our team. He wasn't a problem. He was more of an inspiration."

The "wrong decisions" to which Johnston referred included drug addiction and constant dealings with women of ill repute, both of which got him into trouble on numerous occasions during and after his playing career. Irvin's reputation received one of its biggest hits in 1996, when media reports stated that he and teammate Erik Williams, while under the influence of cocaine, had videotaped their sexual assault on Dallas cheerleader Nina Shahravan, who subsequently reported the incident to police. Although it later surfaced that Shahravan had fabricated the entire incident, forcing her to plead guilty to perjury and spend 90 days in jail, Irvin, nevertheless, suffered the indignity of having his reputation sullied by her accusation.

Still, in spite of his somewhat questionable behavior off the playing field, Irvin remained one of the game's most productive wide receivers for another three years, surpassing 70 receptions and 1,000 receiving yards two more times between 1996 and 1998, while also making nine TD catches in 1997. However, his career came to an abrupt end on October 10, 1999, when, during a 13–10 loss to the Eagles at Philadelphia's Veterans Stadium, he suffered a non-life-threatening cervical spinal cord injury after being driven head-first into the turf by defensive back Tim Hauck following an 8-yard reception. Subsequently carted off the field on a stretcher as the fans in Philadelphia cheered his injury, Irvin later told talk-show host Jim Rome that he accepted the fans' shabby treatment of him because he'd been "killing them for 10 years."

Forced into premature retirement, Irvin ended his playing career with 750 receptions, 11,904 receiving yards, 65 touchdowns, and an average of 15.9 yards per reception. His total of 47 career 100-yard receiving games remains the third most in NFL history, ranking behind only the 65 posted by Jerry Rice and the 50 compiled by Don Maynard.

Irvin continued to tempt fate following his playing days, being arrested twice on charges of drug possession and once on an accusation of sexual assault, although he somehow managed to wriggle out of each situation without doing any jail time. However, his deviant behavior eventually cost him his job at ESPN and kept him out of the Pro Football Hall of Fame until his third year of eligibility. Officially joining the other all-time greats at Canton on August 4, 2007, Irvin delivered an inspirational and tearful acceptance speech in which he referenced his life as a football player and the many mistakes he made off the playing field. Considered by everyone in attendance to be the highlight of the induction ceremonies, Irvin's speech drew praise from many NFL commentators, including those who previously expressed their personal dislike for him.

Irvin has since made a comeback in his professional career, resurfacing as an analyst for NFL Network, whose viewers he informs and entertains with his insights and engaging personality. Inducted into the Cowboys Ring of Honor, along with former teammates Troy Aikman and Emmitt Smith, on September 19, 2005, Irvin received praise during the festivities from Aikman, who stated, "We would never have come close to doing what we did in the 90s had it not been for Michael Irvin." Meanwhile, Irvin

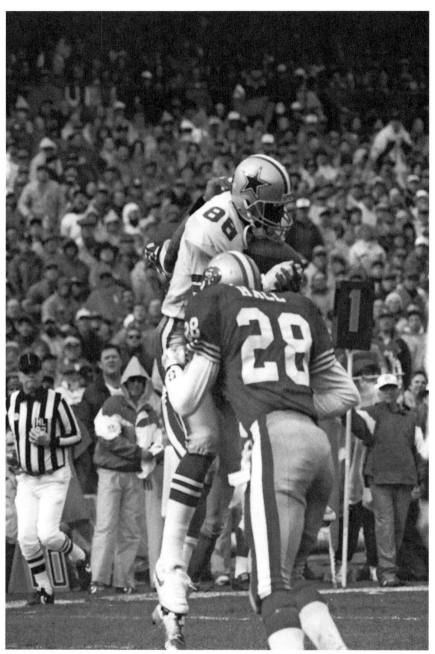

Irvin set single-season franchise records in 1995 for most pass receptions (111) and most pass receiving yards (1,603).
Courtesy of George A. Kitrinos

proclaimed, "I always wanted to be the very best receiver the Cowboys ever had. That was my goal coming in as a rookie and my goal throughout my career: being the best they ever had, going up in the Ring of Honor." He then added, "I can't write my life story without Emmitt and Troy. They can't write their life stories without me. We're tied together forever. This is a day to remember for the rest of our lives."

CAREER HIGHLIGHTS

Best Season

Irvin had a tremendous year for the Cowboys in 1991, earning Pro Bowl honors for the first time and his lone First-Team All-Pro selection by finishing second in the NFL with 93 receptions, leading the league with 1,523 receiving yards, and catching eight touchdown passes. However, he proved to be even slightly more dominant in 1995, establishing single-season franchise records with 111 receptions and 1,603 receiving yards, while also scoring a career-high 10 touchdowns and setting an NFL record by accumulating more than 100 receiving yards in 11 games, including seven times in succession. Irvin continued his exceptional play in the postseason, making seven receptions for 100 yards and two touchdowns during the Cowboys' 38–27 win over Green Bay in the NFC championship game, before making another five catches for 76 yards during their 27–17 victory over Pittsburgh in Super Bowl XXX.

Memorable Moments / Greatest Performances

Irvin made the first TD reception of his career in his very first game, hooking up with quarterback Steve Pelluer on a 35-yard scoring play during a 24–21 loss to the Pittsburgh Steelers in the 1988 regular-season opener.

Irvin recorded the first 100-yard receiving day of his career later that year, torching the Washington secondary for six catches, 149 yards, and three touchdowns during a 24–17 victory over the Redskins on December 11, 1988, with one of his receptions being a season-long 61-yard TD grab. Irvin's outstanding play earned him NFC Offensive Player of the Week honors for the first of four times.

Irvin collaborated with Troy Aikman on a scoring play for the first time on September 17, 1989, when he hauled in a 65-yard TD pass from the rookie quarterback during a 27–21 loss to the Atlanta Falcons. Irvin finished the day with five catches for 115 yards and that one touchdown.

Irvin helped the Cowboys record a 26–14 victory over Cleveland in the 1991 regular-season opener by making nine receptions for 123 yards and one touchdown.

Irvin turned in a similarly impressive performance against Cincinnati later in the year, making six catches for 148 yards during a 35–23 win over the Bengals on October 13, 1991.

Irvin continued his outstanding play six weeks later, helping the Cowboys defeat Washington 24–21 on November 24 by making nine receptions for 130 yards and one touchdown.

Irvin followed that up with another strong performance against Pittsburgh on Thanksgiving, leading the Cowboys to a 20–10 victory over the Steelers by making eight receptions for 157 yards and one touchdown, with his 66-yard, fourth-quarter TD grab sealing the win for Dallas.

Irvin earned NFC Offensive Player of the Week recognition for the second time in the final game of the 1991 regular season, when he helped the Cowboys clinch a playoff berth by making 10 catches for 169 yards and one touchdown during a 31–27 victory over Atlanta.

Irvin again claimed NFC Offensive Player of the Week honors for his performance during a 31–20 win over the Phoenix Cardinals on September 20, 1992, when he made eight receptions for a career-high 210 yards and three touchdowns, with his 87-yard hookup with Troy Aikman in the first quarter representing the longest pass reception of his career.

Irvin turned in one of his finest efforts of the 1993 campaign against Green Bay on October 3, when he made seven catches for 155 yards and one touchdown during a convincing 36–14 victory over the Packers.

Irvin again came up big for the Cowboys two weeks later, when, during a rematch of the 1992 NFC championship game, he made 12 receptions for 168 yards and one touchdown, in helping them defeat San Francisco 26–17. Putting the Cowboys ahead to stay late in the third quarter by hauling in a 36-yard TD pass from Troy Aikman, Irvin ended up capturing NFC Offensive Player of the Week honors for the fourth and final time in his career.

A nemesis of Green Bay through the years, Irvin made eight receptions for 150 yards and one touchdown during a 34–24 win over the Packers on October 8, 1995.

Irvin had another huge game three weeks later, making 10 catches for 135 yards and one touchdown during a 28–13 victory over the Atlanta Falcons on October 29, 1995.

Irvin turned in another outstanding effort almost exactly one year later, when he made 12 receptions for 186 yards and one touchdown, in helping the Cowboys defeat Miami 29–10 on October 27, 1996.

Irvin played a big part in another Cowboys win several weeks later, when he made eight catches for 198 yards and one touchdown during a 10–6 victory over the Arizona Cardinals on December 8, 1996, with his 50-yard TD connection with Troy Aikman midway through the third quarter giving the Cowboys their only touchdown of the game.

Irvin contributed to a lopsided 37–7 victory over the Pittsburgh Steelers in the 1997 regular-season opener by making seven receptions for 153 yards and two touchdowns, with his scoring plays covering 42 and 15 yards.

Irvin topped the 100-yard mark for the final time in his career in the opening game of the 1999 regular season, when he made five receptions for 122 yards and two touchdowns during a 41–35 overtime victory over the Washington Redskins. Irvin's two TD grabs, both of which came in the final four minutes of regulation, enabled the Cowboys to overcome a 35–14 deficit heading into the fourth quarter. Dallas eventually won the contest less than five minutes into the overtime session, when Troy Aikman and Rocket Ismail collaborated on a 76-yard TD catch-and-run.

Known for his ability to excel in big games, Irvin performed extremely well during the Cowboys' 52–17 rout of Buffalo in Super Bowl XXVII, making six receptions for 114 yards and two touchdowns, with his TD grabs coming just 18 seconds apart in the second quarter, making them the fastest pair of touchdowns ever scored by one player in Super Bowl history.

Irvin turned in one of his many outstanding efforts against the Packers in the opening round of the 1993 postseason tournament, helping the Cowboys record a 27–17 victory over Green Bay by making nine receptions for 126 yards and one touchdown.

Although the Cowboys ended up losing the 1994 NFC championship game to the San Francisco 49ers 38–28, Irvin had one of the most productive offensive games in NFL playoff history, making 12 receptions for 192 yards and two touchdowns.

NOTABLE ACHIEVEMENTS

- Surpassed 70 receptions seven times, topping 90 catches twice and 100 catches once (111 in 1995).
- Surpassed 1,000 receiving yards seven times, topping 1,500 yards twice.

- Made at least eight touchdown receptions three times, catching 10 TD passes in 1995.
- Averaged more than 20 yards per reception twice.
- Led NFL with 1,523 receiving yards in 1991.
- Finished second in NFL in pass receptions once and receiving yards twice.
- Led Cowboys in pass receptions and receiving yards eight straight seasons (1991–1998).
- Holds Cowboys single-season records for most pass receptions (111 in 1995) and most pass receiving yards (1,603 in 1995).
- Holds Cowboys career records for most receiving yards (11,904) and 100-yard receiving games (47).
- Ranks among Cowboys career leaders in: pass receptions (2nd); touchdown receptions (3rd); touchdowns scored (5th); and points scored (7th).
- Ranks third in NFL history in career postseason receptions (87).
- Ranks second in NFL history in career postseason receiving yards (1,315).
- Three-time NFC champion (1992, 1993, and 1995).
- Three-time Super Bowl champion (XXVII, XXVIII, and XXX).
- Four-time NFC Offensive Player of the Week.
- Five-time Pro Bowl selection (1991, 1992, 1993, 1994, and 1995).
- 1991 First-Team All-Pro selection.
- Two-time Second-Team All-Pro selection (1992 and 1993).
- 1991 First-Team All-NFC selection.
- NFL 1990s All-Decade Team.
- Pro Football Hall of Fame All-1990s Second Team.
- Pro Football Reference All-1990s First Team.
- Named to Cowboys' 50th Anniversary Team in 2009.
- Inducted into Cowboys Ring of Honor in 2005.
- Elected to Pro Football Hall of Fame in 2007.

6

LARRY ALLEN

The greatest offensive lineman in Cowboys history, Larry Allen is also generally considered to be one of the handful of greatest guards ever to play the game. Excelling as both a run-blocker and pass-protector, Allen used his great physical strength and massive 6'3", 325-pound frame to manhandle his opponent, creating gaping holes in the running game for backs such as Emmitt Smith, Julius Jones, and Marion Barber, while also providing ample protection for quarterbacks Troy Aikman, Quincy Carter, Vinny Testaverde, and Drew Bledsoe. Although primarily a guard, Allen also spent a significant amount of time at each tackle position during his 12 seasons with the Cowboys, dominating his opponent to such an extent wherever he played that he earned seven All-Pro nominations and 10 Pro Bowl selections as a member of the team, with the second figure representing a franchise record for offensive players. And, following the conclusion of his playing career, Allen received the additional honors of being inducted into the Cowboys Ring of Honor and being elected to the Pro Football Hall of Fame.

Born in Los Angeles, California, on November 27, 1971, Larry Christopher Allen lived through a troubling childhood while growing up on the mean streets of Compton. After nearly losing his life at only six weeks of age after contracting meningitis, Allen suffered multiple stab wounds at the hands of a teenage neighbor while trying to protect his brother at the age of 11. In discussing the latter ordeal, Allen revealed, "This guy was messing with my brother and I was trying to protect him. I confronted him and we started fighting. His mother actually gave him the knife. After he stabbed me, my mother made me fight him for three straight days until I won. Yes, I lost the first two days. But I come home from school and she is waiting on the corner, saying 'let's go.' She took me to him."

Surrounded by turf wars and drive-by shootings in his gang-infested neighborhood, Allen claimed that only the local drug-dealers went mostly unscathed, stating, "The drug dealers had all the nice cars. They had everything. They had all the jewelry. . . . Everybody looked up to them. That's

Larry Allen starred at both guard and tackle over the course of his 12 seasons in Dallas.
Courtesy of MainlineAutographs.com

who I looked up to and wanted to be like until I found this football. Before that, I was just running around in the streets."

Steered away from gang violence by his strong-willed mother, who raised him and his younger brother alone after their father left, Allen credited his mom with guiding him in the right direction, recalling, "She found out I wanted to join a gang and was messing around with gangbangers, so she said, 'We are going to see how tough you are.' We had two high schools in Compton—Compton High and Centennial. All the Crips went to Compton and all the Bloods went to Centennial. She sent me to the Blood school. But I lived in the Crip neighborhood. She nipped that in the bud real quick."

Living a nomadic existence as a teenager, Allen attended five middle schools and four different high schools, spending his freshman year at Centennial High School in Compton, where he lettered in football, before splitting the next three years between Tokay High School in Lodi, Edison High School in Stockton, and, finally, Vintage High School in Napa.

After Allen started 48 straight games for them at left guard from 2003 to 2005, the Cowboys decided to release him due to salary cap reasons on March 21, 2006. Upon making the announcement, team owner Jerry Jones stated, "Larry has been the best in pro football for a long time. His ability and performance set a standard for excellence at his position in the NFL for many years, and we are grateful for his contributions to the Dallas Cowboys."

Signed by the San Francisco 49ers three days later, Allen spent the next two years in San Francisco, earning the last of his 11 Pro Bowl selections in 2006, before signing a one-day contract with the Cowboys prior to the start of the 2008 campaign, thereby allowing him to retire as a member of the organization that first drafted him. Voted into the Pro Football Hall of Fame on February 2, 2013, Allen further distinguished himself by being named to the NFL's All-Decade Team for both the 1990s and 2000s.

COWBOYS CAREER HIGHLIGHTS

Best Season

Although Allen's lack of a reputation prevented him from receiving First-Team All-Pro recognition his second year in the league, he performed brilliantly in 1995, earning his first trip to the Pro Bowl by helping Emmitt Smith gain a franchise record 1,773 yards on the ground from his right guard position. Allen also contributed significantly to the Dallas passing game by serving as part of an offensive line that allowed only 18 sacks, which represents the lowest total in franchise history. Allen had another tremendous year in 2001, when, as the team's left guard, he played a key role in the Cowboys finishing third in the league with 2,184 yards rushing. Nevertheless, Allen made his greatest overall impact in 1998, when, starting at left tackle for the entire year, he helped protect Troy Aikman's blind side, contributing to a unit that allowed an NFL-low 19 sacks. Allen's superb blocking also helped Emmitt Smith amass 1,332 rushing yards, earning him consensus First-Team All-Pro honors for one of six straight times.

Memorable Moments / Greatest Performances

After being pressed into action on October 2, 1994, when left tackle Mark Tuinei found himself unable to take the field due to back spasms,

Allen performed extremely well in his first pro start, receiving the game ball for helping to keep the Redskins sackless during a 34–7 victory over Washington.

Allen's teammates presented him with another game ball later that year following a 24–16 win over the New Orleans Saints on December 19. In addition to blocking brilliantly throughout the contest, the 325-pound Allen provided the game's highlight by running down linebacker Darion Conner from behind on an interception return early in the game.

Allen turned in a dominant performance from his right tackle position in his first playoff start, receiving another game ball after helping the Cowboys compile 457 yards of total offense during a lopsided 35–9 victory over the Green Bay Packers in the opening round of the 1994 postseason tournament.

Allen and the rest of the Dallas offensive line turned in a similarly dominant effort against Arizona in the 1995 regular-season finale, helping the Cowboys record 474 yards of total offense during a 37–13 win over the Cardinals.

Playing magnificently throughout the 1998 campaign, Allen performed particularly well during the month of November, when, despite facing four of the NFC's top defensive ends in Hugh Douglas, Chad Bratzke, Simeon Rice, and John Randle, he limited the men he lined up against to no sacks and just a handful of tackles, with Douglas, Rice, and Randle all making just one stop.

Allen continued to excel after he moved to left guard the following year, helping to pave the way for 541 yards of total offense during a 41–35 overtime victory over Washington in the 1999 regular-season opener.

Allen also performed exceptionally well against Warren Sapp and the Tampa Bay Buccaneers in the opening game of the 2001 campaign, limiting the All-Pro defensive tackle to one tackle and no sacks during a 10–6 loss to the Bucs.

NOTABLE ACHIEVEMENTS

- Four-time NFC East champion.
- 1995 NFC champion.
- Super Bowl XXX champion.
- Member of 1994 NFL All-Rookie Team.
- Ten-time Pro Bowl selection (1995–2001 and 2003–2005).

- Six-time First-Team All-Pro selection (1996, 1997, 1998, 1999, 2000, and 2001).
- 1995 Second-Team All-Pro selection.
- Six-time First-Team All-NFC selection (1996, 1997, 1998, 1999, 2000, and 2001).
- 1995 Second-Team All-NFC selection.
- NFL 1990s All-Decade Team.
- NFL 2000s All-Decade Team.
- Pro Football Hall of Fame All-1990s Second Team.
- Pro Football Hall of Fame All-2000s Second Team.
- Named to Cowboys' 50th Anniversary Team in 2009.
- Inducted into Cowboys Ring of Honor in 2011.
- Elected to Pro Football Hall of Fame in 2013.

7

MEL RENFRO

One of the greatest athletes to ever don a Cowboys uniform, Mel Renfro spent 14 years in Dallas, earning All-Pro honors on multiple occasions as both a safety and cornerback during that time. The Cowboys' all-time leader in interceptions and interception-return yardage, Renfro spent his first six seasons starring at free safety, before moving to cornerback, where he continued to perform at a Pro Bowl level. Excelling on special teams as well, Renfro returned one punt and two kickoffs for touchdowns during his career, en route to also establishing franchise records for highest career and single-season kickoff-return average. Renfro's exceptional all-around play, which helped Dallas win nine division titles, four NFC championships, and two Super Bowls, earned him 10 straight trips to the Pro Bowl, six All-Pro selections, seven All-Conference nominations, and eventual induction into the Cowboys Ring of Honor and the Pro Football Hall of Fame.

Born in Houston, Texas, on December 30, 1941, Melvin Lacy Renfro spent much of his youth in Portland, Oregon, where he starred in football and track while attending Jefferson High School. Named *Track and Field News* High School Athlete of the Year as a senior in 1960 after setting Oregon junior AAU championship records in the broad jump, 120-yard high hurdles, and 180-yard low hurdles, Renfro also excelled on the football field, playing cornerback on defense, while splitting his time on offense between halfback and quarterback.

Continuing to star in multiple sports after enrolling at the University of Oregon, Renfro remained a force to be reckoned with in track and field, although his exploits on the football field gained him far more notoriety. Playing halfback on offense and defensive back on defense, the speedy Renfro earned All–Pacific Coast Conference recognition three times and All-America honors twice, ending his college career with 1,540 yards rushing and 23 touchdowns.

Mel Renfro earned All-Pro honors on multiple occasions as both a safety and a cornerback during his time in Dallas.
Courtesy of Steve Liskey, Retrocards.net

Subsequently selected by the Oakland Raiders in the 10th round of the 1964 AFL Draft, Renfro instead chose to sign with the Cowboys, who selected him in the second round of that year's NFL Draft, with the 17th overall pick. In truth, Renfro's name would have come off the board much earlier had he not suffered a wrist injury some weeks earlier that caused his draft stock to drop considerably. But, after having a doctor examine his wrist, the Cowboys elected to take a chance on Renfro, with team president and general manager Tex Schramm recalling years later, "Renfro was by far the best player in the draft."

Even though Renfro made a name for himself in college primarily as a running back, Tom Landry's desire to build a dominating defense prompted him to move the team's second-round draft pick to safety shortly after he arrived at his first training camp. Adapting extremely well to his new position, as a rookie Renfro went on to earn Second-Team All-NFL honors and the first of his 10 consecutive Pro Bowl selections by ranking among the league leaders with seven interceptions and 110 interception-return yards, recovering two fumbles, scoring one touchdown on defense and another on special teams, and topping the circuit in both punt-return and kickoff-return yardage. Renfro followed that up with an exceptional 1965 campaign in which he earned First-Team All–Eastern Conference honors and his second straight Second-Team All-NFL selection by picking off two passes, one of which he returned 90 yards for a touchdown, recovering two fumbles, and averaging a franchise-best 30 yards per kickoff return.

Renfro continued to perform at an elite level in each of the next four seasons, recording a total of 22 interceptions, en route to earning four more Pro Bowl nominations, another Second-Team All-NFL selection, and his lone First-Team All-Pro nomination in 1969, when he recorded a career-high and league-leading 10 interceptions, prompting Tom Landry, who usually withheld praise from his players, to pronounce him "the best in the league at free safety."

Yet, in spite of the success Renfro experienced at safety, the Cowboys elected to move him to right cornerback in 1970—a position he ended up manning his final eight years in the league. During that time, Renfro established himself as one of the NFL's best cover corners, using his speed, athleticism, and intelligence to shut down many of the league's top wide receivers. In discussing the technique he used to blanket opposing wideouts, Renfro explained:

> I got out there and got comfortable to the point where you know receivers, the game, and what's happening; you can function well. I studied my opponents and their mannerisms, and I had a great backpedal. I kept receivers in front of me without turning my shoulders. . . . I would look at the guard's, the back's, or the quarterback's body, and I'd break it down in my head what was going to happen. At a certain point, he could only do so many different things, and I'd be ready for it. . . . My whole game was beating the man in front of me. It was a matter of studying the opponent as well as you can and knowing the tendencies. You had to have the speed, agility, and quickness to get the job done.

The fact that Renfro recorded fewer interceptions as a cornerback than he did as a safety can be attributed primarily to the reluctance of opposing quarterbacks to throw in his direction. Charlie Waters, who spent his first eight years in the league playing alongside Renfro in the Dallas secondary, said of his longtime teammate, "He had phenomenal feet. I've never seen anybody with feet as smooth and fluid, with that change of direction. I hate to use the word 'beautiful,' but he was graceful. I never saw him fall, rarely stumble, he was just so graceful."

Renfro's physical gifts, which once caused Tom Landry to suggest that he had the ability to play any skill position on the field at a Pro Bowl level, enabled him to earn four more Pro Bowl selections, two more All-Pro nominations, and All-NFC honors four times as a cornerback, helping the Cowboys win five division titles, four conference championships, and two Super Bowls in the process. And, even after his speed began to desert him during the latter stages of his career, Renfro relied on guile to remain a key contributor to the Dallas defense.

After spending the previous seven seasons starting at right cornerback for the Cowboys, Renfro found himself reduced to a backup role in 1977, prompting him to announce his retirement following the conclusion of the campaign. He ended his career with 52 interceptions, 626 interception-return yards, 3,249 all-purpose yards, three defensive touchdowns, and three touchdowns on special teams, with his totals in each of the first two categories representing franchise records. Meanwhile, Renfro's 10 Pro Bowl appearances rank second only to Bob Lilly's 11 in team annals, earning him induction into the Cowboys Ring of Honor in 1981, 15 years before the Pro Football Hall of Fame opened its doors to him.

Unfortunately, Renfro initially experienced very little success off the field once his playing career ended, eventually being forced to file for bankruptcy after spending two years serving as a defensive backs coach for two different teams at the professional level and losing a considerable amount of money on failed business ventures. In discussing the difficulties he faced in retirement, Renfro revealed, "During my era, we didn't have the large amounts of money that players could fall back on or rely on to survive. I was totally unprepared. I struggled with what to do with my life."

However, after doing a considerable amount of soul-searching, Renfro turned things around, with much of his motivation coming from his late brother, who he remembered as a great athlete who made many bad decisions during his life. Reflecting back on the personal transformation he underwent at the time, Renfro said, "Something was missing. I prayed a lot, and I guess God told me to give back to the community. . . . My brother got

Seen here breaking up a pass intended for Hall of Fame wide receiver Paul Warfield, Mel Renfro recorded more career interceptions (52) than any other player in Cowboys history.
Courtesy of SportsMemorabilia.com

lost in the shuffle, fell through the cracks, and passed away at a young age. Instead of people helping him, they turned their backs on him. I decided to get involved."

Making it his goal to help children, Renfro established the Mel Renfro Bridge Foundation in 1996. The foundation, which works in conjunction with a church in Portland, Oregon, mixes religion, mentoring, counseling, athletics, and the arts to provide assistance to at-risk kids. It also offers substance abuse help. Renfro, who is cancer-free after undergoing prostate cancer surgery in 2002, currently works as a motivational speaker as well.

CAREER HIGHLIGHTS

Best Season

Renfro had a tremendous year for the Cowboys in 1969, earning his lone First-Team All-Pro nomination by leading the NFL with a career-high 10 interceptions, while also finishing fourth in the league with 118 interception-return yards. However, he made his greatest overall impact as a rookie in 1964, earning Second-Team All-Pro and Pro Bowl honors by ranking among the league leaders with seven interceptions, 110 interception-return yards, 1,435 all-purpose yards, and averages of 25.4 yards per kickoff return and 13.1 yards per punt return, while also scoring two touchdowns (one on defense, and the other on a punt return) and topping the circuit with 418 punt-return yards and 1,017 kickoff return yards.

Memorable Moments / Greatest Performances

Renfro made the first interception of his career a memorable one, picking off a George Izo pass early in the fourth quarter and returning it 39 yards for what proved to be the winning score in a 24–18 victory over the Washington Redskins on September 20, 1964.

Renfro recorded the first multiple-interception game of his career later that year, picking off Chicago quarterback Billy Wade twice during a 24–10 victory over the Bears on November 1, 1964.

Although the Cowboys lost their November 22, 1964, rematch with the Redskins 28–16, Renfro turned in a tremendous all-around effort, intercepting a pass and amassing a total of 210 yards on special teams (168 yards on four kickoff returns and 42 yards on three punt returns).

However, Renfro topped that performance the following week, when, during a 45–21 loss to the Packers, he accumulated a franchise-record 273 return yards, collecting a big chunk of that yardage on a 69-yard TD punt return in the second quarter.

Although the St. Louis Cardinals defeated the Cowboys 20–13 on October 4, 1965, Renfro gave Dallas its only touchdown of the game when he picked off a Charley Johnson pass in the second quarter and returned it 90 yards for the longest such return of his career.

Renfro recorded another spectacular touchdown a little over one month later, on November 7, 1965, when he gave the Cowboys an early 7–0 lead over the 49ers by returning the game's opening kickoff 100 yards. Dallas went on to win the contest by a score of 39–31.

Renfro scored his final touchdown on special teams on October 30, 1966, when he returned the second-half kickoff 87 yards during a 52–21 mauling of the Pittsburgh Steelers.

En route to amassing a league-leading 10 interceptions in 1969, Renfro picked off two passes in one game twice, accomplishing the feat for the first time during a 41–28 win over Washington on November 16, before turning the trick again during a 27–10 victory over the Baltimore Colts on December 13.

Renfro had a tremendous 1970 postseason for the Cowboys, recording an interception in each of their three playoff games. After sealing the Cowboys' 5–0 victory over Detroit in the opening round by picking off a Bill Munson pass during the latter stages of the contest, Renfro helped preserve their 10–3 third-quarter lead over the 49ers in the NFC championship game by picking off a John Brodie pass deep in Cowboys territory and returning the ball 19 yards, to the Dallas 38. The Cowboys subsequently drove the ball down the field and scored what proved to be the game-winning TD of a 17–10 victory over the 49ers. Renfro followed that up by squelching a Baltimore scoring threat in Super Bowl V, intercepting a second-quarter Johnny Unitas pass at the Dallas 15 yard line.

Renfro continued his outstanding play in that year's Pro Bowl, earning co-MVP honors by putting on display for all to see his exceptional athletic ability. In addition to doing an excellent job of blanketing AFC receivers from his cornerback position, Renfro returned two punts for touchdowns, leading the NFC to a 27–6 win in the process.

Renfro scored the last of his six regular-season touchdowns on October 14, 1973, when he intercepted a John Hadl pass and ran it back 30 yards for a TD during a 37–31 loss to the Los Angeles Rams.

Renfro recorded the final interception of his Hall of Fame career during a 24–14 victory over the Eagles on December 4, 1977, picking off a Ron Jaworski pass and returning it 25 yards.

NOTABLE ACHIEVEMENTS

- Led NFL with 10 interceptions in 1969.
- Recorded seven interceptions two other times (1964 and 1967).
- Accumulated more than 100 interception-return yards twice (1964 and 1969).
- Returned three interceptions for touchdowns during career.

- Led NFL in: punt returns (32); punt-return yardage (418); kickoff returns (40); kickoff-return yardage (1,017); and total punt and kick-off-return yardage (1,435) in 1964.
- Finished second in NFL with punt-return average of 13.1 yards in 1964.
- Finished third in NFL with kickoff-return average of 30 yards in 1965.
- Returned one punt and two kickoffs for touchdowns during career.
- Led Cowboys in interceptions three times.
- Holds Cowboys single-season record for highest kickoff-return average (30 yards per return in 1965).
- Holds Cowboys career records for: most interceptions (52); most interception-return yards (626); most kickoff-return touchdowns (2); and highest kickoff-return average (26.4 yards per return).
- Ranks among Cowboys career leaders in interception-return touch-downs (tied-2nd) and seasons played (tied-4th).
- Two-time NFL Eastern Conference champion (1966 and 1967).
- Four-time NFC champion (1970, 1971, 1975, and 1977).
- Two-time Super Bowl champion (VI and XII).
- 1970 Pro Bowl Co-MVP.
- 10-time Pro Bowl selection (1964–1973).
- 1969 First-Team All-Pro selection.
- Five-time Second-Team All-Pro selection (1964, 1965, 1966, 1972, and 1973).
- Three-time First-Team All-Eastern Conference selection (1965, 1967 and 1968).
- Three-time First-Team All-NFC selection (1970, 1971, and 1973).
- 1972 Second-Team All-NFC selection.
- Named to Cowboys' 25th Anniversary Team in 1984.
- Named to Cowboys' 50th Anniversary Team in 2009.
- Inducted into Cowboys Ring of Honor in 1981.
- Elected to Pro Football Hall of Fame in 1996.

8

TROY AIKMAN

The third and final member of the brilliant trio of players otherwise known as "The Triplets" that helped create a dynasty in Dallas during the 1990s, Troy Aikman joined Emmitt Smith and Michael Irvin in leading the Cowboys to six division titles, three NFC championships, and three Super Bowl victories. Establishing himself as one of the league's top signal-callers over the course of his 12 seasons in Dallas, Aikman compiled a total of 90 victories as starting quarterback of the Cowboys during the 1990s, giving him the third most wins of any QB in NFL history in any single decade. An outstanding leader with an extremely accurate arm, Aikman passed for more than 3,000 yards five times and completed more than 60 percent of his passes six times, finishing either first or second in the league in the last category on five separate occasions en route to earning six Pro Bowl nominations. The Cowboys' all-time leader in pass completions, Aikman also ranks second in franchise history in passing yardage, touchdown passes, and completion percentage, with his excellent play earning him the number 95 spot on the *Sporting News*'s 1999 list of the 100 Greatest Players in NFL History and eventual induction into both the Cowboys Ring of Honor and the Pro Football Hall of Fame.

Born in West Covina, California, on November 21, 1966, Troy Kenneth Aikman spent his formative years growing up in Cerritos, California, before moving with his family at the age of 12 to Henryetta, Oklahoma. After earning All-State honors in both baseball and football at Henryetta High School, Aikman received a contract offer from the New York Mets. However, with football being his first love, he instead chose to attend the University of Oklahoma, where he spent the next two years playing under head coach Barry Switzer, before transferring to UCLA after a broken ankle caused him to lose his starting job to Jamelle Holieway, who subsequently led the Sooners to the 1985 National Championship. Forced to sit out one year due to college transfer rules, Aikman did not play at all in 1986. But, after returning to the field the following year, he went on to lead the Bruins

Troy Aikman completed more passes over the course of his career than any
other quarterback in Cowboys history.
Courtesy of MearsOnlineAuctions.com

to a composite record of 20-4 over the course of the next two seasons, earning Pac-10 Offensive Player of the Year honors as a junior, before winning
the 1988 Davey O'Brien Award as the nation's top quarterback and being
named a consensus All-American and UPI West Coast Player of the Year
as a senior.

Aikman's exceptional play at the collegiate level, strong arm, and impressive 6'4", 219-pound frame prompted the Cowboys, who finished with an NFL-worst 3-13 record the previous year, to select him with the first overall pick of the 1989 NFL Draft. Surrounded by very little talent his first season in Dallas, Aikman struggled as a rookie, completing just under 53 percent of his passes for 1,749 yards, while throwing nine touchdowns and 18 interceptions for a Cowboys team that finished the season with a record of 1-15 under first-year head coach Jimmy Johnson.

Both Aikman and the Cowboys made significant strides following the arrival of Emmitt Smith in 1990, with Dallas compiling a record of 7-9 and Aikman completing 56.6 percent of his passes for 2,579 yards, although he threw only 11 touchdown passes and 18 interceptions. Aikman truly began to come into his own the following year, with his performance being aided immeasurably by the simultaneous maturation of Michael Irvin into one of the league's premier wide receivers. Completing 65.3 percent of his passes for 2,754 yards and 11 touchdowns despite missing four games due to injury, Aikman led the Cowboys to a record of 11-5 that earned them their first playoff berth in six years. Ranking among the league leaders in both completion percentage and passer rating (86.7), Aikman earned Pro Bowl honors for the first time in his career. He followed that up with five more Pro Bowl nominations in succession, clearly establishing himself during that time as one of the NFL's top quarterbacks. Here are the numbers he posted over the course of the next five seasons:

SEASON	YARDS PASSING	TD PASSES	INTS	COMP. PCT.	QBR
1992	3,445	23	14	63.8	89.5
1993	3,100	15	6	**69.1**	99.0
1994	2,676	13	12	64.5	84.9
1995	3,304	16	7	64.8	93.6
1996	3,126	12	13	63.7	80.1

While those numbers might seem modest by today's standards, it must be considered that Aikman compiled them during the 1990s while playing under the restraints of the Cowboys' run-oriented offense. In addition to leading all NFL quarterbacks with a career-high 69.1 completion percentage in 1993, Aikman finished second in the league in that category in each of the next three seasons. He also placed near the top of the league rankings in passing yardage once, touchdown passes once, and quarterback rating four times during the period. Meanwhile, the Cowboys captured the NFC East title all five years, advancing to the NFC championship game four times, and winning the Super Bowl at the end of the 1992, 1993, and 1995 seasons. Aikman displayed his passing accuracy during the 1992 playoffs, breaking Joe Montana's postseason record of 83 passes without an interception by completing 89 consecutive passes without throwing a pick. He also earned Super Bowl XXVII MVP honors by completing 22 of 30 passes for 273 yards and four touchdowns during the Cowboys' lopsided 52–17 victory over the Buffalo Bills.

Yet, in spite of the superb job Aikman did of directing the Dallas offense during that time, he never made All-Pro, earning just a pair of Second-Team All-NFC nominations over the course of his career. Certainly, competing against the likes of Steve Young, Brett Favre, Dan Marino, Jim Kelly, and John Elway for postseason honors had something to do with the lack of recognition he received. But Aikman presented another theory, suggesting, "If I had played in an offense that threw the ball like the offense Dan Marino, Steve Young, or Brett Favre played in—not taking anything away from the things those guys have done—they were all great players; There are those who don't put me in that same category because that's not the system that I played in. I don't think people ever truly got to see the ability that I had as a passer."

Aikman added, "I had an ability to throw the pass pretty much where I wanted. I was always very accurate. I took a great deal of pride in my ability to stay in the pocket and get hit, and deliver the football."

But Drew Brees, who grew up rooting for the Cowboys, admired Aikman more for the many intangible qualities he brought to the team, observing, "Troy had, first of all, that fiery, competitive nature; that will to win, that will to work hard and do whatever it takes to succeed; to be able to make sure that he's spreading the ball around and that he's playing within the offense and playing within himself and giving everybody the opportunities, knowing when he's called upon to make the play, and he's going to make that big throw."

Brees continued, "There are going to be those times when maybe they're frustrated, and you just have to manage a lot of those personalities from time to time. It's your leadership ability that makes sure you're getting the best out of those guys."

Although Aikman posted solid numbers once again in 1997, concluding the campaign with 3,283 yards passing, 19 TD passes, and a completion percentage of 56.4, the Cowboys stumbled to a 6-10 record, leaving them out of the playoffs for the first time in seven years. Dallas advanced to

Aikman passed for more than 3,000 yards five times as a member of the Cowboys.
Courtesy of George A. Kitrinos

the postseason tournament in each of the next two seasons, with Aikman performing relatively well, completing close to 60 percent of his passes both years, while totaling 5,294 yards through the air, 29 touchdown passes, and 17 interceptions. But, with Aikman missing more and more games each season as the number of concussions he suffered continued to mount, he lost some of his effectiveness. Aikman found his performance further compromised by persistent back pain he experienced his final year in the league. After suffering his 10th concussion in 2000 following a hit by Washington linebacker LaVar Arrington, Aikman elected to call it quits, announcing his retirement at season's end. He ended his career as the Cowboys' all-time leading passer, having thrown for a total of 32,942 yards. Aikman also threw 165 touchdown passes and 141 interceptions, completed 61.5 percent of his passes, and posted a quarterback rating of 81.6.

Following his retirement, Aikman embarked on a successful career in broadcasting that has seen him spend most of the last two decades serving as a color commentator on the Fox network's NFC telecasts. He also hosts a weekly sports radio show on Sporting News Radio and is a part-owner of the San Diego Padres.

Inducted into the Pro Football Hall of Fame on August 5, 2006, Aikman stated during his acceptance speech that he considered himself to be merely a beneficiary of the Cowboys' system and the outstanding play of teammates such as Emmitt Smith and Michael Irvin. However, former Dallas head coach Jimmy Johnson disagreed, claiming that Aikman's MVP performance against Buffalo in Super Bowl XXVII cemented him as "a championship quarterback; the greatest team player I was ever associated with." Johnson went on to say, "In my mind, I always judge a quarterback by how he plays in the big games. How does he perform in the playoffs? Troy Aikman always came up big in the big games."

Emmitt Smith also praised Aikman upon learning of his former team-mate's Hall of Fame selection, saying, "Troy's leadership and focus are what made us the team we were in the 1990s. I am happy for him because I know that he put in the time and hard work during his career to get to this point."

Meanwhile, fellow Hall of Fame Cowboys quarterback Roger Staubach commented, "I appreciate Troy Aikman because he resurrected the Dallas Cowboys in the 1990s, and he made it fun to watch them again."

CAREER HIGHLIGHTS

Best Season

Aikman compiled arguably the most impressive stat-line of his career in 1992, when he completed 63.8 percent of his passes, posted a passer rating of 89.5, and established career-high marks in passing yardage (3,445) and touchdown passes (23) during the regular season, before directing the Cowboys offense to a total of 116 points in their three playoff victories. However, he performed more efficiently the following season, concluding the 1993 campaign with 3,100 yards passing, 15 touchdown passes, only six interceptions, a league-leading and career-best 69.1 completion percentage, and a 99.0 passer rating that also represented the highest mark of his career. Although the Associated Press failed to accord Aikman "official" All-Pro honors either year, the Dallas quarterback received "unofficial" First-Team All-Pro recognition from the *Sporting News* in the second of those campaigns. All things considered, Aikman had the finest season of his career in 1993.

Memorable Moments / Greatest Performances

Although the Cowboys lost their November 12, 1989, meeting with the Phoenix Cardinals 24–20, Aikman had a huge game, tossing a pair of touchdown passes and setting an NFL rookie record by throwing for 379 yards.

Aikman again excelled in defeat a few weeks later, completing four touchdown passes during a 35–31 loss to the Los Angeles Rams on December 3, 1989.

Aikman turned in another strong performance against the Rams on November 18, 1990, leading the Cowboys to a 24–21 win over Los Angeles by passing for 303 yards and three touchdowns, with one of those being a 61-yard scoring strike to Michael Irvin.

Aikman earned NFC Offensive Player of the Week honors for the first time in his career for his performance against the Giants on September 29, 1991, when he led the Cowboys to a 21–16 victory over New York by completing 20 of 27 passes for 277 yards and one touchdown. Aikman helped wipe out a second-half comeback by the Giants that saw them overcome an 11-point deficit by tossing a 23-yard TD pass to Michael Irvin late in the fourth quarter.

Aikman celebrated Christmas early the following year, leading the Cowboys to a 41–17 pasting of Atlanta on December 21, 1992, by completing 18 of 21 passes for 239 yards and three touchdowns. The Dallas QB hooked up with three different receivers for scores, connecting with Kelvin Martin from 11 yards out, Jay Novacek from 18 yards out, and Alvin Harper from 23 yards out.

After leading the Cowboys to a 30–20 win over San Francisco in the 1992 NFC championship game by passing for 322 yards and two touchdowns, Aikman turned in an epic performance against Buffalo in Super Bowl XXVII, earning game MVP honors by completing 73.3 percent of his passes and throwing for 273 yards and four touchdowns, en route to compiling a passer rating of 140.7.

Aikman continued his outstanding play in 1993, earning NFC Offensive Player of the Week honors for his performance against Green Bay on October 3, when he passed for 317 yards and one touchdown during a 36–14 win over the Packers.

Aikman again received NFC Offensive Player of the Week recognition after leading the Cowboys to a 38–3 trouncing of the Arizona Cardinals on October 9, 1994, by passing for 231 yards and two touchdowns.

Continuing his trend of excelling against Green Bay, Aikman led the Cowboys to a lopsided 35–9 victory over the Packers in their 1994 divisional playoff matchup by completing 23 of 30 passes for 337 yards and two touchdowns, with his 94-yard hookup with Alvin Harper representing the second longest pass completion in NFL postseason history.

Aikman once again outplayed Brett Favre on October 8, 1995, leading the Cowboys to a 34–24 win over the Packers by passing for 316 yards and two touchdowns, with his longest completion of the day being a 48-yard TD pass to Michael Irvin.

Aikman closed out the 1995 regular season in style, throwing for 350 yards and two touchdowns during a 37–13 victory over the Arizona Cardinals on Christmas Day.

Aikman delivered one of the more memorable touchdown passes of his career on October 20, 1996, when he hooked up with Kelvin Martin from 60 yards out with only 1:42 left in the game, to give the Cowboys a 32–28 win over the Atlanta Falcons.

Aikman followed that up with a strong performance against Miami one week later, earning NFC Offensive Player of the Week honors by passing for 363 yards and three touchdowns during a 29–10 victory over the Dolphins.

Aikman turned in his finest effort of the 1997 campaign in the regular-season opener, passing for 295 yards and four touchdowns during a 37–7 win over the Pittsburgh Steelers that earned him NFC Offensive Player of the Week honors for the fifth time in his career.

Although the Cowboys lost their 1998 Thanksgiving Day matchup with the Minnesota Vikings 46–36, Aikman had a huge game, completing 34 of 57 passes for a career-high 455 yards.

The opening game of the 1999 regular season proved to be a memorable one for Aikman and the Cowboys, who overcame a 21-point, fourth-quarter deficit to the arch-rival Washington Redskins to eventually triumph 41–35 in overtime. With Washington holding a 35–14 lead heading into the final period, Aikman led the Cowboys on three scoring drives that tied the score at 35–35 at the end of regulation, connecting with Michael Irvin on a pair of TD passes with less than four minutes remaining on the clock. Aikman then completed the comeback by hitting Rocket Ismail with a 76-yard scoring strike less than five minutes into the overtime session, giving the Cowboys the unlikely victory. Aikman finished the game with 362 yards passing and a career-high five touchdown passes, earning in the process NFC Offensive Player of the Week honors for the sixth and final time in his career.

NOTABLE ACHIEVEMENTS

- Passed for more than 3,000 yards five times.
- Threw more than 20 touchdown passes once (23 in 1992).
- Completed more than 60 percent of his passes six times, topping 65 percent twice.

- Posted touchdown-to-interception ratio of better than 2–1 three times.
- Posted quarterback rating above 90.0 twice, finishing with mark of 99.0 in 1993.
- Rushed for more than 300 yards once (302 in 1989).
- Averaged 7.9 yards per carry in 1989.
- Led NFL quarterbacks in: completion percentage once; interception percentage once; game-winning drives once; and fourth-quarter comebacks twice.
- Finished second in NFL in: pass completions once; passer rating once; completion percentage four times; and interception percentage twice.
- Holds Cowboys career records for most pass completions (2,898) and most pass attempts (4,715).
- Ranks among Cowboys career leaders in: passing yardage (2nd); touchdown passes (2nd); completion percentage (2nd); and quarterback rating (4th).
- Three-time NFC champion (1992, 1993, and 1995).
- Three-time Super Bowl champion (XXVII, XXVIII, and XXX).
- MVP of Super Bowl XXVII.
- 1997 NFL Walter Payton Man of the Year Award winner.
- Six-time NFC Offensive Player of the Week.
- Six-time Pro Bowl selection (1991, 1992, 1993, 1994, 1995, and 1996).
- Two-time Second-Team All-NFC selection (1994 and 1995).
- Number 95 on the *Sporting News*'s 1999 list of 100 Greatest Players in NFL History.
- Inducted into Cowboys Ring of Honor in 2005.
- Elected to Pro Football Hall of Fame in 2006.

9

TONY DORSETT

An explosive runner who had the ability to score from anywhere on the field anytime he touched the ball, Tony Dorsett spent 11 of his 12 NFL seasons in Dallas, establishing himself during that time as arguably the most dynamic offensive player in franchise history. Blessed with blinding speed, Dorsett gained more than 70 yards from scrimmage on one play six times during his career, en route to rushing for more than 1,000 yards eight times and surpassing 1,500 yards from scrimmage in five different seasons. The second-leading rusher in NFL history at the time of his retirement in 1988, Dorsett has since slipped to ninth-place all-time, although he continues to rank second only to Emmitt Smith in team annals in virtually every rushing category. Also a solid pass-receiver, Dorsett made at least 40 receptions in a season four times, placing him among the Cowboys' all-time leaders in that category as well. Dorsett's stellar all-around play helped the Cowboys win five division titles, two NFC championships, and one Super Bowl, earning him in the process four trips to the Pro Bowl, three All-Pro selections, five All-NFC nominations, and a spot on the Cowboys' 25th Anniversary Team. And, following the conclusion of his playing career, Dorsett received the additional honors of being named to the Pro Football Reference All-1980s Team and being inducted into both the Cowboys Ring of Honor and the Pro Football Hall of Fame.

Born in Rochester, Pennsylvania, on April 7, 1954, Anthony Drew Dorsett Sr. grew up in nearby Aliquippa, some 25 miles northwest of Pittsburgh. Starring in football and basketball while attending Hopewell High School, Dorsett earned All-State honors twice on the gridiron by excelling as a running back on offense and as both a cornerback and linebacker on defense. After leading the Vikings to a composite record of 18-2 his final two seasons at Hopewell by rushing for a total of 2,272 yards, Dorsett enrolled at the University of Pittsburgh, where he became the first freshman in 29 years to be named an All-American. Dorsett continued his brilliant play for the Panthers the next three seasons, finishing his college career with

Tony Dorsett retired as the second-leading rusher in NFL history.
Courtesy of George A. Kitrinos

6,082 yards rushing, which established a new NCAA record (later broken by Ricky Williams). Particularly dominant as a senior in 1976, Dorsett won the Heisman Trophy and the Maxwell Award, earned Walter Camp Player of the Year honors, and also received UPI Player of the Year recognition after leading Pittsburgh to the national title by rushing for 2,150 yards, which represented the highest total compiled by any running back in the nation.

Even though some pro scouts expressed the belief that Dorsett's somewhat smallish 5'11", 192-pound frame might lead to durability issues once he entered the NFL, the Cowboys made him their number one priority heading into the 1977 NFL Draft, feeling that he had the ability to rejuvenate their sluggish ground game. Looking back years later at the overall view held toward him at that time, Dorsett said, "A lot of people said I wouldn't last in this league. I was the skinny little kid from Aliquippa, Pennsylvania who wasn't supposed to make it." Feeling confident in Dorsett's ability to remain on the field, the Cowboys completed a draft-day deal with the Seahawks in which they sent their first-round pick (#14 overall) and three second-round picks to Seattle for the second overall pick of the draft, which they subsequently used to select Dorsett.

In spite of the king's ransom the Cowboys paid to acquire Dorsett, the rookie running back began his time in Dallas somewhat ignominiously, seeing very little action the first few weeks of the regular season, as he and Tom Landry clashed over his running style. However, the strictly regimented Landry, who initially designed precise running plays, eventually became convinced that Dorsett represented a different type of running back for whom he needed to alter his coaching philosophy. Instructing his offensive linemen to block and hold their men at the point of attack, Landry gave Dorsett the freedom to use his extraordinary vision and instincts to choose his running lane. Performing magnificently from that point on, Dorsett concluded his first NFL season with 1,007 yards rushing, 29 receptions for another 273 yards, and 13 touchdowns, earning in the process NFL Offensive Rookie of the Year and Second-Team All-NFC honors. In discussing the impact Dorsett made on the Dallas offense his first year in the league, Roger Staubach recalled, "When he came to us, we hadn't had a strong running attack for about three years. . . . Tony Dorsett made a big difference when he came in 1977. Getting Dorsett was a real shot in the arm. This guy was a sensational player. He had speed, he was tough, could run inside. He took a lot of pressure off me. With him, we had a very balanced game."

Dorsett followed up his brilliant rookie campaign by finishing third in the NFL with 1,325 yards rushing, placing second in the league with 1,703 yards from scrimmage, and scoring nine touchdowns in 1978, en route to earning First-Team All-NFC honors and his first trip to the Pro Bowl. Dorsett posted excellent numbers in each of the next two seasons as well, surpassing 1,100 yards rushing and 1,400 yards from scrimmage in both 1979 and 1980, while scoring seven touchdowns in the first of those campaigns and 11 in the second. He then put together the most dominant season of his career in 1981, earning consensus First-Team All-Pro honors by finishing second in the league with 1,646 yards rushing and 1,971 yards from scrimmage.

In discussing his team's most dynamic offensive player, Tom Landry said, "Surprisingly enough, he's a better north-south runner than he is east-west runner. He has great feel and recognition when he heads into the line as an inside runner. But you don't think of him about being an inside runner because he only weighs 190 pounds. But it's his great acceleration and speed that make him what he is today."

Commenting on Dorsett's ability to go the distance anytime he touched the ball, Philadelphia Eagles cornerback Herman Edwards noted, "He can find the open crack and, once he hits that crack, if he has daylight, there's not too many people in pro football that will be able to catch him."

Roger Staubach later marveled at his former teammate's extraordinary all-around ability, stating, "I would have loved to have played more years with Tony Dorsett. I played just three years with him, and he was just a phenomenal football player. Tony had moves, so he made a lot of big plays, but he had exceptional speed. . . . He wasn't just running outside, and running away from people. He was very tough inside. . . . He could do everything."

Staubach added, "I threw an 8-yard pass out to him, and I got credit for a 95-yard touchdown. There's not too many guys that can do that. . . . He was a great football player. The things he did were special."

Dorsett remained one of the NFL's top running backs for another four years, earning two more trips to the Pro Bowl, two more All-Pro selections, and another two All-NFC nominations between 1982 and 1985. After a players' strike shortened the 1982 regular season to just nine games, limiting Dorsett to 745 yards on the ground, he resumed his annual practice of rushing for more than 1,000 yards the following year, earning All-Pro, All-Conference, and Pro Bowl honors for the final time by placing among the league leaders with 1,321 yards rushing and 1,608 yards from scrimmage. He followed that up by surpassing 1,100 yards rushing and 1,600 yards from scrimmage in each of the next two seasons, establishing career-high marks with 51 receptions and 459 receiving yards in 1984, before amassing more than 1,700 yards from scrimmage for the third time in his career the following year.

However, Dorsett's performance began to fall off somewhat after the Cowboys signed star running back Herschel Walker to a five-year, $5 million contract prior to the start of the 1986 campaign. Upset over the size of Walker's deal, troubled by his own reduced role in the Dallas offense, and plagued by ankle and knee injuries that forced him to miss three games, Dorsett rushed for only 748 yards in 1986, failing to reach the 1,000-yard mark for just the second time in his career. With Walker becoming the Cowboys' featured running back the following year, Dorsett started just six games, rushing for only 456 yards and averaging a career-low 3.5 yards per carry. After Dorsett demanded a trade at season's end, the Cowboys dealt him to the Denver Broncos for a conditional fifth-round draft choice on June 2, 1988, bringing to an end his 11-year stay in Dallas. Dorsett left the Cowboys with career totals of 12,036 yards rushing, 72 rushing

Dorsett rushed for more than 1,000 yards eight times.
Courtesy of RMYAuctions.com

touchdowns, 382 receptions, 3,432 receiving yards, 13 receiving touchdowns, 15,468 yards from scrimmage, and an average of 4.4 yards per carry, making him the franchise's all-time leading rusher and second-leading all-time scorer at the time.

Dorsett ended up spending just one season in Denver, rushing for 703 yards as a member of the Broncos in 1988, before announcing his retirement after suffering a knee injury the following summer. While playing for the Broncos, though, he moved into second place on the NFL's all-time rushing list, amassing a total of 12,306 yards on the ground that placed him behind only the great Walter Payton.

Unfortunately, some 25 years after Dorsett left the game, doctors diagnosed him with CTE, a degenerative brain disease linked to head trauma that is characterized by memory loss, aggression, and depression. In discussing how his malady affects his life during a 2015 radio interview, Dorsett revealed:

I got diagnosed with CTE and it's very frustrating at times for me. I've got a good team of people around me, my wife and kids, who work with me. When you've been in this town [Dallas] for so long and I have to go to some place I've been going to for many, many, many years, and then all of a sudden I forget how to get there.

"I signed up for this when, I guess, I started playing football so many years ago. But, obviously, not knowing that the end was going to be like this. But I love the game. The game was good to me. It's just unfortunate that I'm going through what I'm going through. I'm in the fight, man. I'm not just laying around letting this overtake me. I'm fighting. I'm in the battle. I'm hoping we can reverse this thing somehow.

COWBOYS CAREER HIGHLIGHTS

Best Season

Dorsett had a magnificent rookie campaign of 1977, averaging a career-high 4.8 yards per carry, rushing for 1,007 yards, and scoring 13 touchdowns, even though he only started the final few games of the regular season. He also performed brilliantly in 1978, 1983, and 1985, rushing for more than 1,300 yards, scoring at least nine touchdowns, and accumulating more than 1,600 yards from scrimmage each year. Nevertheless, the 1981 season proved to be the greatest of Dorsett's career. In addition to establishing a new franchise record (since broken) by gaining 1,646 yards on the ground, Dorsett scored six touchdowns, amassed a career-best 1,971 yards from scrimmage, and equaled his career-high rushing average of 4.8 yards per carry, earning in the process his lone First-Team All-Pro selection and *Football Digest* NFL Running Back of the Year honors.

Memorable Moments / Greatest Performances

Dorsett scored the first two touchdowns of his career in just his second game, recording TD runs of 11 and 34 yards during a 41–21 victory over the New York Giants on September 25, 1977.

Dorsett rushed for more than 100 yards for the first time two weeks later, when he carried the ball 14 times for 141 yards and two touchdowns during a 30–24 win over the St. Louis Cardinals on October 9, with his

77-yard TD run early in the second quarter proving to be the highlight of the contest.

Dorsett established a new franchise record on December 4, 1977, when he rushed for 206 yards, in leading the Cowboys to a 24–14 victory over the Philadelphia Eagles. Dorsett also scored two touchdowns during the contest, opening the scoring with a 1-yard run in the first quarter, before putting the game away with an 84-yard TD scamper in the final period.

Dorsett helped the Cowboys record a resounding 38–0 victory over the Baltimore Colts in their 1978 regular-season opener by rushing for 147 yards on just 15 carries and collaborating with Roger Staubach on a 91-yard TD catch-and-run. He finished the game with a total of 254 yards from scrimmage.

Dorsett turned in another exceptional effort three weeks later, leading the Cowboys to a 21–12 win over the St. Louis Cardinals on September 24 by carrying the ball 21 times for 154 yards and one touchdown.

Dorsett posted a similarly impressive stat-line against Green Bay later in the year, carrying the ball 23 times for 149 yards and two touchdowns during a 42–14 victory over the Packers on November 12, 1978.

Dorsett followed that up with a strong outing against New Orleans, leading the Cowboys to a convincing 27–7 win over the Saints on November 19 by gaining 152 yards on 25 carries and scoring a touchdown, with his 63-yard run from scrimmage proving to be easily the longest gain of the day for either team.

Dorsett scored three touchdowns in one game for the only time in his career on October 7, 1979, when he accomplished the feat during a 36–20 win over the Minnesota Vikings. Dorsett finished the game with 145 yards on the ground, another 47 yards through the air, and those three TD runs, which came from 5, 3, and 30 yards out.

Although the Cowboys lost their November 9, 1980, matchup with the Giants 38–35, Dorsett had a huge day, carrying the ball 24 times for 183 yards and two touchdowns.

Dorsett helped lead the Cowboys to a 34–13 victory over the Los Angeles Rams in the first round of the 1980 postseason tournament by rushing for 160 yards and scoring a pair of touchdowns, one of which came on a 12-yard run, and the other on a 10-yard pass from Danny White.

Dorsett turned in a number of exceptional performances during his banner year of 1981, with the first of those coming on September 21, when he carried the ball 19 times for 162 yards and one touchdown during a 35–21 win over the New England Patriots. Dorsett scored his TD from

75 yards out, which represented his longest run of the season. Dorsett had another big game against Los Angeles on October 18, rushing for 159 yards and one touchdown during a 29–17 victory over the Rams. In addition to rushing for 117 yards during a 27–17 win over the Buffalo Bills on November 9, Dorsett collaborated with Danny White on a 73-yard TD catch-and-run early in the second half that began a string of 20 unanswered Dallas points. Dorsett also led the Cowboys to a 37–13 victory over the Baltimore Colts on December 6 by rushing for a season-high 175 yards.

Although the Cowboys ended up losing their January 3, 1983, Monday Night Football matchup with the Minnesota Vikings 31–27, Dorsett experienced arguably the most memorable moment of his career early in the fourth quarter, when he took a handoff from Danny White on the Dallas 1 yard line, burst through the middle of the Vikings defense, cut to his right, picked up an escort from Drew Pearson, and tiptoed down the sidelines past two Minnesota defenders, to become the only player in NFL history to ever record a 99-yard touchdown run. In describing the play, Dorsett offered, "I was just thinking about getting out of the backfield. I saw a hole open up and went around my block to the right when I saw Drew Pearson downfield. The key to long runs is downfield blocking."

Dorsett broke off another long run in the 1983 regular-season opener, gaining 77 yards on one play during a 31–30 victory over the Washington Redskins in which the Cowboys overcame a 23–3 halftime deficit to their NFC East rivals. He finished the game with 151 yards on only 14 carries.

Dorsett rushed for more than 100 yards for the final time in his career on November 9, 1986, when he carried the ball 22 times for 101 yards and one touchdown during a 17–13 loss to the Los Angeles Raiders.

NOTABLE ACHIEVEMENTS

- Rushed for more than 1,000 yards eight times, topping 1,500 yards once (1,646 in 1981).
- Surpassed 1,500 yards from scrimmage five times.
- Rushed for more than 10 touchdowns twice.
- Scored at least 10 touchdowns four times.
- Averaged more than 4.5 yards per carry four times.
- Caught more than 40 passes four times, surpassing 50 receptions once (51 in 1984).
- Led NFL with 177 carries in 1982.

- Finished second in NFL in: rushing yardage twice; rushing touchdowns once; touchdowns scored once; and yards from scrimmage twice.
- Finished third in NFL in: rushing yardage once; rushing touchdowns once; yards per rushing attempt once; and all-purpose yards once.
- Led Cowboys in rushing yardage 10 times.
- Ranks among Cowboys career leaders in: rushing yardage (2nd); total yardage (2nd); rushing touchdowns (2nd); rushing average (3rd—minimum 500 attempts); rushing attempts (2nd); touchdowns scored (2nd); points scored (4th); and pass receptions (7th).
- Ranks ninth in NFL history in rushing yardage (12,739).
- Ranks 11th in NFL history in yards from scrimmage (16,293).
- Holds NFL record for longest touchdown run (99 yards vs. Minnesota on 1/3/83).
- Two-time NFC champion (1977 and 1978).
- Super Bowl XII champion.
- 1977 Associated Press NFL Offensive Rookie of the Year.
- 1981 *Football Digest* NFL Running Back of the Year.
- 1985 Week 6 NFC Offensive Player of the Week.
- Four-time Pro Bowl selection (1978, 1981, 1982, and 1983).
- 1981 First-Team All-Pro selection.
- Two-time Second-Team All-Pro selection (1982 and 1983).
- Three-time First-Team All-NFC selection (1978, 1981, and 1982).
- Two-time Second-Team All-NFC selection (1977 and 1983).
- Pro Football Reference All-1980s Second Team.
- Named to Cowboys' 25th Anniversary Team in 1984.
- Number 53 on the *Sporting News*'s 1999 list of 100 Greatest Players in NFL History.
- Inducted into Cowboys Ring of Honor in 1994.
- Elected to Pro Football Hall of Fame in 1994.

10

JASON WITTEN

One of the greatest tight ends in NFL history, Jason Witten has served as the cornerstone of the Cowboys' offense for the past 14 seasons. The holder of numerous franchise records, including most career receptions, most receptions in a single game, and most consecutive games played, Witten has surpassed 90 receptions and 1,000 receiving yards four times each during his time in Dallas, en route to making more catches and amassing more receiving yards than anyone else ever to play his position, with the exception of Tony Gonzalez. More than just an outstanding receiver, Witten is a throwback of sorts, taking as much pride in his blocking ability as he does in his pass-receiving skills. A consummate pro and a true iron man who has missed just one game his entire career, Witten has brought a sense of stability to the Cowboys that has helped them capture four division titles, with his many contributions to the team earning him 10 Pro Bowl selections, four All-Pro nominations, and an eventual place in the Pro Football Hall of Fame.

Born in Elizabethton, Tennessee, on May 6, 1982, Christopher Jason Witten spent his early years living in Washington, DC, before moving back to his place of birth at the age of 11 to live with his grandparents after his alcoholic father became abusive toward his mother and two older brothers a few years earlier. An outstanding two-way player at Elizabethton High School, Witten excelled as a tight end on offense and a linebacker on defense, helping his team advance to the state semifinals three straight times. Particularly effective on the defensive side of the ball as a senior, Witten recorded 163 tackles, nine sacks, two interceptions, five forced fumbles, and three fumble recoveries, earning in the process numerous accolades, including All-America and All-State honors and recognition as *USA Today* Player of the Year for the state of Tennessee. Doing a solid job on offense as well, Witten made 26 receptions and scored 14 touchdowns. An outstanding all-around athlete, Witten also starred on the basketball court, averaging 15 points and 12 rebounds per game in his senior year.

Jason Witten's 110 receptions in 2012 established a single-season NFL record for tight ends.
Courtesy of Keith Allison

After accepting a scholarship offer from the University of Tennessee, Witten began his college career as a backup defensive end, before moving to tight end due to a number of injuries at that position. He subsequently spent most of the next two seasons learning the position and serving primarily as a blocker, before having a breakout year as a junior, when he made 39 receptions, amassed 493 receiving yards, and scored five touchdowns, en route to earning All-SEC and Academic All-SEC honors.

Electing to forgo his final year of college eligibility, Witten entered the 2003 NFL Draft, where the Cowboys selected him in the third round, with the 69th overall pick. Sharing playing time with fellow tight end Dan Campbell as a rookie, Witten started only seven games his first year in the league. Nevertheless, he contributed to the Dallas cause by making 35 receptions for 347 yards and one touchdown. Missing the only game of his career that year, Witten sat out the Cowboys' Week 6 meeting with Philadelphia after breaking his jaw on a hit by Arizona's Ronald McKinnon and Ray Thompson one week earlier. However, after undergoing surgery to have three plates inserted to assist the healing process, Witten displayed his toughness by returning to action the following week, remaining on the field the rest of the year.

Laying claim to the starting job the following season, Witten had a breakout year, earning First-Team All-NFC honors and the first of his 10 Pro Bowl selections by making 87 receptions for 980 yards and six touchdowns. He returned to the Pro Bowl in each of the next two seasons as well, totaling 130 receptions, 1,511 receiving yards, and seven touchdowns from 2005 to 2006. Witten's outstanding play prompted former Cowboys tight end Billy Joe DuPree to suggest that he had already established himself as the best player ever to man the position for the team, with the former All-Pro stating during an interview prior to the start of the 2007 campaign, "Jason has a combination of Doug Cosbie, Billy Joe DuPree and Jay Novacek put together. Each one of those guys had specific talents. He's a lot larger than Jay, bulk-wise. Maybe a little better blocker than Jay. He also has quick feet and most people, defenders, don't really understand he may be a little quicker and faster than what they anticipate. Jason Witten is the best tight end who's played here."

Giving credence to DuPree's claim, Witten subsequently embarked on an extraordinary six-year run during which he posted the following numbers:

SEASON	RECEPTIONS	YARDS	TOUCHDOWNS
2007	96	1,145	7
2008	81	952	4
2009	94	1,030	2
2010	94	1,002	9
2011	79	942	5
2012	110	1,039	3

In addition to earning five more trips to the Pro Bowl during that time, Witten made First-Team All-Pro twice and Second-Team All-Pro another two times. By accumulating more than 1,000 receiving yards on four separate occasions, Witten became the first tight end in franchise history to reach that magical mark even once. Meanwhile, his 110 receptions in 2012 established a single-season NFL record for tight ends. Witten also continued to display his ability to play in pain during that time, making those 110 catches in 2012 after suffering a lacerated spleen in the preseason opener that doctors initially expected to keep him out of action for the first several weeks of the regular season.

An old-school type player, the 6'5", 257-pound Witten takes great pride in excelling in all facets of the game, describing his on-field mentality thusly:

> Just to be a complete pro. And what I mean by that is, I really believe in you prepare yourself throughout offseason, throughout training camp; you gotta lay out expectations for yourself. Nobody more critical on yourself than you can be as an individual. And then, when the game comes, you gotta go own it. If it's a block at the point of attack, that's what I want to do. I don't want 'em to bring another tackle in, I want to be the guy that can do that. If it's catching a 10-yarder for a hook route for a first down on third-and-10, that's what I want to do. I think just doing your job, doing it with integrity and consistency that guys should know like, "Hey, that's how you do it." And I hope that doing it that way, and doing it the right way, is the way I want to be remembered on the field.

The completeness of Witten's game prompted former teammate Darren Woodson to identify him as the finest all-around tight end in NFL history, with Woodson commenting:

> You cannot tell me there's a better tight end to ever play the game. I look at Tony Gonzalez. He wouldn't block a soul. A soul. Great, dynamic in the passing game, runs great routes, but won't block a soul. Antonio Gates, turn the film on of him. He won't touch a soul. You already know Jimmy Graham won't block anybody. This guy [Witten], not only is he a great pass catcher, but he'll do everything. He lines up on the Edge. He'll reach block you. He'll cut you off. He'll motion in the backfield. He'll lead draw you as a fullback. He does everything. He's a complete tight end.

Kansas City Chiefs All-Pro tight end Travis Kelce agrees with Woodson's assessment, stating:

> I realized early on that there's no perfect way to play tight end. Actually, that's not true. Jason Witten is perfect. When Witten's on the field, every step is right. Every route is crisp. Everything catchable is grabbed. Every single ball, every single play. Jason Witten

Witten holds Cowboys career records for most pass receptions (1,089) and most consecutive games played (219).
Courtesy of Keith Allison

is a model of consistency. But, in the likely scenario that you are not Jason Witten, there are certain ways to improve at the position so you can at least get a bit closer to being like him (but still not like him because nobody is as good as Jason Witten). The first step towards that is to become as proficient at blocking as you are at catching the ball.

Although advancing age has diminished Witten's production somewhat over the course of the last four seasons, he has remained one of the league's better players at his position and an integral part of the Dallas offense, earning two more Pro Bowl selections, while helping the Cowboys capture the division title in both 2014 and 2016. During that time, Witten established himself as the franchise's all-time iron man, extending his string of consecutive games played to 219, while also surpassing Michael Irvin as the team's all-time leader in pass receptions (1,089). Witten will enter the 2017 campaign with those 1,089 receptions, 63 of which went for touchdowns, and a total of 11,888 receiving yards that leaves him just 16 yards shy of Michael Irvin's franchise record.

In assessing the career of his longtime teammate and close friend, Tony Romo speculated, "He [Witten] might be the best Dallas Cowboy of all time. Literally, his career has been exceptional. He's hit every mark you could ever have, and he's going to go down as the first or second-greatest tight end of all time. I've just been lucky enough to play with him."

CAREER HIGHLIGHTS

Best Season

Witten had a tremendous year for the Cowboys in 2012, establishing a single-season NFL record for tight ends by making 110 receptions, while also amassing 1,039 receiving yards and scoring three touchdowns. He also performed brilliantly in 2010, earning one of his two First-Team All-Pro selections by finishing third in the league with 94 receptions, accumulating 1,002 receiving yards, and scoring a career-high nine touchdowns. Nevertheless, Witten had his finest all-around season in 2007, when he earned First-Team All-Pro honors by making 96 receptions, gaining a career-high 1,145 yards, and scoring seven touchdowns.

Memorable Moments / Greatest Performances

Witten made the first touchdown reception of his career during a 19–3 victory over the New York Giants on December 21, 2003, hooking up with quarterback Quincy Carter on a 36-yard TD connection late in the first quarter of a game that also featured four Billy Cundiff field goals.

Although the Cowboys lost their October 24, 2004, meeting with the Packers 41–20, Witten accumulated more than 100 receiving yards for the first time in his career, making eight receptions for 112 yards and one touchdown, which came on a 42-yard hookup with quarterback Vinny Testaverde.

Witten again starred in defeat three weeks later, catching nine passes for 133 yards and two touchdowns during a 49–21 loss to the Philadelphia Eagles on November 15, 2004.

Witten helped the Cowboys begin the 2007 regular season on a promising note, making six receptions for 116 yards and one touchdown during a 45–35 win over the Giants in Week 1.

Exactly three months later, on December 9, 2007, Witten tied an NFL record held by Kellen Winslow Sr. for the most receptions in a game by a tight end, when he caught 15 passes for 138 yards and one touchdown during a 28–27 victory over the Detroit Lions. Witten punctuated his superb performance by hauling in a game-winning 16-yard TD pass from Tony Romo with only 18 seconds remaining in regulation.

Witten helped lead the Cowboys to a lopsided 34–9 victory over the Seattle Seahawks on Thanksgiving Day 2008 by making nine receptions for 115 yards and one touchdown.

Although the Cowboys suffered a 31–24 defeat at the hands of the Giants on December 6, 2009, Witten had a huge game, finishing the contest with 14 receptions for 156 yards.

Witten turned in another strong effort three weeks later, making six receptions for 117 yards, including a career-long 69-yard catch-and-run, during a 17–0 victory over the Redskins on December 27, 2009.

Witten again torched the Washington defense on December 19, 2010, making 10 receptions for 140 yards and one touchdown during a 33–30 win over the Redskins.

Proving to be an exceptional clutch performer over the course of his career, Witten has made a number of game-winning touchdown receptions for the Cowboys through the years, with one of those coming in the final game of the 2010 regular season, when he scored from 4 yards out on a pass thrown by backup quarterback Stephen McGee with just 55 seconds left in regulation, giving the Cowboys a 14–3 victory over Philadelphia. Witten again came up big for the Cowboys in the 2015 regular-season opener, hauling in an 11-yard TD pass from Tony Romo with just seven seconds remaining in the fourth quarter, to give Dallas a 27–26 win over the New York Giants. Witten provided further heroics on October 30, 2016, when he gave the Cowboys a 29–23 victory over Philadelphia by hooking up with Dak Prescott on a 5-yard scoring play nearly halfway through the overtime session.

Although the Cowboys ended up losing to the Giants 29–24 on October 28, 2012, Witten turned in the most prolific pass-receiving performance of his career, setting a single-game franchise record by making 18 receptions, while also amassing a personal-best 167 receiving yards.

Yet, when asked what he considered to be his best moment as a member of the Cowboys, Witten responded: "I would have to say in 2007, when we finished 13-3 and made it to the second round [of the playoffs]. I guess a specific play would be the Philadelphia Eagles play when my helmet came off—not because of the publicity that came with that play—rather, if there's a play in which you wanted to be defined on how you play, I hope that play kinda represents it. That '07 team was a special team to be on."

NOTABLE ACHIEVEMENTS

- Has surpassed 80 receptions six times, topping 90 catches four times and 100 catches once (110 in 2012).

- Has surpassed 1,000 receiving yards four times, topping 900 yards three other times.
- Has made at least seven touchdown receptions three times.
- Finished third in NFL with 94 receptions in 2010.
- Finished fifth in NFL with 110 receptions in 2012.
- Has led Cowboys in receptions eight times and receiving yards once.
- Holds NFL single-season record for most receptions by a tight end (110 in 2012).
- Holds Cowboys single-game record for most pass receptions (18 vs. Giants on 10/28/12).
- Holds Cowboys career records for most pass receptions (1,089) and most consecutive games played (219).
- Ranks among Cowboys career leaders with: 11,888 receiving yards (2nd); 63 touchdown receptions (4th); 63 touchdowns (6th); 382 points scored (9th); and 223 games played (2nd).
- Ranks second among active players and seventh in NFL history with 1,089 career receptions.
- Ranks sixth among active players with 11,888 receiving yards.
- Ranks second in NFL history for most receptions and receiving yards by a tight end.
- Four-time division champion (2007, 2009, 2014, and 2016).
- 2009 NFL Iron Man Award winner.
- 2010 NFL Alumni Association Tight End of the Year.
- 2012 NFL Walter Payton Man of the Year Award winner.
- Ten-time Pro Bowl selection (2004–2010 and 2012–2014).
- Two-time First-Team All-Pro selection (2007 and 2010).
- Two-time Second-Team All-Pro selection (2008 and 2012).
- 2004 First-Team All-NFC selection.

11

DREW PEARSON

One of the truly great clutch receivers in NFL history, Drew Pearson developed a reputation during his time in Dallas for making big plays in crucial situations. Establishing himself as Roger Staubach's (and, later, Danny White's) "go-to" guy on offense, Pearson always seemed to come up with the big catch, making him a vital member of Cowboys teams that won six division titles, three NFC championships, and one Super Bowl. A two-time 1,000-yard receiver in an era when few players typically reached that lofty mark. Pearson annually ranked among the league leaders in receptions and receiving yardage, earning in the process three trips to the Pro Bowl, three All-Pro selections, and four All-Conference nominations. Meanwhile, Pearson's ability to excel under pressure earned him spots on the Cowboys' 25th and 50th Anniversary Teams, and eventual induction into the Cowboys Ring of Honor.

Born in South River, New Jersey, on January 12, 1951, Drew Pearson attended local South River High School, where he began his football career as a quarterback, succeeding Joe Theismann as the school's starter at that position. In 1969 Pearson enrolled at the University of Tulsa, where he started four games behind center as a sophomore, before being converted into a wide receiver prior to the start of his junior year. Excelling at wideout for the Golden Hurricane over the course of the next two seasons, Pearson made a total of 55 receptions for 1,119 yards and six touchdowns, averaging in the process just over 20 yards per catch.

Considered by most scouts to be too skinny and too slow to succeed in the NFL, the 6-foot, 184-pound Pearson began his pro career with the Cowboys as an undrafted free agent after all 26 NFL teams bypassed him in the 1973 Draft. However, after making just 22 receptions for 388 yards and two touchdowns in a part-time role his first year in the league, Pearson emerged as the Cowboys' top offensive threat in 1974, ranking among the NFL leaders with 62 receptions and 1,087 receiving yards, en route to earning Pro Bowl, First-Team All-NFC, and First-Team All-Pro honors. He

Drew Pearson led the Cowboys in pass receptions and receiving yardage four straight times.
Courtesy of MearsOnlineAuctions.com

followed that up by making First-Team All-NFC again in 1975, concluding the campaign with a team-leading 46 receptions and 822 receiving yards, while also finishing sixth in the league with a career-high eight TD catches. Pearson then earned Pro Bowl and consensus First-Team All-Pro and First-Team All-NFC honors in both 1976 and 1977 by making 58 receptions for

806 yards and six touchdowns in the first of those campaigns, before hauling in 48 passes for a league-leading 870 receiving yards the following year.

Although Pearson lacked elite speed, he ran precise routes and possessed excellent quickness, smooth, silky moves, and superb hands. But the thing that truly set him apart from most other players in the league was his ability to make big plays and rise to the occasion when his team needed him the most. Pearson first began to earn his nickname "Mr. Clutch" in 1974, when he caught a long touchdown pass from backup quarterback Clint Longley in the closing moments of the Cowboys' annual Thanksgiving Day game, giving Dallas a thrilling 24–23 come-from-behind victory over the Washington Redskins. Pearson again came through in the clutch for the Cowboys in their 1975 divisional playoff matchup with Minnesota, hauling in a desperation Hail Mary pass from Roger Staubach in the closing seconds, to give the Cowboys a stunning 17–14 victory over the Vikings. Pearson continued his heroics against Atlanta in the divisional round of the 1980 playoffs, making two touchdown catches in the final four minutes, to rally the Cowboys past the Falcons, 30–27. And Pearson nearly rendered "The Catch" irrelevant, when, in the waning moments of the 1981 NFC championship game against San Francisco, he caught a long pass from Danny White that likely would have gone for a touchdown and won the game for the Cowboys had 49ers cornerback Eric Wright not made a one-handed tackle that brought Pearson down just outside field goal range. Unfortunately, White fumbled the ball on the very next play, ending Dallas hopes of a last-second comeback and sending the 49ers to their first Super Bowl. Reflecting back on that loss and the other playoff defeats the Cowboys suffered during his time in Dallas, Pearson stated, "I played in seven NFC championship games in 11 years and lost four of them. You're happy that you played in that many big games, but it's disappointing when you reflect on them. We played to win it all. Getting close wasn't enough for us."

Although Pearson never again earned Pro Bowl or All-Pro honors after 1977, he continued to perform at a high level the remainder of his career, having one of his finest seasons in 1979, when he made 55 receptions for 1,026 yards and equaled his career high with eight touchdown grabs. However, Pearson's career ended abruptly in March of 1984, when he fell asleep behind the wheel of his Dodge Daytona, causing his vehicle to crash into a parked tractor-trailer. The accident, which cost his younger brother his life, forced him to retire from the game due to the internal injuries he suffered. Looking back on the incident, Pearson said, "It was devastating because I wasn't about to retire. I was about to sign a new contract when the accident

Pearson's "Hail Mary" touchdown reception against Minnesota in the 1975
playoffs remains one of the most memorable plays in NFL history.
Courtesy of MearsOnlineAuctions.com

happened. It was tough to give up, but my brother gave up his life, so I had
to keep it in perspective."

Announcing his retirement at only 32 years of age, Pearson, who served
as an offensive captain for the Cowboys his final two seasons, ended his
career with 489 receptions, 7,822 receiving yards, 48 touchdown catches,
and an average of 16 yards per reception. He also carried the ball 21 times
for 189 yards, completed three touchdown passes, and scored a pair of

touchdowns on fumble recoveries. More than 30 years after he caught his last pass for the Cowboys, Pearson continues to rank among the franchise's all-time leaders in several statistical categories, including pass receptions (third), receiving yardage (fourth), and touchdown receptions (seventh).

Following his playing days, Pearson spent one year working as a broadcaster at CBS, before joining the Dallas coaching staff for one year. After leaving the Cowboys, Pearson returned to broadcasting, working extensively for such networks as CBS and HBO, before becoming head coach of the Arena Football League's Dallas Texans in 1991. After guiding the Texans to a record of 4-6 in his one season at the helm, Pearson left football for good, choosing instead to start his own business, Drew Pearson Marketing, which has proven to be highly successful.

Although Pearson has yet to be inducted into the Pro Football Hall of Fame, he has earned the distinctions of being named to the NFL 1970s All-Decade Team and being identified as one of the Top 20 Pro Football All-Time wide receivers. Roger Staubach, who spent seven years playing alongside Pearson in the Dallas offense, certainly believes those honors are well deserved, saying on one occasion, "If you look at his productivity and the quality of his catches, it was phenomenal."

Staubach added, "Every time I threw it to Drew, I had a lot of confidence. He wasn't afraid of anything. That had a lot to do with a lot of the big plays he made."

CAREER HIGHLIGHTS

Best Season

Pearson had a big year for the Cowboys in 1977, earning First-Team All-Pro, First-Team All-Conference, and Pro Bowl honors by making 48 receptions for a league-leading 870 receiving yards. However, he posted better overall numbers in both 1974 and 1979, concluding the first of those campaigns with 62 catches and 1,087 receiving yards, before making 55 receptions for 1,026 yards and a career-high eight touchdowns in 1979. Yet, in spite of Pearson's outstanding numbers, he finished just eighth in the league in receiving yards and failed to earn any postseason honors in 1979. On the other hand, Pearson placed in the league's top three in both receptions and receiving yardage in 1974, earning in the process Pro Bowl and consensus First-Team All-Pro and First-Team All-NFC honors. All things considered, Pearson had the finest all-around season of his career in 1974.

Memorable Moments / Greatest Performances

Pearson had his breakout game as a rookie on December 2, 1973, when he made four receptions for 93 yards during a 22–10 victory over the Denver Broncos.

Pearson topped that performance two weeks later, though, making five receptions for 140 yards and two touchdowns during a convincing 30–3 win over the St. Louis Cardinals in the 1973 regular-season finale. Pearson's scoring plays, which came on 28- and 17-yard hookups with Roger Staubach, represented the first two touchdowns of his career.

Although the Cowboys lost their September 23, 1974, matchup with the Philadelphia Eagles 13–10, Pearson had a huge game, making 10 receptions for 161 yards and also carrying the ball once for 6 yards.

Pearson helped the Cowboys record a lopsided 36–10 victory over the Detroit Lions on October 6, 1975, by making six receptions for 188 yards and two touchdowns, which came on a 46-yard hookup with running back Robert Newhouse and a 37-yard connection with Roger Staubach.

Pearson proved to be the difference in a 17–10 win over the Buffalo Bills on November 15, 1976, catching nine passes for 135 yards, and scoring the Cowboys' final touchdown on a 21-yard collaboration with Roger Staubach late in the first half.

Pearson had a big day against the hated Washington Redskins on October 16, 1977, leading the Cowboys to a 34–16 victory over their NFC East rivals by making six receptions for 157 yards and one touchdown, with his TD coming on a 59-yard connection with Roger Staubach.

Pearson helped the Cowboys overcome a 14–6 fourth-quarter deficit to the upset-minded New York Giants on November 4, 1979, by hauling in a 32-yard TD pass from Roger Staubach midway through the period. Rafael Septien gave Dallas the 16–14 win minutes later when he split the uprights from 22 yards out. Pearson finished the game with six catches for 124 yards and that all-important TD grab.

Pearson again proved to be a thorn in the side of New York four weeks later, when, during a 28–7 win over the Giants on December 2, he made five receptions for 88 yards and three touchdowns, collaborating with Staubach on scoring plays that covered 7, 8, and 44 yards.

Pearson helped lead the Cowboys to a 59–14 thrashing of the San Francisco 49ers on October 12, 1980, by once again scoring three touchdowns, with his TD grabs, all of which came on throws from Danny White, covering 16, 22, and 17 yards.

Occasionally reverting back to his days as a quarterback, Pearson completed three touchdown passes during his career, with the longest of those coming during a 21–7 victory over the Giants on October 27, 1974, when he hooked up with wide receiver Golden Richards on a 46-yard scoring play.

Nevertheless, Pearson will always be remembered most fondly by Cowboys fans for the many late-game heroics he provided them through the years, with the first of those coming against the Los Angeles Rams in the first round of the 1973 playoffs, when his 83-yard touchdown reception more than halfway through the fourth quarter gave the Cowboys a 24–16 lead in a game they went on to win 27–16.

Pearson again displayed his ability to come up big in the clutch on Thanksgiving Day in 1974, when, with the Cowboys trailing the Washington Redskins 23–17 late in the fourth quarter and backup quarterback Clint Longley subbing for an injured Roger Staubach, he got behind a Washington defender and hauled in a 50-yard TD pass to lift the Cowboys to a 24–23 victory.

Pearson also helped the Cowboys stave off elimination in the divisional round of the 1980 postseason tournament, when he scored two touchdowns in the final 3:40 to lift his team to a 30–27 win over the Atlanta Falcons. Pearson's TD grabs covered 14 and 23 yards, with the second of those coming with only 42 seconds left on the clock.

Still, the play for which Pearson is best remembered took place in the closing moments of the Cowboys' opening-round playoff matchup with Minnesota in 1975. With Dallas in possession of the ball near midfield and trailing Minnesota 14–10 in the game's final minute, Roger Staubach lofted a high-arching pass deep downfield to the Vikings 5 yard line. Pearson, who drew close one-on-one coverage from cornerback Nate Wright on the play after Staubach pump-faked Minnesota free safety Paul Krause to the other side of the field, later described the events that followed:

> I had one more gear left. If Roger had thrown it to the back of the end zone, I could have shifted into that last gear, done the toe dance in the back of the end zone, and walked away untouched. As I looked back and saw the ball coming, I saw it was going to be short, and then I did that swim move to get inside position. In doing that, I made contact with Nate, but there was no deliberate push. With that contact, he went down and I was able to swing my arms around. The ball hit my hands as I brought them around, and

it went through my hands. I ended up catching the Hail Mary with my elbow and my hip. The ball slithered through my hands and stuck between my elbow and my hip. That adds to the mystique and aura of the Hail Mary.

Pearson's 50-yard Hail Mary touchdown reception, which gave the Cowboys a 17–14 victory over the Vikings, was named one of the Top 75 plays in NFL history by NFL Films in 1994. The voters also included his Thanksgiving Day game-winning TD catch against Washington on that list.

NOTABLE ACHIEVEMENTS

- Surpassed 50 receptions three times, topping 60 catches once (62 in 1974).
- Surpassed 1,000 receiving yards twice.
- Made eight touchdown receptions twice.
- Led NFL with 870 receiving yards in 1977.
- Finished second in NFL with 1,087 receiving yards in 1974.
- Finished third in NFL with 62 receptions in 1974.
- Led Cowboys in pass receptions and receiving yardage four straight seasons (1974–1977).
- Ranks among Cowboys career leaders in: pass receptions (3rd); touchdown receptions (7th); receiving yardage (4th); total yardage (7th); and yards per reception (5th).
- Three-time NFC champion (1975, 1977, and 1978).
- Super Bowl XII champion.
- 1977 *Football Digest* NFL Receiver of the Year.
- Three-time Pro Bowl selection (1974, 1976, and 1977).
- Three-time First-Team All-Pro selection (1974, 1976, and 1977).
- Four-time First-Team All-NFC selection (1974, 1975, 1976, and 1977).
- 1978 Second-Team All-NFC selection.
- Pro Football Hall of Fame All-1970s First Team.
- Named to Cowboys' 25th Anniversary Team in 1984.
- Inducted into Cowboys Ring of Honor in 2011.

12

RAYFIELD WRIGHT

One of the premier offensive tackles of his time, Rayfield Wright spent 13 seasons in Dallas, starring at right tackle for the Cowboys for most of his career, after earlier failing to distinguish himself at two other positions. A member of Cowboy teams that won 10 division titles, five NFC championships, and two Super Bowls, Wright anchored the offensive line for squads that finished either first or second in the NFL in total offense five times during the 1970s, helping to pave the way for the first five 1,000-yard rushers in franchise history in the process. Along the way, Wright earned six trips to the Pro Bowl, five All-Pro selections, six All-NFC nominations, a spot on the NFL 1970s All-Decade Team, and eventual induction into the Cowboys Ring of Honor and the Pro Football Hall of Fame.

Born in Griffin, Georgia, on August 23, 1945, Larry Rayfield Wright attended local Fairmont High School, where he lettered in basketball, before continuing to star on the hardwood after enrolling at nearby Fort Valley State College. Yet, even though basketball remained Wright's first love throughout his college years, he also began to develop his football skills, playing free safety, defensive end, and tight end for the Wildcats at different times, at the behest of head coach Stan Lomax, who became very much a father figure to him.

Subsequently selected by the Cowboys in the seventh round of the 1967 NFL/AFL Draft, with the 182nd overall pick, Wright arrived in Dallas as a long and lean 6'6", 225-pound tight end who possessed only marginal pass-catching skills. However, after finding himself unable to unseat Pettis Norman as the starter at the position, Wright gradually bulked up to 255 pounds, enabling him to receive a brief trial at defensive end, before finally settling in at right tackle after he replaced an injured Ralph Neely during the latter stages of the 1969 campaign.

Although the ability Wright displayed while filling in for Neely convinced the Cowboys to move the latter to the left side of the line the following year, Wright's development into a top blocker did not occur

Rayfield Wright played for Cowboys teams that won 10 division titles, five NFC championships, and two Super Bowls.
Courtesy of RMYAuctions.com

overnight. In discussing the adjustments he had to make, Wright revealed, "I struggled with the position. I got the game film and studied all night, but I couldn't do what they said. I'd get knocked down at practice. I needed my own style."

Wright ultimately turned to his experience on the basketball court to develop his blocking technique, explaining, "When I defend you as a basketball player, I don't care where you go as long as I stay between you and the basket. I do that by shuffling my feet quickly from side to side. It doesn't matter which way you go because you can't get by me. I went out on the field the next day, and I was fine."

Wright added, "The only thing I had to do was develop my upper-body strength. When a guy came in close, I'd give him a quick punch—like a karate chop—to his shoulder. If you hit him with enough force, he turns. You can't run forward if you're turned sideways. While he was straightening back up, I'd hit him on the other shoulder."

With Wright having perfected his technique, he soon emerged as one of the NFL's elite right tackles, which, at the time, represented the most important spot on the offensive line since opposing teams generally placed their best pass-rusher at left defensive end. In addition to providing outstanding protection for quarterbacks Craig Morton and Roger Staubach in his first full season as a starter, Wright helped open up huge holes for running backs Calvin Hill, Duane Thomas, and Walt Garrison, enabling the Cowboys to lead the league in rushing, en route to capturing their first NFC title. Wright subsequently earned Pro Bowl honors for the first of six straight times and All-Pro recognition for the first of five times in 1971, when his superb blocking at the point of attack helped the Cowboys win their first world championship.

Nicknamed the "Big Cat" for his nimble feet, Wright broke every time-honored mold previously held for men of his size, with his athleticism and quickness afoot making him a precursor of the "modern" offensive tackle. Wright also possessed a certain "meanness" that all offensive linemen must have in order to excel, stating on one occasion, "I love blocking, love the contact. There's a lot of satisfaction in knowing that you're moving your man out of there. Biggest of all is to put my man on the ground—I'm on top of him and the ball carrier is 10–15 yards downfield. That's satisfaction."

In discussing his longtime adversary, Hall of Fame defensive end Carl Eller once suggested, "An all-day fight with Rayfield Wright definitely is not my idea of a pleasant Sunday afternoon. I think he is pretty much of a composite of an All-Pro tackle. He has size, strength, and quickness. The big thing in Rayfield's favor is that he has a lot of range. He moves faster than most tackles. He's just difficult to play against."

Roger Staubach expressed his appreciation for the work Wright did in front of him when he said, "He was absolutely the best. Rayfield was a big, strong guy that was able to transfer his size and strength from tight end to tackle. He also had such quick feet that he was able to deal with some of the faster defensive ends and even the linebacker blitzes. If he got beat, I don't remember it."

Wright earned 1972 Offensive Lineman of the Year honors from the NFL Players Association.
Courtesy of Dallas Cowboys

Following Wright's election to the Pro Football Hall of Fame, Calvin Hill stated, "Rayfield could do it all. He could pull. He could run in the open field. He could finesse-block and power-block in the run game. And there was no one better in pass-blocking. He was dominant."

Even though Wright's string of three straight First-Team All-Pro selections ended in 1974, he remained one of the NFL's best offensive tackles the next few seasons, earning three more Pro Bowl selections, three All-Conference nominations, and two Second-Team All-Pro selections, before missing virtually all of the 1977 campaign after undergoing knee surgery during the previous offseason. Returning to action in 1978, Wright spent another two years in Dallas, helping the Cowboys capture one more NFC title, before being released by the team in March 1980. Although Wright subsequently signed with division rival Philadelphia, he never appeared in a single game with the Eagles, choosing instead to announce his retirement early in training camp. He ended his 13-year career having appeared in more than 200 games for the Cowboys, including the playoffs, spending his last seven seasons in Dallas serving as a team co-captain. Named to the Cowboys' 25th Anniversary Team in 1984, Wright later received the additional distinctions of being inducted into the team's Ring of Honor in 2004 and being elected to the Pro Football Hall of Fame in 2006.

In retirement, Wright briefly served as an assistant coach to the Arizona Rattlers of the Arena Football League, before deciding to give back to the community by providing assistance to at-risk, inner city youth and serving as president of the NFL Alumni Chapter "Caring for Kids" program in the mid-90s. More recently, Wright has found himself struggling with early-onset dementia caused by the many concussions he suffered during his playing career. Discussing his malady with the *New York Times* in 2014, Wright told that newspaper that he had been "too proud" to tell anybody of his condition until recently, stating, "You don't want people to look at you any differently. When you've been at the top of the NFL, you don't want people to know. You're supposed to be tough and invincible."

CAREER HIGHLIGHTS

Best Season

Although Wright failed to earn All-Pro honors for the first time in five years in 1975, it could be argued that he played his best ball for the Cowboys that year, when, coming off knee surgery, he helped them capture the NFC title with his superb blocking. Particularly effective during the postseason, Wright turned in three consecutive exceptional performances against legendary defensive ends Carl Eller, Jack Youngblood, and L. C. Greenwood, with Youngblood summarizing his opponent's play by stating, "He was truly outstanding." Meanwhile, in discussing Wright's performance against Eller, longtime Dallas offensive line coach Jim Myers proclaimed that he "played as well, or even better, in that game." Nevertheless, it would be extremely difficult to disagree with the notion that Wright had the finest season of his career in 1972, when he earned consensus First-Team All-Pro honors and recognition as the NFL Players Association NFC Offensive Lineman of the Year by helping to pave the way for Calvin Hill to become the first 1,000-yard rusher in team history.

Memorable Moments / Greatest Performances

Wright experienced one of the most memorable moments of his career during a 34–14 win over Philadelphia on October 13, 1968, when he made the only touchdown reception of his career, gathering in a 15-yard pass from Don Meredith.

However, Wright later identified a 24–23 loss to the Los Angeles Rams on November 23, 1969, as the turning point of his career. Making his first NFL start at right tackle against Deacon Jones, Wright battled the league's best pass-rusher to a standstill, stating years later, "I never worried about football after that game. I knew I could play."

NOTABLE ACHIEVEMENTS

- 1967 NFL Eastern Conference champion.
- Five-time NFC champion (1970, 1971, 1975, 1977, and 1978).
- Two-time Super Bowl champion (VI and XII).
- NFL Players Association 1972 NFC Offensive Lineman of the Year.
- Six-time Pro Bowl selection (1971, 1972, 1973, 1974, 1975, and 1976).
- Three-time First-Team All-Pro selection (1971, 1972, and 1973).
- Two-time Second-Team All-Pro selection (1974 and 1976).
- Four-time First-Team All-NFC selection (1971, 1972, 1973, and 1974).
- Two-time Second-Team All-NFC selection (1975 and 1976).
- Named to 1990 NFL All–Super Bowl Team.
- NFL 1970s All-Decade Team.
- Pro Football Hall of Fame All-1970s First Team.
- Pro Football Reference All-1970s Second Team.
- Named to Cowboys' 25th Anniversary Team in 1984.
- Inducted into Cowboys Ring of Honor in 2004.
- Elected to Pro Football Hall of Fame in 2006.

13

DeMARCUS WARE

An elite pass-rusher who also did an excellent job of defending against the run, DeMarcus Ware proved to be one of the NFL's most dominant defensive players over the course of his nine seasons in Dallas. Finishing in double digits in sacks seven straight times at one point, Ware led the league in that category twice, en route to establishing himself as the Cowboys' all-time sack leader. A solid run defender as well, Ware accumulated more than 70 tackles in a season three times, with many of his stops resulting in losses for the opposing team. Ware's stellar all-around play helped the Cowboys win two division titles, earning him in the process seven trips to the Pro Bowl, seven All-Pro selections, recognition as the 2008 NFC Defensive Player of the Year, and a spot on the NFL 2000s All-Decade Team.

Born in Auburn, Alabama, on July 31, 1982, DeMarcus Omar Ware starred in multiple sports while attending Auburn High School, excelling in football, baseball, basketball, and track. An outstanding two-way player on the football field, Ware led his school to an undefeated record as a senior, prompting the members of the team to name him the squad's Most Valuable Wide Receiver and Most Valuable Linebacker.

Choosing to remain in-state following his graduation from Auburn, Ware accepted a scholarship offer from Troy University, where he spent three seasons starting at defensive end, amassing a total of 27½ sacks, 74 quarterback hurries, 201 tackles, 54½ tackles for loss, and 10 forced fumbles during that time. Particularly dominant in his senior year, Ware earned Sun Belt Defensive Player of the Year honors and consideration for the Hendricks Award, which is presented annually to the top defensive end in college football, by recording 10½ sacks, 53 tackles, 19 tackles for loss, and four forced fumbles.

Considered by most pro scouts to be perfectly suited to assume the role of a "tweener" (i.e., a combination defensive end / outside linebacker) in a 3-4 defense, Ware entered the 2005 NFL Draft being targeted by Dallas

Ware recorded double-digit sacks for the Cowboys seven straight times.
Courtesy of PristineAuction.com

scrimmage 19½ times in 2011. Despite being plagued by numerous injuries in 2012 that included a torn hamstring, a fractured right wrist, and a hyper-extended right elbow, Ware put together another solid season, concluding the campaign with 11½ sacks and five forced fumbles.

However, after undergoing shoulder surgery at the end of the year and being switched to defensive end in the Cowboys' new 4-3 defense by first-year defensive coordinator Monte Kiffin, Ware failed to perform at the same lofty level in 2013, finishing the season with just six sacks and 40 tackles. Convinced that the 31-year-old Ware had seen his best days as an NFL player, the Cowboys released him on March 11, 2014, making him a free agent for the first time in his career. Ware left Dallas having recorded a franchise-record 117 sacks and 32 forced fumbles. He also made 574 tackles (442 solo), recovered seven fumbles, intercepted two passes, and scored three defensive touchdowns.

Just one day after being released by the Cowboys, Ware signed a three-year, $30 million contract with the Denver Broncos, for whom he compiled a total of 21½ sacks from 2014 to 2016, earning in the process two more

Pro Bowl nominations. Ware played his best ball for the Broncos in 2014, recording 10 sacks and 45 tackles, before making 7½ sacks for Denver's 2015 NFL championship team. After recording just four sacks for the Broncos this past season, Ware chose to announce his retirement, ending his career with a total of 138½ sacks that places him eighth in NFL history. He also recorded 659 tackles (505 solo), 35 forced fumbles, and three interceptions.

Although Ware spent his final three seasons in Denver, his heart never really left Dallas. Speaking during a 2016 telephone interview, Ware promised to retire as a member of the organization that first drafted him, stating, "That's where everything started for me. I was part of the Cowboys' organization for nine years and put in a lot of sweat and tears there. Jerry Jones is a great owner, and it's a great organization. Coming back there and maybe being able to be in the Ring of Honor and being able to do some things for the community, it'll be awesome. It's home for me and for my kids."

COWBOYS CAREER HIGHLIGHTS

Best Season

Ware had a huge year for the Cowboys in 2011, earning First-Team All-Pro honors by finishing second in the NFL with 19½ sacks, recording 58 tackles, forcing two fumbles, and deflecting two passes. However, he performed even better in 2008, when, in addition to leading the league with 20 sacks, he established career-high marks in forced fumbles (six) and tackles (84), making nine stops behind the line of scrimmage. Ware's 20 sacks tied Derrick Thomas for the sixth-highest official single-season total in league history, earning him in the process consensus First-Team All-Pro honors and recognition as the NFC Defensive Player of the Year and the NFL Alumni Pass Rusher of the Year.

Memorable Moments / Greatest Performances

Ware recorded the first sack of his career on September 25, 2005, getting to San Francisco quarterback Tim Rattay for a 2-yard loss during a 34–31 win over the 49ers.

Ware earned NFC Defensive Player of the Week honors for the first of four times later in the year, recording three sacks, making six tackles, and forcing three fumbles during a 24–20 victory over the Carolina Panthers on December 24, 2005.

Exhibiting the same quickness he possessed before injuring his knee, Howley became an immediate starter in Dallas, spending most of his first two seasons with the Cowboys playing weak-side (right) linebacker. However, with the arrival of Dave Edwards in 1963, the 6'3", 228-pound Howley assumed strong-side linebacker responsibilities. Embracing his new role, Howley did an exceptional job of blanketing tight ends and covering running backs coming out of the backfield, with his 10.1 speed enabling him to stay with even the league's swiftest backs. In fact, Tom Landry once stated that Howley might have succeeded in the NFL as a running back himself had he not been so valuable to the team at linebacker.

Howley's pass-coverage skills prompted many opposing quarterbacks to avoid his area of the field when seeking out a potential target. Howley's quickness also allowed him to provide underneath coverage on the opposing team's best wide receiver. Blessed with an ability to anticipate and diagnose plays, Howley always seemed to be in the right place at the right time, making him an excellent ball-hawk and an outstanding run-stopper.

Howley's unique skill set, which helped him earn Pro Bowl honors each year from 1965 to 1969, prompted the Dallas coaching staff to allow him an opportunity to freelance more on defense than most of his teammates, with Coach Landry once stating, "Sometimes we allow certain people like Chuck or Bob Lilly to vary from our defensive pattern. People like Chuck can often do this and get away with it because of their outstanding athletic ability."

Opposing wide receivers Gary Collins and Roy Jefferson attested to Howley's coverage skills, with both men identifying him as one of the two best linebackers they ever played against. Meanwhile, Dallas wideout Lance Rentzel suggested, "What separated Chuck Howley from the vast majority of other linebackers in the NFL at the time he played was his athletic ability. He had speed and quickness that was quite unusual."

A sure tackler and excellent blitzer as well, Howley accumulated a total of 26½ sacks over the course of his career, with his single-season high coming in 1969, when he brought down opposing quarterbacks behind the line of scrimmage 5½ times. Howley shifted back to the right side of the Dallas defense that year, after spending the previous six seasons playing left-side linebacker. Continuing his string of five consecutive First-Team All-Pro selections that began in 1966 and his streak of 98 consecutive games played that began one year earlier, Howley also earned Pro Bowl honors for the fifth straight time.

Howley made First-Team All-Pro for the fifth and final time in 1970, when he helped the Cowboys capture their first NFC championship, before earning Super Bowl MVP honors even though his team suffered a

In Super Bowl V, Howley became the only player ever to be named MVP of the contest as a member of the losing team.
Courtesy of Malcolm Emmons

devastating 16–13 defeat at the hands of the Baltimore Colts. He followed that up by intercepting five passes and recovering three fumbles for the Cowboys' 1971 Super Bowl–winning team, earning in the process Pro Bowl, Second-Team All-Pro, and Second-Team All-Conference honors.

Howley spent one more full season in Dallas, performing well for the Cowboys in 1972, before suffering a serious injury to his left knee on a crackback block by wide receiver Charley Taylor during a late-season victory over the Washington Redskins. After appearing in one game the following year, Howley announced his retirement, ending his career with more takeaways (43) than any other outside linebacker in NFL history, with the exception of Pittsburgh's Jack Ham (52). During his time in Dallas, Howley played for six division champions, two NFC champions, and one Super Bowl champion. The Cowboys inducted him into their Ring of Honor in 1977, making him the fourth player to be so honored.

In paying tribute to one of the key members of the Doomsday Defense, Tom Landry stated, "I don't know that I've ever seen anybody better at linebacker than Chuck Howley."

Meanwhile, Rams Hall of Fame defensive end Jack Youngblood suggested, "He [Howley] was one of the first linebackers to play bigger than his size. He played above his natural ability."

Following his retirement, Howley opened a uniform rental business in the Dallas area, before eventually getting involved in the cattle industry. Unfortunately, he has spent the last few years suffering from dementia—a condition brought on by the many collisions he endured over the course of 14 NFL seasons. Looking back at his playing career several years after he left the game, Howley said, "I just hope I can be considered the best at my position. I gave what I could. You look back on life and think, 'Was there more I could have done?' I don't know that I could have."

COWBOYS CAREER HIGHLIGHTS

Best Season

Howley performed extremely well for the Cowboys in 1966, 1967, 1969, and 1970, earning First-Team All-Pro honors each year. Particularly effective in 1969 and 1970, Howley recorded two interceptions and a career-high 5½ sacks in the first of those campaigns, before picking off another two passes and recovering three fumbles the following year. Howley also made Second-Team All-Pro in 1971, when he recovered three fumbles and intercepted five passes, which he returned for a total of 122 yards. Nevertheless, Howley had his finest all-around season in 1968, when, en route to earning consensus All-Pro honors, he recorded a career-high six interceptions, which he returned for 115 yards and one touchdown.

Memorable Moments / Greatest Performances

Howley helped the Cowboys earn their first win of the 1963 campaign in a Week 5 matchup with the Detroit Lions on October 13, recording two interceptions during a hard-fought 17–14 victory.

Howley, who scored three regular-season touchdowns over the course of his career, tallied his first points on October 2, 1966, when, during a 47–14 thrashing of the Atlanta Falcons, he recorded a 97-yard fumble return that proved to be longest in the NFL the entire year.

Howley recorded the first pick-six of his career in the 1967 regular-season opener, intercepting a Frank Ryan pass and returning it 28 yards for what proved to be the game-winning score in a 21–14 victory over the Cleveland Browns.

Howley again crossed the opponent's goal line in the 1968 regular-season opener, returning one of his two interceptions on the day 35 yards for a TD during a 59–13 mauling of the Lions.

Howley turned in another outstanding performance during a 45–13 win over the Eagles two weeks later, leading a Dallas defense that allowed just 40 yards rushing and forced seven turnovers by recording another two interceptions, one of which he ran back 58 yards, which represented the longest such return of his career.

Continuing to display a penchant for making big plays on Opening Day, Howley helped lead the Cowboys to a 49–37 victory over the Buffalo Bills in the 1971 regular-season opener by recording a 53-yard interception return.

Although the Cowboys ended up losing their 1968 divisional playoff matchup with the Cleveland Browns 31–20, Howley exhibited his ability to excel in big games, giving Dallas an early 7–3 lead by recovering a fumble, which he returned 44 yards for a touchdown. Howley also recorded a sack during the contest.

Howley also performed well during the Cowboys' 20–12 win over Minnesota in the 1971 divisional playoff round, recording a 26-yard interception return.

Yet, there is little doubt that Howley turned in the most memorable performance of his career in Super Bowl V, when he earned game MVP honors by making four tackles and intercepting two passes during the Cowboys' heartbreaking 16–13 loss to the Baltimore Colts. In discussing his feat of becoming the only player ever to be named Super Bowl MVP while playing for the losing team, Howley revealed, "It was hard to enjoy being MVP of that game. How do you celebrate that? I remember some of the other guys saying, 'Chuck, that's fantastic.' But it was very difficult to be enthusiastic. I just felt like we left some unfinished business out there."

The Cowboys took care of that unfinished business the following year, when they recorded a 24–3 victory over the Miami Dolphins in Super Bowl VI. Howley contributed to the cause by recovering a Larry Csonka fumble and intercepting a Bob Griese pass, which he returned 41 yards to the Miami 9 yard line before stumbling and falling. His two takeaways gave the Dallas offense short fields, leading to 10 of the Cowboys' 24 points.

NOTABLE ACHIEVEMENTS

- Scored three career touchdowns (two interception returns and one fumble return).
- Recorded 5½ sacks in 1969.
- Recorded at least five interceptions twice (1968 and 1971).
- Accumulated more than 100 interception-return yards twice (1968 and 1971).
- Led NFL with 97 fumble-return yards in 1966.
- Ranks among Cowboys career leaders in: interceptions (10th); interception-return yardage (8th); and fumbles recovered on defense (tied-5th).
- Ranks second all-time among NFL outside linebackers in career take-aways (43).
- Two-time NFL Eastern Conference champion (1966 and 1967).
- Two-time NFC champion (1970 and 1971).
- Super Bowl VI champion.
- Only player to be named MVP of Super Bowl as member of losing team (Super Bowl V).
- Six-time Pro Bowl selection (1965, 1966, 1967, 1968, 1969, and 1971).
- Five-time First-Team All-Pro selection (1966, 1967, 1968, 1969, and 1970).
- 1971 Second-Team All-Pro selection.
- Three-time First-Team All-Eastern Conference selection (1963, 1967, and 1968).
- 1970 First-Team All-NFC selection.
- 1971 Second-Team All-NFC selection.
- Pro Football Reference All-1960s Second Team.
- Named to Cowboys' 25th Anniversary Team in 1984.
- Named to Cowboys' 50th Anniversary Team in 2009.
- Inducted into Cowboys Ring of Honor in 1977.

15

RALPH NEELY

Perhaps the best player yet to be inducted into the Cowboys Ring of Honor, Ralph Neely spent 13 seasons in Dallas, excelling on both ends of the Cowboys' offensive line during that time. After earning two Pro Bowl, three All-Conference, and four All-Pro selections as a right tackle over the course of his first five seasons, Neely moved to the left side of the Dallas offensive line, where he spent his final eight years in the league starring at left tackle. Along the way, Neely started every game for the Cowboys nine times, missing more than two contests in just one of his 13 seasons. Neely's durability and exceptional blocking helped the Cowboys win nine division titles, four conference championships, and two Super Bowls, eventually earning him spots on the NFL 1960s All-Decade Team and the Cowboys' 25th Anniversary Team.

Born in Little Rock, Arkansas, on September 12, 1943, Ralph Eugene Neely attended Farmington High School in New Mexico, where he starred in basketball as a center and football as a two-way tackle, earning All-State honors twice for his outstanding play on the gridiron. After being courted by several colleges, Neely elected to accept a football scholarship from the University of Oklahoma, where he spent the next few years playing under head coaches Bud Wilkinson and Gomer Jones. Continuing to excel on both sides of the ball for the Sooners, Neely earned Big Eight Sophomore Lineman of the Year honors, two All-Conference selections, and a pair of All-America nominations during his time at Oklahoma.

Subsequently declared ineligible to play in the 1965 Gator Bowl after he accepted a contract offer from the Houston Oilers, who selected him in the second round of that year's AFL Draft, Neely sat out the contest, which Oklahoma ended up losing to Florida State University 36–19. However, Neely began to have second thoughts about his earlier decision after the Baltimore Colts, who selected him in the second round of the 1965 NFL Draft, with the 28th overall pick, traded his rights to the Cowboys in exchange for punter Billy Lothridge and a fourth-round selection in the

Ralph Neely starred at both offensive tackle positions during his time in Dallas.
Courtesy of Steve Liskey, Retrocards.net

1966 Draft. Preferring to play for an NFL team, and upset with Houston for having leaked the news of his signing, Neely began negotiating with the Cowboys and ultimately returned his check to the Oilers, setting off a stream of litigation between the two franchises that eventually led to Dallas sending four future draft picks to Houston and paying all of the court costs involved in the case.

Neely played for four NFC championship teams and two Super Bowl champions as a member of the Cowboys.
Courtesy of Dallas Cowboys

Although the price the Cowboys ended up paying for Neely might have seemed a bit exorbitant at the time, they later came to view his acquisition as a bargain. Immediately anointed the starter at right tackle upon his arrival in Dallas, Neely appeared in every game for the Cowboys for the first of four straight times in 1965, earning a spot on the NFL All-Rookie team in the process. He followed that up in 1966 by earning First-Team All–Eastern Conference and Second-Team All-NFL honors for a Cowboys team that boasted the league's most potent offense—one that topped the circuit in both total yardage and points scored (445). Neely then earned the first of his two Pro Bowl selections in 1967 by helping the Cowboys advance to the NFC title game for the second straight year. That same season, he began a string of three straight seasons in which he made First-Team All-Pro.

Much of the success the 6'6", 265-pound Neely experienced during that time could be attributed to his exceptional quickness, which enabled him to dominate opposing defensive linemen. The Cowboys also benefited from Neely's outstanding strength and versatility, which allowed him to move to left tackle in 1970, to create room on the right side for burgeoning star Rayfield Wright.

With Neely sliding over to play left tackle and Wright assuming his former post, the Dallas offensive line featured the best set of tackles in the NFL for much of the 1970s. Although Neely never again appeared in the Pro Bowl or earned All-Pro honors, he remained one of the league's top offensive linemen, earning his fourth and final All-Conference selection in 1975, when he helped lead the Cowboys to their second NFC title. Neely also proved to be extremely durable during that time, starting 83 out of a possible 84 games from 1972 to 1977. In fact, Neely missed more than two games for the only time in his career in 1971, when an off-road, in-season motorcycle accident left him with a fractured left leg that shelved him for the final seven games of the regular season and the entire postseason, preventing him from participating in the team's successful run to the world championship. However, Neely started every game for the Cowboys at left tackle when they won the Super Bowl six years later, before announcing his retirement at season's end. Although Neely has chosen to maintain a low profile since leaving the game, he has returned to the spotlight once or twice, most notably when the NFL named him to its 1960s All-Decade Team, and when the Cowboys named him to their 25th Anniversary Team in 1984.

CAREER HIGHLIGHTS

Best Season

Although Neely continued to perform extremely well after he moved to the left side of the Dallas offensive line in 1970, he played his best ball for the Cowboys from 1966 to 1969, earning All-Pro honors all four years, while also making All-Conference three times and appearing in two Pro Bowls. While any of those seasons would make a good choice, the 1968 campaign perhaps proved to be the most dominant of Neely's career. En route to earning consensus First-Team All-Pro and First-Team All-Conference honors, Neely contributed significantly to the NFL's most potent offense—one that led the league in points scored (431) and total yardage. The 431 points scored by the Cowboys that year represented the second-highest total ever compiled by the team prior to the advent of the 16-game schedule in 1978.

Memorable Moments / Greatest Performances

Neely experienced one of his more memorable moments on December 3, 1972, when, during a 27–6 win over St. Louis, he carried the ball for the only time in his career, registering a 10-yard gain on the ground against the Cardinals.

Neely turned in a pair of exceptional performances against Green Bay's Willie Davis in the 1966 and 1967 NFL championship games, totally neutralizing the Hall of Fame defensive end, who failed to record a single sack in either contest. Neely's stellar play prompted Davis to later call him "the finest offensive tackle I've ever played against."

NOTABLE ACHIEVEMENTS

- 1967 NFL Eastern Conference champion.
- Four-time NFC champion (1970, 1971, 1975, and 1977).
- Two-time Super Bowl champion (VI and XII).
- Member of 1965 NFL All-Rookie Team.
- Two-time Pro Bowl selection (1967 and 1969).
- Three-time First-Team All-Pro selection (1967, 1968, and 1969).
- 1966 Second-Team All-Pro selection.
- Three-time First-Team All–Eastern Conference selection (1966, 1967, and 1968).
- 1975 Second-Team All-NFC selection.
- NFL 1960s All-Decade Team.
- Pro Football Hall of Fame All-1960s First Team.
- Named to Cowboys' 25th Anniversary Team in 1984.

16

HARVEY MARTIN

Perhaps the best pure pass-rusher ever to play for the Cowboys, Harvey Martin spent his entire 11-year career in Dallas, leading the team in sacks in seven of those 11 seasons. En route to compiling the second-highest sack total in franchise history, Martin finished in double digits in that category on six separate occasions, leading the NFL with an unofficial total of 23 quarterback sacks in 1977 that remains the highest single-season mark ever posted by a member of the team. More than just a pass-rusher, Martin also did an excellent job of defending against the run, amassing as many as 85 tackles one season. Extremely durable as well, Martin missed just one game his entire career, appearing in every game for the Cowboys in each of his last eight seasons. Martin's stellar play helped the Cowboys win six division titles, three NFC championships, and one Super Bowl, earning him in the process four Pro Bowl nominations, four All-Pro selections, three All-NFC nominations, recognition as the 1977 NFL Defensive Player of the Year, and a spot on the NFL 1970s All-Decade Team.

Born in Dallas, Texas, on November 16, 1950, Harvey Banks Martin grew up dreaming of one day playing for his hometown team, although he didn't play organized football until his junior year of high school. Spending most of his free time as a teenager working at a department store, Martin envisioned eventually becoming a manager at the establishment. However, his plans changed after he overheard his father expressing to his mother his dissatisfaction with young Harvey's inability to excel on the football field to the same degree as most of his friends' sons.

Wounded by his father's words, the sensitive Martin decided to try out for his school's football team after he transferred to South Oak Cliff High School in his junior year. Although Martin saw very little action as a backup offensive lineman his first season, he emerged as a force to be reckoned with after the coaching staff moved him to defensive end prior to the start of his senior year. Applying constant pressure to opposing quarterbacks, Martin helped lead his team to a 12-1 record and the Dallas city championship.

Harvey Martin led the Cowboys in sacks in seven of his 11 years with the team.
Courtesy of Steve Liskey, Retrocards.net

Yet, in spite of the success Martin experienced during his final year of high school, college recruiters expressed little interest in him due to his relative lack of experience. With few suitors knocking on his door, Martin ultimately accepted a scholarship offer from East Texas State University (now known as Texas A&M University–Commerce), whose coaches saw a considerable amount of potential in the wiry 6'5" defensive end. After two mostly uneventful seasons at East Texas State, Martin evolved into the best defensive end in school history as a senior, earning NAIA All-America, All-Texas, and All-LSC honors, en route to leading his team to a national title.

Subsequently selected by the Cowboys in the third round of the 1973 NFL Draft, with the 53rd overall pick, Martin spent most of his rookie campaign backing up starting defensive ends Larry Cole and Pat Toomay, although he saw enough action as a third-down pass-rushing specialist to lead the team with nine quarterback sacks. Fulfilling a similar role the following year, Martin brought down opposing quarterbacks behind the line of scrimmage another 7½ times.

Although Martin performed well over the course of his first two seasons, the members of the Dallas coaching staff, who considered him to be "too nice" when he first entered the league, worked hard at instilling in him a sense of aggressiveness, confidence, and mental toughness that didn't come naturally to him. Heeding the advice of his coaches, improving his technique by going up against future Hall of Fame tackle Rayfield Wright in practice each day, and adding some much needed weight to his lean frame, the 6'5", 260-pound Martin took over as the team's starting right defensive end in 1975, by which time he had transformed himself into an intense and fierce competitor to whom his teammates referred as "Too Mean."

Acquitting himself extremely well in his first year as a full-time starter, Martin helped the Cowboys advance to the Super Bowl by recording 9½ sacks during the regular season. He followed that up with an exceptional 1976 campaign in which he registered a team-leading 15½ sacks, earning in the process Second-Team All-Pro honors and the first of his four consecutive trips to the Pro Bowl. Martin topped that performance, though, in 1977, earning NFL Defensive Player of the Year and consensus First-Team All-Pro honors by recording 85 tackles and a league-leading 23 quarterback sacks, which, although unofficial, remains the highest single-season total in franchise history. Making Martin's extraordinary campaign even more impressive is the fact that he amassed those 23 sacks in only 14 games. (The NFL did not adopt a 16-game schedule until the following year.)

Employing a repertoire of moves that included a quick swim move to the inside and a forearm club with his right arm that enabled him to go past the left tackle's outside shoulder, Martin developed into arguably the NFL's most feared sack artist, with both Tom Landry and Tex Schramm calling him the best pass-rusher they ever saw. In discussing Martin's pass-rushing skills years later, sportswriter Ron Borges noted, "Harvey Martin was a sack machine before they created the sack. He was the 'Doom' in the Doomsday Defense."

Commenting on his former teammate's ability to harass opposing quarterbacks, Robert Newhouse stated, "He was so big and so strong that he could run right past the tackles. He was strong and fast, and you couldn't stop him. It didn't matter how many guys you tried to put over there, he would get to the quarterback."

Meanwhile, even though Ed "Too Tall" Jones gained general recognition as being the Cowboys' better run-defending end, Martin did a solid job against the run as well. He also contributed to the success of the team with his dedication and professionalism, which earned him the admiration and respect of his peers, teammates, and coaches.

After undergoing surgery on his lower jaw to correct a serious underbite following the conclusion of the 1977 campaign, Martin found himself unable to eat solid food for several weeks, causing him to lose more than 40 pounds. Yet, even though he entered training camp weak and well under his normal playing weight of 260 pounds, Martin managed to tie Randy White for the team lead with 16 sacks in 1978.

Unfortunately, Martin developed addictions to cocaine and alcohol over the course of the next few seasons, causing his on-field performance to gradually decline. His level of play further diminished by growing financial problems, Martin recorded 32 sacks from 1979 to 1981, before seeing his sack total fall off to eight in 1982 and, finally, just two in 1983.

Claiming that the Cowboys forced him to play while injured, Martin elected to announce his retirement in 1983 after refusing to take a team-ordered drug test. However, he later admitted in his 1986 autobiography that he did indeed suffer from cocaine addiction at the time. Martin ended his playing career with an unofficial total of 114 quarterback sacks—a figure that currently places him second only to DeMarcus Ware in team annals.

Martin's inner demons only grew worse after he retired, with the former NFL Defensive Player of the Year hitting rock-bottom in 1996, when charges of domestic violence and cocaine usage briefly landed him in prison, before forcing him to enter an eight-month court-ordered rehabilitation program. Although Martin eventually turned his life around, securing a job as a salesman for Dallas company Arrow-Magnolia and spending much of his time speaking to children about the evils of drug abuse, he lived just five more years, dying of pancreatic cancer at only 51 years of age on December 24, 2001. Following Martin's passing, Tex Schramm commented, "He'll be remembered as one of the great Cowboys of the golden years. . . . He was a great player, one of the first great pass rushers."

Martin earned 1977 NFL Defensive Player of the Year honors by leading the league with 23 quarterback sacks.
Courtesy of Dallas Cowboys

CAREER HIGHLIGHTS

Best Season

Martin played his best ball for the Cowboys from 1976 to 1978, surpassing 15 sacks in each of those seasons, en route to earning three straight Pro Bowl selections. Yet, while Martin performed extremely well all three years, he clearly reached the apex of his career in 1977, when he recorded 85 tackles and a franchise-record and league-leading 23 unofficial quarterback sacks, earning in the process consensus First-Team All-Pro and NFL Defensive Player of the Year honors. Martin capped off his brilliant season by recovering two fumbles against Minnesota in the NFC championship game, before earning co-MVP honors of Super Bowl XII by registering two sacks against Denver.

Memorable Moments / Greatest Performances

Martin played well in the first postseason game of his career, recording 1½ sacks and recovering a fumble during the Cowboys' 27–16 win over the Los Angeles Rams in their 1973 divisional playoff matchup.

Although there is no official record of how many times he got to the opposing quarterback during the contest, Martin led a Dallas onslaught that sacked Detroit signal-callers Greg Landry and Bill Munson a total of 11 times during a 36–10 victory over the Lions on October 6, 1975.

Martin recorded two safeties during his career, with the first of those coming on September 9, 1979, when he sacked San Francisco quarterback Steve DeBerg in the end zone during a 21–13 win over the 49ers. Martin again put up two points for the Cowboys on October 18, 1981, when he tackled Los Angeles quarterback Pat Haden in the end zone during a 29–17 victory over the Rams.

Martin turned in an outstanding performance on September 19, 1982, helping to lead the Cowboys to a 24–7 win over the Cardinals by sacking St. Louis QB Neil Lomax three times.

After earning co-MVP honors in Super Bowl XII by sacking Denver quarterbacks twice, Martin continued his exceptional postseason play the following year, recording a sack and recovering a fumble during the Cowboys' 28–0 victory over the Los Angeles Rams in the NFC championship game.

Martin again performed well throughout the 1980 postseason, recording two sacks of Steve Bartkowski during Dallas's 30–27 win over Atlanta in the divisional playoff round, before getting to Ron Jaworski twice during the Cowboys' 20–7 loss to Philadelphia in the NFC championship game.

NOTABLE ACHIEVEMENTS

- Finished in double digits in sacks six times, recording franchise-record 23 unofficial sacks in 1977.
- Led NFL with 23 quarterback sacks in 1977.
- Led Cowboys in sacks seven times.
- Missed just one game entire career.
- Holds Cowboys unofficial single-season record for most quarterback sacks (23 in 1977).
- Ranks second in Cowboys history with 114 career sacks (104 unofficial).
- Three-time NFC champion (1975, 1977, and 1978).
- Super Bowl XII champion.
- Co-MVP of Super Bowl XII.
- 1977 Associated Press Defensive Player of the Year.
- 1977 *Football Digest* NFL Defensive Lineman of the Year.
- Four-time Pro Bowl selection (1976, 1977, 1978, and 1979).
- 1977 First-Team All-Pro selection.
- Three-time Second-Team All-Pro selection (1976, 1979, and 1982).
- 1977 First-Team All-NFC selection.
- Two-time Second-Team All-NFC selection (1976 and 1979).
- NFL 1970s All-Decade Team.
- Pro Football Hall of Fame All-1970s Second Team.

17

ED "TOO TALL" JONES

An excellent run-stuffer who also did an outstanding job of applying pressure to opposing quarterbacks, Ed "Too Tall" Jones spent his entire 15-year NFL career in Dallas, appearing in more games during that time (224) than anyone else in franchise history. Serving as an anchor on the left side of the Cowboys' defensive line for well over a decade, Jones helped lead the team to five division titles, three conference championships, and one Super Bowl victory, earning in the process three Pro Bowl selections, three All-Pro nominations, and five All-NFC selections. Recovering a franchise-record 19 fumbles on defense over the course of his career, Jones also ranks among the team's all-time leaders in sacks (106) and tackles (1,032). Yet, it is for the manner in which he altered the game with his ability to knock down passes at the line of scrimmage that the 6'9" Jones is perhaps remembered most.

Born in Jackson, Tennessee, on February 23, 1951, Edward Lee Jones attended local Central Merry High School, where he starred in multiple sports, earning All-America honors in basketball, while also excelling as a first baseman on the baseball diamond. Limited to only three games of football because his high school did not support the sport until his senior year, Jones found himself being recruited by several Division I colleges for his basketball skills as he neared graduation. He also fielded offers from a few MLB teams that expressed interest in having him play first base in their minor league systems. Yet, Jones, who fought a Golden Gloves boxing match as a senior, knocking out his opponent in less than a minute, retained thoughts in the back of his mind of one day becoming a professional fighter.

After accepting a scholarship offer from Tennessee State University, Jones continued to play basketball for two more years, before finally choosing to focus exclusively on football. Developing into a star on the gridiron, Jones earned All-America honors twice, helping his team capture the black college football national championship in both 1971 and 1973. It was also during his time at Tennessee State that Jones acquired his rather unusual

Ed "Too Tall" Jones ranks among the Cowboys all-time leaders in both sacks and tackles.
Courtesy of PristineAuction.com

moniker of "Too Tall," with the nickname becoming affixed to him after his first football practice, when a teammate commented that his pants didn't fit because he was "too tall to play football."

Jones's exceptional play at the collegiate level made him one of the most sought-after commodities heading into the 1974 NFL Draft. Ordinarily, the Cowboys, who finished the previous season with a record of 10-4, would not have been in a position to draft someone with his credentials. However, they had earlier traded Tody Smith and Billy Parks to the Houston Oilers for the rights to the number 1 overall pick, which they used to select Jones, making him the first player from a historically black college to go that high in the NFL Draft.

Jones spent most of his rookie campaign serving as a backup, before laying claim to the starting left defensive end job in his second season. Although Jones performed well in that role over the course of the next few seasons, doing a solid job opposite Harvey Martin, who terrorized opposing quarterbacks from his right defensive end position, he proved to be something of a disappointment, failing to attain the level of greatness the Cowboys expected from him when they made him the first overall pick of the draft. Jones later explained that his inability to reach his full potential stemmed mostly from a secret desire to re-enter the boxing ring, telling *Sports Illustrated* in 1981, "The only reason I was playing football before was just because I had the talent to play. Football was great. It just didn't happen to be No. 1 with me."

Ultimately succumbing to his first love, Jones decided to leave the Cowboys after five seasons, announcing his retirement following the conclusion of the 1978 campaign to pursue a career in boxing. However, after winning six bouts against mostly overmatched opponents, Jones lost his thirst for pugilism and elected to return to the Cowboys, with whom he began a second tour of duty in 1980 that lasted 10 years.

Rededicating himself to his chosen profession following his return to the gridiron, the 6'9", 270-pound Jones finally reached a level of focus that matched his considerable physical gifts. Performing better than he did in his earlier stint with the Cowboys, Jones developed into one of the NFL's best run-stopping linemen, earning Pro Bowl, All-Conference, and All-Pro honors three straight times from 1981 to 1983. Teaming up with Harvey Martin, Jones helped give the Cowboys one of the top defensive-end tandems in all of football, with Dallas safety Michael Downs later noting, "Ed was probably the most consistent guy we had. Harvey would lead the team in sacks, but he seldom made tackles at the line of scrimmage because he was always in the starting block [to rush the passer]; that put Ed in position to make a lot of plays."

In discussing his role on the team, Jones stated, "My job was to keep linemen off our linebackers. Often times, I would keep two players, sometimes three; and my job was just to disrupt the linemen up front, blow things up, and our linebackers would clean up."

Still, Jones proved to be considerably more than just a space-eater and run-stuffer. After compiling a total of 21 sacks from 1982 to 1984, Jones recorded a team-leading and career-high 13 sacks in 1985—a figure that placed him in the league's top 10 for the first time. He also led the Cowboys with 10 quarterback sacks in 1987, once again ranking among the league leaders in that category. Furthermore, Jones became extremely adept at using his 6'9" frame to bat down passes, with one of his more memorable deflections coming during a critical late-season contest against the Giants in 1985, when he batted a Phil Simms pass into the air, enabling teammate Jim Jeffcoat to come up with the ball and return it 65 yards for a touchdown. In fact, Jones's ability to knock down passes prompted the NFL to begin keeping pass deflections as an official statistic.

Jones remained the Cowboys' starting left defensive end until midway through the 1989 campaign, when Tony Tolbert replaced him as the starter at the position. The 38-year-old Jones subsequently announced his retirement at season's end, concluding his career with unofficial totals of 106 sacks and 1,032 tackles, with both figures placing him among the Cowboys' all-time leaders. Jones also is credited with nine blocked kicks, with seven of those coming on field-goal attempts and the other two on extra points. Extremely durable, Jones never missed a game due to injury, playing in a franchise-record 224 games and 15 seasons, although Jason Witten appears destined to surpass the first of those marks in 2017.

CAREER HIGHLIGHTS

Best Season

Jones had a big year for the Cowboys in 1985, when he recorded a career-high 13 sacks. Yet, even though he sacked opposing quarterbacks just six times in 1982, Jones had his finest all-around season, earning his lone First-Team All-Pro selection and NFL Most Valuable Defensive Player of the Year honors.

Memorable Moments / Greatest Performances

Jones intercepted three passes during his career, with the first of his picks coming against former Cowboys teammate Craig Morton during a 14–3 victory over the Giants on November 30, 1975.

Jones had to wait seven years before making his second interception, picking off a Ken Stabler pass during a 21–7 win over the New Orleans Saints on December 19, 1982. He also registered a sack during the contest.

Jones recorded the final interception of his career on October 23, 1983, when he picked off a Marc Wilson aerial during a 40–38 loss to the Oakland Raiders.

Jones earned NFC Defensive Player of the Week honors on three separate occasions, doing so for the first time on November 16, 1986, when he sacked Dan Fouts three times during a 24–21 victory over the San Diego Chargers.

Jones again came away with NFC Defensive Player of the Week honors on November 2, 1987, when he recorded a career-high four sacks during a 33–24 win over the Giants.

Jones garnered Player of the Week honors for the third and final time on September 25, 1988, by recording a sack and applying constant pressure to Atlanta quarterbacks Chris Miller and Steve Dils during a 26–20 victory over the Falcons.

An outstanding postseason performer over the course of his career, Jones recorded 12 sacks and one interception in a total of 20 playoff contests, with perhaps his finest effort coming against Atlanta in the divisional round of the 1978 postseason tournament, when he sacked Steve Bartkowski twice during the Cowboys' 27–20 victory over the Falcons.

Jones also came up big against Tampa Bay in the divisional round of the playoffs three years later, picking off a Doug Williams pass during a lopsided 38–0 Cowboys win.

NOTABLE ACHIEVEMENTS

- Finished in double digits in sacks twice.
- Led Cowboys in sacks twice.
- Never missed a game entire career.
- Holds Cowboys records for most: fumbles recovered on defense (19); seasons played (15); and games played (224).
- Ranks fourth in Cowboys history with 106 career sacks (57½ official).
- Ranks fifth in Cowboys history with 1,032 career tackles.
- Three-time NFC champion (1975, 1977, and 1978).
- Super Bowl XII champion.
- Three-time NFC Defensive Player of the Week.
- Three-time Pro Bowl selection (1981, 1982, and 1983).
- 1982 First-Team All-Pro selection.
- Two-time Second-Team All-Pro selection (1981 and 1983).
- Two-time First-Team All-NFC selection (1981 and 1983).
- Three-time Second-Team All-NFC selection (1978, 1982, and 1985).
- Pro Football Reference All-1980s First Team.

for a touchdown. Woodson's outstanding play earned him praise from *Sports Illustrated*, which described him in an October 31, 1994, article as "a masher who doubles as an outside linebacker in passing situations" and "the most productive player on the best defense in the NFL." The author continued to flatter Woodson by writing, "A combination of strength, brute-force hitting, and speed—4.35 seconds in the 40—makes Woodson the most versatile player on the Super Bowl champions."

The 6'1", 220-pound Woodson did indeed possess a tremendous amount of versatility, with his combination of size and speed enabling him to assume various roles on the Dallas defense. Although Woodson typically played strong safety in the Cowboys' base defensive alignment, he often lined up as an outside linebacker in the team's nickel pass defense, frequently covering the opposing team's slot receiver in that particular scheme. In discussing Woodson's ability to play multiple positions, Gerry Fraley wrote in the *Dallas Morning News*, "Woodson had the run-stopping skills of a strong safety and the pass-coverage ability of a free safety. His ability to cover slot receivers made a significant difference for the defense."

Meanwhile, an article on DallasCowboys.com from July 3, 2009, stated, "While Woodson delivered his share of big-time hits from the safety position, he was always the team's slot cornerback, covering receivers inside, which is considered to be the toughest spot on the field. In today's game, most teams put their best cover corner in the slot, but Woodson did that for years from the safety position. With that, it helped the Cowboys stop the run as well, having a safety that close to the line of scrimmage without being a liability in coverage."

Also excellent at covering kickoffs and punts, Woodson recorded a total of 134 tackles on special teams over the course of his career, placing him second in franchise history only to Bill Bates. An outstanding leader as well, Woodson served as the quarterback of the Dallas secondary, becoming known to his teammates as the "Sheriff" in spite of his quiet demeanor. Meanwhile, Woodson's character and strong work ethic added that much more to his overall value to the team.

Defensive tackle La'Roi Glover, who joined the Cowboys as a free agent in 2002, acknowledged the influence that Woodson had on his decision when he said, "Part of the reason I came to the Cowboys was to play with Woody. He was a big hitter and seemed like the leader of the defense. . . . He showed up every day in the offseason to try and improve his game. He didn't take anything for granted."

Former Cowboys head coach Jimmy Johnson praised Woodson for the many contributions he made to the team by describing him as "a player

Woodson's exceptional play against both the run and the pass made him the finest all-around safety in franchise history.
Courtesy of PristineAuction.com

who could hit, tackle and take charge of a secondary. He did all those things with authority. He made his presence known on the football field, but played within the scheme and played smart."

New York Giants cornerback Jason Sehorn also expressed his admiration for Woodson when he suggested, "Woodson might have been their best player. When we were on offense, the Cowboys didn't have to substitute because he could just walk up and man the slot. That's special."

Woodson continued to perform at an elite level for several more years, playing particularly well from 1995 to 1998, when he accumulated more than 100 tackles three times, earned Pro Bowl honors each season, and received All-Pro recognition twice. Although Woodson never again appeared in the Pro Bowl or made All-Pro, he remained one of the Cowboys' best defensive players until a herniated disk forced him to sit out the entire 2004 campaign. He announced his retirement at season's end, concluding his career with 1,350 tackles, which represents a franchise record.

Present at Woodson's retirement press conference, then-Cowboys head coach Bill Parcells said, "Woodson is the kind of guy that makes this profession something that you like to engage in. He's the epitome of a professional. He does epitomize that in every sense; what he did in playing and his approach to the game."

Cowboys owner Jerry Jones added, "For 13 years, he was everything you could ask for—unselfish, reliable, dependable, a team player first and a team leader always. He's a living, breathing example of the saying that character does matter."

In making his announcement, Woodson stated, "When I put that helmet on, I laid it on the line. Not just for this team, but for everyone here. I laid it on the line every time I put that helmet on. I wanted to win so bad that nothing else really mattered. The most important thing was giving everything I had each time I stepped out on the field. And I think I did that." Since leaving the game, Woodson has taken on the role of football analyst for ESPN, appearing regularly on shows such as NFL Live and SportsCenter.

In summing up the overall impact Woodson made on the Cowboys during his 12 seasons in Dallas, Troy Aikman stated, "He was committed to being the best player he could be. The reason we were able to do the things we did is because of guys like Darren Woodson."

CAREER HIGHLIGHTS

Best Season

Although Woodson failed to intercept any passes in 1993, he established a single-season franchise record for defensive backs by recording 155 tackles. He had another big year for the Cowboys in 1995, earning Pro Bowl and All-Pro honors for the second straight time by leading the team with 144 tackles and returning one of his two interceptions for a touchdown. However, Woodson had his finest all-around season in 1994, when, in addition to finishing second on the team with well over 100 tackles, he established career-high marks in interceptions (five) and interception-return yards (140), returning one of his picks 94 yards for his first career touchdown. Woodson's outstanding performance earned him Pro Bowl and All-Pro recognition for the first time in his career.

Memorable Moments / Greatest Performances

Woodson recorded the first interception of his career during a 20–17 win over the Houston Oilers on September 11, 1994.

Nearly one month later, on October 9, 1994, Woodson picked off two passes during a convincing 38–3 victory over the Arizona Cardinals, helping to set up one Dallas touchdown by returning one of his interceptions 17 yards to the Arizona 23 yard line.

Woodson proved to be the hero of a 31–19 win over Philadelphia on December 4, 1994, by making a game-saving interception with just under seven minutes remaining in the fourth quarter and returning the ball 94 yards for a touchdown that sealed the Cowboys' victory over the Eagles. Woodson's pick and subsequent return, which squelched a Philadelphia drive that brought the Eagles all the way down to the Cowboys' 8 yard line, earned him NFC Defensive Player of the Week honors.

Woodson scored the only other touchdown of his career on October 1, 1995, when he picked off a pass thrown by Washington quarterback Gus Frerotte and returned the ball 37 yards for a TD during a 27–23 loss to the Redskins. Woodson also made 10 tackles during the contest.

Displaying his tremendous versatility, Woodson recorded an interception and a sack during a 20–17 overtime victory over the San Francisco 49ers on November 10, 1996.

Woodson nearly crossed the opponent's goal line again on December 15, 1996, when he helped lead the Cowboys to a 12–6 win over the Patriots by recording a pair of interceptions, one of which he returned 21 yards to the New England 4 yard line.

Although the Cowboys lost their September 7, 1997, meeting with the Arizona Cardinals 25–22 in overtime, Woodson turned in a tremendous all-around effort, recording seven tackles, one sack, two forced fumbles, and one fumble recovery.

Woodson recorded two sacks in one game for the only time in his career on November 8, 1998, when he brought down New York quarterback Danny Kanell behind the line of scrimmage twice during a 16–6 victory over the Giants.

NOTABLE ACHIEVEMENTS

- Returned two interceptions for touchdowns during career.
- Recorded five interceptions in a season twice (1994 and 1996).
- Amassed more than 100 interception-return yards once (140 in 1994).
- Recorded more than 100 tackles nine times.
- Led Cowboys in interceptions twice (1994 and 1996) and tackles twice (1995 and 1998).
- Holds Cowboys single-season record for most tackles by a defensive back (155 in 1993).
- Holds Cowboys career record for most total tackles (defense + special teams: 1,350).
- Ranks second in Cowboys history with 1,216 tackles on defense.
- Ranks second in Cowboys history with 134 special-teams tackles.
- Ranks 11th in Cowboys history with 23 career interceptions.
- Three-time NFC champion (1992, 1993, and 1995).
- Three-time Super Bowl champion (XXVII, XXVIII, and XXX).
- 1994 Week 14 NFC Defensive Player of the Week.
- Five-time Pro Bowl selection (1994, 1995, 1996, 1997, and 1998).
- Three-time First-Team All-Pro selection (1994, 1995, and 1996).
- Three-time First-Team All-NFC selection (1994, 1995, and 1996).
- Named to Cowboys' 50th Anniversary Team in 2009.
- Inducted into Cowboys Ring of Honor in 2015.

LEE ROY JORDAN

An outstanding leader and tremendous competitor, Lee Roy Jordan spent most of his 14 years in Dallas serving as captain of the Cowboys' fabled Doomsday Defense. Despite being one of the league's smallest middle linebackers, Jordan used his quickness, intelligence, and intensity to amass more tackles on defense than any other player in franchise history. An exceptional ball-hawk as well, Jordan compiled 32 interceptions and 18 fumble recoveries over the course of his career, with both figures placing him among the club's all-time leaders. Jordan's leadership and strong all-around play helped the Cowboys win three NFC championships and one Super Bowl, earning him two All-Pro selections, four All-Conference nominations, and five trips to the Pro Bowl in the process. And, following the conclusion of his playing career, Jordan received the additional honors of being named to the Cowboys' 25th Anniversary Team in 1984 and being inducted into the team's Ring of Honor in 1989.

Born in Excel, Alabama, on April 27, 1941, Lee Roy Jordan grew up picking cotton and tending cattle on his family's farm, before enrolling at local Excel High School, where he starred on the gridiron as a fullback. After also being courted by Auburn University, Jordan ultimately accepted a scholarship offer to play football at the University of Alabama under legendary head coach Paul "Bear" Bryant. Excelling as both a linebacker and center during his time at Alabama, Jordan helped the Crimson Tide capture one national championship and compile a composite record of 29-2-2 over the course of his three varsity seasons, earning in the process All–Southeastern Conference honors twice and All-America status as a senior in 1962, when he also earned the distinction of being named College Lineman of the Year. The highlight of Jordan's collegiate career proved to be his performance in the 1963 Orange Bowl, when he earned game MVP honors by recording 31 tackles during a 17–0 victory over Oklahoma that President Kennedy attended.

Jordan's exceptional play during his time at Alabama later drew him high praise from Coach Bryant, who stated, "He was one of the finest

Lee Roy Jordan amassed more tackles on defense than any other player in Cowboys history.
Courtesy of Steve Liskey, Retrocards.net

football players the world has ever seen. If runners stayed between the sidelines, he tackled them. He never had a bad day, he was 100 percent every day in practice and in the games."

Subsequently selected by Dallas in the first round of the 1963 NFL Draft, with the sixth overall pick, Jordan chose to sign with the Cowboys instead of the Boston Patriots, who selected him in the second round of the AFL Draft, with the 14th overall pick. After being named the Cowboys' starting weak-side linebacker during the 1963 preseason, Jordan performed well as a rookie, intercepting three passes and placing among the team's leading tacklers, even though he missed seven games due to injury. Jordan remained on the right side of the Dallas defense the following year, before gradually transitioning to middle linebacker over the course of the 1965 campaign.

Taking over at middle linebacker full time in 1966, Jordan began an exceptional 11-year run during which he annually led the team in tackles and never missed a game. Appearing in 154 consecutive contests from 1966 to 1976, Jordan ended up amassing a franchise-record 1,236 tackles on defense, with 743 of those being of the solo variety. Combining with fellow linebackers Chuck Howley and Dave Edwards to form the backbone of coach Tom Landry's Flex Defense, Jordan directed his teammates with unmatched intensity and efficiency, calling all the signals on that side of the ball while serving as defensive captain. And, even though Bob Lilly remained the team's greatest player throughout most of the period, Jordan established himself as the unit's unquestioned emotional leader.

Nicknamed "Killer" by his teammates, Jordan accomplished all he did even though he remained the league's smallest middle linebacker for virtually his entire career. Listed at 6'1" and 220 pounds, Jordan later admitted to weighing closer to 205 pounds most of the time. Yet, his intelligence and competitiveness enabled him to compensate for his lack of size, with Tom Landry saying of his defensive captain, "He was a great competitor. He was not big for a middle linebacker, but, because of his competitiveness, he was able to play the game and play it well. His leadership was there, and he demanded a lot out of the people around him, as he did of himself."

Gil Brandt added, "The way he went all out, he probably weighed 200 pounds by the end of the game."

Amassing as many as 100 solo tackles in a season, Jordan proved to be one of the league's best run-stoppers, although he excelled against the pass as well, recording six interceptions in two separate campaigns. Jordan also had a penchant for scooping up loose footballs, recovering 18 fumbles during his career—a figure that ties him for the second-most recoveries in franchise history.

Named to the Pro Bowl three straight times from 1967 to 1969 and accorded his lone First-Team All-Pro selection in the last of those campaigns, Jordan subsequently showed no signs of slowing down with age,

Jordan also ranks among the Cowboys all-time leaders in interceptions and fumble recoveries.
Courtesy of Dallas Cowboys

earning two more Pro Bowl nominations in 1973 and 1974, while also earning All-Conference honors in both 1973 and 1975. Nevertheless, with Jordan approaching his 36th birthday following the conclusion of the 1976 campaign, he elected to announce his retirement, ending his career with more solo tackles (743), assisted tackles (493), and total tackles (1,236) than any other player in franchise history, to that point. The Cowboys won eight division titles and three conference championships with Jordan serving as their middle linebacker.

Following his retirement, Jordan became a successful entrepreneur, purchasing the Redwood Lumber Company of Dallas and renaming it Lee Roy Jordan Lumber. Under Jordan's leadership, the company grew tremendously, allowing him to later expand his operation to the Hillsboro, Texas, region. Although Jordan still travels to Texas on business from time to time, he currently resides in the Baldwin County section of Alabama, choosing to return to his original home state after he built up his business.

CAREER HIGHLIGHTS

Best Season

Jordan performed extremely well in both 1968 and 1969, helping the Cowboys limit the opposition to a franchise-best 186 points and a league-best 1,195 yards rushing in the first of those campaigns by making 97 solo tackles, before earning his lone First-Team All-Pro nomination the following year. Nevertheless, it could be argued that he had his two finest seasons during the latter stages of his career. En route to earning one of his two First-Team All-NFC selections, Jordan amassed a career-high 100 solo tackles in 1975—a figure that remains the third-highest single-season total in franchise history. However, he excelled even more two years earlier, when, in addition to captaining a defense that held the opposition to a total of just 203 points, he recorded a career-high six interceptions, one of which he returned 31 yards for a touchdown. Jordan's outstanding all-around play earned him recognition as the *Kansas City Committee of 101*'s NFC Defensive Player of the Year and *Football Digest*'s 1973 NFL Linebacker of the Year.

Memorable Moments / Greatest Performances

Jordan scored three touchdowns during his career, with the first of those coming on October 30, 1966, when, during a lopsided 52–21 victory over the Pittsburgh Steelers, he put the Cowboys ahead to stay early in the second quarter by picking off a George Izo pass and returning it 49 yards for a touchdown.

Jordan again lit the scoreboard a little over one year later, on November 5, 1967, when he intercepted a Randy Johnson pass and returned it 33 yards for a touchdown during a 37–7 blowout of the expansion Atlanta Falcons.

Bob Hayes helped change the game forever with his blinding speed.
Public Domain/Wikipedia

that the *Los Angeles Times* described 20 years later as the "most astonishing sprint of all time."

However, before Hayes traveled to Tokyo, the Cowboys selected him in the seventh round of the 1964 NFL Draft (88th overall) with a future draft pick, enabling them to draft him before his college eligibility expired.

Although the Denver Broncos also claimed Hayes with a future pick in that year's AFL Draft, "Bullet Bob," as he came to be known, ultimately chose to sign with the Cowboys, who hoped to develop his previously unrefined football skills.

Joining the Cowboys after he completed his senior year at Florida A&M, Hayes later recalled the circus-like atmosphere that surrounded him when he arrived at his first pro training camp, telling the *Florida Times-Union* in 1999, "I got more exposure in my rookie year with the Cowboys than a Heisman Trophy winner would have gotten. There was a negative aspect to me being there. A lot of people didn't think a world-class sprinter of my stature would make the team, never mind revolutionize the passing game of Pro Football."

Hayes did indeed revolutionize the pro football passing game, making an enormous impact his first few years in the NFL. Taking the league by storm, Hayes earned Pro Bowl, First-Team All–Eastern Conference, and Second-Team All-NFL honors as a rookie in 1965 by catching 46 passes for 1,003 yards, topping the circuit with 12 touchdown receptions, and ranking among the leaders with 13 touchdowns, 1,598 all-purpose yards, and an average of 21.8 yards per reception. Hayes followed that up with a similarly productive 1966 season in which he earned his second straight Pro Bowl selection and consensus First-Team All-Pro honors by placing near the top of the league rankings with 64 receptions, 1,232 receiving yards, 1,337 all-purpose yards, and an average of 19.3 yards per reception, while leading the league with 13 TD catches.

Hayes's blazing speed made it impossible for any defensive back in the league to contain him one-on-one, forcing opposing teams to disregard traditional man-to-man coverages whenever they played the Cowboys and resort to zone coverages instead. Opposing d-backs also attempted to slow down the 6-foot, 187-pound Hayes by employing the bump-and-run against him. Commenting on the overall impact Hayes made after he joined the Cowboys, Roger Staubach stated, "I watched him with Don Meredith while I was in the Navy, and he and Don really changed things in the NFL. They were a fantastic combination, and Bob literally changed the way you had to defend that kind of speed. He got these guys from man-to-man, they played a lot more zone, and I think he was kind of a game changer."

Revealing the manner in which Hayes altered the thought process of opposing teams, legendary Miami Dolphins head coach Don Shula offered, "He changed the game because of his speed. He wasn't just the world's fastest human, he was a great athlete and football player. Put that together, and he made you change everything on your defense when you played the Cowboys."

Hall of Fame wide receiver Tommy McDonald said of Hayes, "This guy was just too much. The defensive halfbacks were scared to death of him. It was absolutely fantastic. . . . He was one heckuva football player."

Confirming McDonald's assessment, seven-time Pro Bowl cornerback Roger Wehrli noted, "You really had to watch where Bob was all the time on the field because he had the ability to break a game wide open on every play. . . . He was fast. . . . I could say that he never beat me deep on a pass to the end zone, but it wasn't because I could run as fast as he did. You always had to give him a little more cushion than you did other players."

Meanwhile, St. Louis Cardinals Hall of Fame safety Larry Wilson, who went up against Hayes on a number of occasions, observed that the league's fastest player differed from other track stars who later pursued a career in the NFL in that he had the ability to use his speed "in a football sense," rather than just trying to run as fast as he could. Wilson explained, "He had several speeds, all of them fast. But defensive backs had to figure out which one he was using, and which one he was going to use."

Hayes continued his string of four straight seasons in which he made at least 10 touchdown receptions in 1967, when he made the Pro Bowl for the third and final time and earned First-Team All–Eastern Conference and Second-Team All-Pro honors by catching 49 passes for 998 yards, scoring 10 touchdowns, averaging 20.4 yards per reception, and amassing 1,291 all-purpose yards. He followed that up with another outstanding season, concluding the 1968 campaign with 53 receptions, 909 receiving yards, 10 touchdowns, and 1,243 all-purpose yards, earning in the process First-Team All-Conference and First-Team All-Pro recognition.

Despite being plagued by injuries in each of the next two seasons, Hayes remained arguably the league's top deep threat, performing particularly well in 1970, when he accumulated 889 yards through the air, scored 10 touchdowns, and averaged a career-high 26.1 yards per reception. Charlie Waters, who joined the Cowboys that year, later said of his onetime teammate, "His speed was mind-boggling. When he got even with you, you'd already lost the race. . . . Most of the track guys I ever knew were kind of lean. When I met Bob, the first thing I noticed was he had such a developed chest and upper-body strength. Almost a barrel chest for a small man. He used that piston action, with the pumping of his arms, to drive his legs. I'd never seen that."

Hayes had his last big year for the Cowboys in 1971, when he caught 35 passes for 840 yards, scored eight touchdowns, and led the league with an average of 24 yards per reception, leaving a lasting impression on the team's new starting quarterback, Roger Staubach, who recalled during a

2014 interview, "He wasn't just a guy with great speed, he had very good hands, and I wish I could have played with him longer. I don't know of any other world class sprinter who can take that speed and transform it into football. Because speed is really, really a great asset, but there's still more to it, and Bob had that world class speed and he played enough football where he knew how to run routes."

Staubach added, "The receivers today, there's really a lot of fast receivers, but Bob Hayes would fit in with anybody today and still be the fastest guy on the team. I don't know of anybody who was any faster than Bob, and if he was healthy and in his prime, I'd put him up against anybody today."

Hayes spent three more years in Dallas, serving the Cowboys primarily as a part-time player during that time, before being dealt to San Francisco for a third-round draft choice on July 17, 1975. Failing to perform up to expectations in his four games with the 49ers, Hayes suffered the indignity of being released by them on October 23, forcing him to subsequently announce his retirement. Hayes ended his career with 371 receptions, 7,414 receiving yards, 9,221 all-purpose yards, 71 touchdown receptions, and 74 total touchdowns, compiling virtually all those numbers as a member of the Cowboys.

Sadly, Hayes drifted into drug and alcohol addiction following his playing days, landing him in prison for 10 months after he pled guilty to delivering narcotics to an undercover officer in 1979. Yet, Roger Staubach maintains that his former teammate should not be defined by his post-playing career struggles, stating, "I liked the heck out of Bob. He got himself into some trouble . . . but he wasn't that kind of person. The personal addiction he had to fight didn't help him, but it was something he had to deal with, and I think, because he would do anything for anyone else, everyone wanted to be there to help him when he had his challenges."

Unfortunately, Hayes's conviction did not sit well with the Hall of Fame voters, who failed to elect him during his normal period of eligibility, prompting Hall of Fame teammate Mel Renfro to say on one occasion, "It's tragic that Bob Hayes is not in the Pro Football Hall of Fame. I played with Bob. I played against him in practice, and he was better than any receiver that I ever faced in my career. He revolutionized the way the NFL played pass defense back in the '60s and '70s. He was just a fabulous player."

However, Hayes eventually did gain induction as a senior selection in 2009, seven years after he died of heart failure at the age of 59 following a long battle with prostate cancer and liver ailments. Although Hayes said nary a word about his earlier snub prior to his passing, those closest to him later revealed how much being enshrined at Canton meant to him, with

- Tied with four other players for Cowboys single-season record for most punt-return touchdowns (two in 1968).
- Holds Cowboys records for: most career touchdown receptions (71); longest touchdown reception (95 yards); highest career average per reception (20.0 yards); highest single-season average per reception (26.1 yards in 1970); and highest career punt-return average (11.1).
- Ranks among Cowboys career leaders in: pass receptions (8th); receiving yardage (5th); touchdowns scored (3rd); and points scored (5th).
- Two-time NFL Eastern Conference champion (1966 and 1967).
- Two-time NFC champion (1970 and 1971).
- Super Bowl VI champion.
- Three-time Pro Bowl selection (1965, 1966, and 1967).
- Two-time First-Team All-Pro selection (1966 and 1968).
- Two-time Second-Team All-Pro selection (1965 and 1967).
- Four-time First-Team All-Eastern Conference selection (1965, 1966, 1967, and 1968).
- Named to Cowboys' 25th Anniversary Team in 1984.
- Named to Cowboys' 50th Anniversary Team in 2009.
- Inducted into Cowboys Ring of Honor in 2001.
- Elected to Pro Football Hall of Fame in 2009.

21

EVERSON WALLS

Initially considered to be too slow to play cornerback in the NFL, Everson Walls proved his doubters wrong by establishing himself as one of the best cover corners in the game during his nine years in Dallas. One of only two players in NFL history to lead the league in interceptions three times, Walls accomplished the feat over the course of his first five seasons with the Cowboys, en route to amassing a total of 44 picks as a member of the team that places him second only to the great Mel Renfro in franchise history. Although Walls never had the good fortune to win an NFL championship until after he left the Cowboys following the conclusion of the 1989 campaign, he helped lead them to four playoff appearances and two division titles, earning in the process four trips to the Pro Bowl, three All-Pro selections, and four All-NFC nominations. And, even though Walls has yet to be inducted into the Cowboys Ring of Honor, fans of the team saw fit to vote him onto both the Cowboys' 25th and 50th Anniversary Teams.

Born in Dallas, Texas, on December 28, 1959, Everson Collins Walls grew up in nearby Richardson, just two miles from the Dallas Cowboys practice facility. Preferring basketball over football as a youth, Walls did not compete on the gridiron until his senior year at Lloyd V. Berkner High School, recalling years later, "Once I started to realize my love for basketball, I learned my skills were tailor made for football. A lot of the things I learned about [basketball], being aggressive toward the ball, coincide with being a wide receiver and defensive back. Judging the ball in the air and things of that nature, they just came so naturally."

After leading the district in interceptions in his lone season of high school ball, Walls received a full scholarship from Grambling State University, where he spent his college career playing for legendary head coach Eddie Robinson. Despite earning Division I-AA All-America honors as a senior by leading the nation with 11 interceptions, Walls went undrafted by all 28 NFL teams in 1981 after he posted a disappointing time of 4.72 seconds in the 40-yard dash at the scouting combine. Looking back at the

Everson Walls led the NFL in interceptions in three of his first five seasons in Dallas.
Courtesy of Dallas Cowboys

consensus view held toward Walls at the time, former Cowboys personnel director Gil Brandt stated, "People didn't draft him because he didn't have top speed. But he had a great understanding of how to play the game."

Brandt added, "We had seen him play for Grambling against Boise State and make two interceptions and knock down some passes in a playoff game. He had ball skills. As soon as the draft was over, we got him. Everson was a product of the computer. He wasn't the fastest guy in the world. He ran a 4.6 and that was an OK time. But he had the ability to react to the ball and had a bunch of interceptions."

Having signed with the Cowboys as an undrafted free agent, Walls began the 1981 season as a backup cornerback. However, after impressing the Dallas coaching staff with his cover skills, soft hands, and excellent instincts, Walls laid claim to the starting left cornerback job by Week 5, after which he went on to lead the league with 11 interceptions, which he returned for a total of 133 yards. In addition to landing him a spot on the NFL All-Rookie Team, Walls's outstanding play earned him the first of his four Pro Bowl selections, prompting Cowboys running back Robert

Newhouse to later say, "Every time you looked up, he was on the field making a play. He wasn't the fastest or the quickest, but he made the play. If you weren't careful, he'd pick it off and run it the other way. . . . He was a technician, and he used everything within the rules and some things that weren't that he got away with."

Walls followed up his exceptional rookie season by recording a league-leading seven interceptions during the strike-shortened 1982 campaign, earning in the process First-Team All-NFC, Second-Team All-NFL, and NFL Defensive Back of the Year honors. Although Walls amassed a total of only seven interceptions over the course of the next two seasons, he continued to do an excellent job of blanketing opposing wide receivers, earning two more All-Conference selections and his lone First-Team All-Pro nomination. Limited to those seven picks by the reluctance of opposing quarterbacks to throw to his side of the field, Walls established himself as one of the most feared cover corners in the league, even though his lack of elite speed occasionally allowed opposing wideouts to beat him deep. Displaying a knack for making big plays with his outstanding instincts and superb ball skills, Walls also proved to be an extremely intelligent player, often baiting opposing quarterbacks into thinking his man had broken free, only to break on the ball at the last moment. And, as Gil Brandt noted, "Everson had excellent hands. He didn't drop interceptions."

Walls earned Pro Bowl, All-NFC, and All-Pro honors for the final time in 1985, when he led the league with nine interceptions, becoming in the process the first player to top the circuit in that category on three separate occasions. (Ed Reed later accomplished the feat as well.) After recording another three picks the following year, Walls signed a three-year deal with the Cowboys worth just over $5 million, making him the second-highest-paid cornerback in the league. However, after totaling seven interceptions over the course of the next two seasons, Walls failed to pick off a single pass in 1989, causing him to lose his starting job during the latter stages of the campaign. Subsequently waived by the Cowboys at season's end, Walls ended his time in Dallas with 44 interceptions and 391 interception-return yards.

In explaining his decision to cut Walls, first-year head coach Jimmy Johnson, who objected to the veteran cornerback's fraternization with Phoenix players following a loss to the Cardinals, later said, "Everson Walls was a helluva cornerback in his prime. But, in the fall of 1989, he was past his prime."

Walls, though, offered a different take on his release, suggesting, "Jimmy Johnson was tired of me. He was trying to get rid of older players and money. We knew we were bad. We knew we weren't talented. He was doing the best he could, and I think I just wore out my welcome. It was a new regime, and it wasn't my place."

After leaving the Cowboys, Walls signed as a free agent with the division-rival New York Giants, with whom he won a Super Bowl while playing safety for the first time in his career in 1990. Following a two-year stint in New York, Walls signed with the Browns, spending one year in Cleveland, before announcing his retirement following the conclusion of the 1993 campaign. He ended his career with 57 interceptions, which represents the 13th-highest total in NFL history.

Although Walls chooses to take the high road when discussing his Ring of Honor snub by the Cowboys, he makes it clear that he believes he earned that distinction during his time in Dallas, stating, "Jerry [Jones] has a new regime with their arena and their team. I have an understanding they take care of their own. We all wore the star, but the line between the new and old is pretty clear. I wouldn't be surprised if I was left off it for some time. I can make a case, but I shouldn't have to make a case. The numbers speak for themselves. I carried myself in a manner that fans should be proud of. I shouldn't have to wait for it or argue for it."

Following his playing days, the gregarious Walls entered into a career in broadcasting, eventually emerging as a TV personality and serving as a commentator for various national sports talk shows. He is also involved in real estate development and gives back to the community by donating much of his time to different charitable organizations and events.

Walls, though, made his greatest philanthropic gesture in March 2007, when he donated a kidney to former Cowboys teammate Ron Springs, inspiring him to later write the book, *A Gift for Ron: Friendship and Sacrifice On and Off the Gridiron*. In discussing the sacrifice he made for his close friend, Walls stated, "It really was an easy decision because I had known a young lady that had done it named Lisa Allen. She had done it when she was 17 years old. She showed a lot of courage. You never know when you're going to inspire someone to do something. It took away any hesitation I had because I knew somebody who had done it."

Unfortunately, Springs died of a heart attack in 2011, after being in a coma for four years. Nevertheless, former Cowboys safety Cliff Harris expressed his admiration for Walls and his kind gesture when he said, "He's a man of heart, and passion and compassion. To do what he did makes him a unique person. Not many people would do something like that for a teammate, but Everson did. That tells you the kind of guy he is."

COWBOYS CAREER HIGHLIGHTS

Best Season

Even though Walls intercepted just four passes in 1983, he had an outstanding season for the Cowboys, earning his lone First-Team All-Pro nomination. He also performed exceptionally well over the course of the strike-shortened 1982 campaign, earning First-Team All-NFC, Second-Team All-Pro, and NFL Defensive Back of the Year honors by leading the league with seven interceptions in only nine games. However, Walls made his greatest overall impact as a rookie in 1981, when he led the NFL with 11 interceptions, which he returned for a career-high 133 yards. Walls's total of 11 picks remains the highest single-season mark ever posted by a member of the Cowboys.

Memorable Moments / Greatest Performances

Walls recorded the first of his 57 career interceptions in his very first game as a rookie, picking off a Joe Theismann pass during a 26–10 victory over the Washington Redskins in the 1981 regular-season opener.

Walls intercepted two passes in one game for the first time in his career two weeks later, picking off Matt Cavanaugh twice during a 35–21 Monday night win over the Patriots on September 21.

Walls again recorded two interceptions during a 29–17 victory over the Los Angeles Rams on October 18, 1981.

Turning in another exceptional performance the very next week, Walls intercepted David Woodley twice during a thrilling 28–27 comeback win over the Miami Dolphins.

Walls was at it again two weeks later, picking off Joe Ferguson twice during a 27–14 victory over the Buffalo Bills on November 9.

Walls displayed his pass-coverage skills before a national audience on November 25, 1982, when he recorded two interceptions during the Cowboys' 31–14 Thanksgiving Day win over the Cleveland Browns.

Yet, the play for which Walls is remembered most occurred during the latter stages of the 1981 NFC championship game, when San Francisco's Dwight Clark gave the 49ers a 28–27 victory over the Cowboys by victimizing him in the back of the end zone on a touchdown reception that became known simply as "The Catch." Recalling the events of the day, Walls, who earlier intercepted Joe Montana twice during the contest, stated, to his hand during the scuffle, before being taken to a nearby hospital for a psychiatric examination. Looking back at the experience years later, Niland attributed his actions to the possession of his soul by the devil, revealing that the incident led to a religious conversion that eventually made him a born-again Christian, stating, "The Lord smacked me right on my face and got my attention."

The Cowboys, though, proved to be far less forgiving, retaining Niland's services for one more year, before trading him to the Philadelphia Eagles for a third-round draft pick prior to the start of the 1975 campaign. Niland spent one year with the Eagles, starting 13 games at left guard for them in 1975, before retiring after tearing ligaments in his left knee during training camp the following season. Although Niland later found religion, it took him quite some time to change his ways following his retirement. After seeing his marriage come to an end in 1983, Niland continued to use drugs and alcohol for several more years. He also served an 11-month jail sentence in 1987 for making false statements to obtain a loan. Reflecting back on his many transgressions, Niland stated in *Where Have All Our Cowboys Gone?*: "I've had a very colorful life, both good and bad. I don't think football is very conducive to growing up. I could tell you some dirty stuff, but I really wouldn't want to repeat it. I could write a book myself. In fact, I did write a book, and I'll print it one of these days."

COWBOYS CAREER HIGHLIGHTS

Best Season

Niland earned First-Team All-Pro honors in both 1971 and 1972, with the first of those campaigns proving to be the finest of his career. En route to also earning one of his four First-Team All-NFC selections in 1971, Niland helped the eventual world champions lead the NFL in total yardage, points scored (406), and rushing touchdowns (25). The Cowboys also finished second in the league in passing yardage and placed third in the circuit in yardage gained on the ground.

Memorable Moments / Greatest Performances

Niland scored his lone career touchdown on November 19, 1972, when he recovered a fumble in the end zone during a 28–7 win over the Philadelphia Eagles.

Nevertheless, Niland's performance against the Miami Dolphins in Super Bowl VI would have to be considered the highlight of his career. Going up against Bob Heinz, who recorded 2½ sacks in Miami's previous two playoff games, Niland overwhelmed the Dolphins right tackle, limiting him to no sacks, while helping to pave the way for Cowboy running backs to amass a total of 252 yards on the ground.

NOTABLE ACHIEVEMENTS

- Missed only two games in nine seasons with Cowboys.
- Two-time NFL Eastern Conference champion (1966 and 1967).
- Two-time NFC champion (1970 and 1971).
- Super Bowl VI champion.
- Six-time Pro Bowl selection (1968, 1969, 1970, 1971, 1972, and 1973).
- Two-time First-Team All-Pro selection (1971 and 1972).
- 1969 Second-Team All-Pro selection.
- Four-time First-Team All-NFC selection (1970, 1971, 1972, and 1973).
- 1974 Second-Team All-NFC selection.
- Named to Cowboys' 25th Anniversary Team in 1984.

CAREER HIGHLIGHTS

Best Season

Hill performed exceptionally well for the Cowboys in both 1979 and 1980, compiling nearly identical numbers those two seasons. After earning Pro Bowl and Second-Team All-NFC honors in the first of those campaigns by making 60 receptions and ranking among the league leaders with 1,062 receiving yards and a career-high 10 TD catches, Hill caught 60 passes for 1,055 yards and eight touchdowns in 1980. However, Hill had his finest all-around season in 1985, when he earned Pro Bowl and All-Conference honors for the final time by establishing career-high marks in receptions (74) and receiving yards (1,113), while also scoring seven touchdowns.

Memorable Moments / Greatest Performances

Although the Cowboys suffered a 27–14 defeat at the hands of the Los Angeles Rams on September 17, 1978, Hill scored his first career touchdown during the contest, hauling in an 18-yard TD pass from Roger Staubach early in the fourth quarter.

Hill recorded the first 100-yard receiving day of his career a few weeks later, when he made seven receptions for 112 yards and two touchdowns during a 24–3 victory over the Giants on October 8, 1978, with his TD grabs covering 17 and 30 yards.

Hill came up big for the Cowboys on September 16, 1979, making five receptions for 91 yards and two touchdowns during a 24–20 win over the Chicago Bears, with his 22-yard TD grab in the fourth quarter providing the margin of victory.

Although the Cowboys lost their November 12, 1979, matchup with the Philadelphia Eagles 31–21, Hill had a huge game, making seven receptions for 213 yards and two touchdowns, with his scoring plays covering 48 and 75 yards.

A little over one month later, Hill capped off a memorable Cowboys comeback in Roger Staubach's final regular-season game by hooking up with his quarterback on an 8-yard scoring play in the closing moments of a 35–34 win over the Washington Redskins. Hill finished the game with eight receptions for 113 yards.

Hill provided further heroics on November 2, 1980, when his 28-yard TD grab with 45 seconds left in regulation gave the Cowboys a 27–24 victory over the St. Louis Cardinals.

Hill proved to be a thorn in the side of St. Louis once again two weeks later, when he made seven receptions for 126 yards and one touchdown during a 31–21 win over the Cardinals, with his TD coming on a 58-yard hookup with Danny White late in the first half.

Hill turned in one of his finest postseason performances against Green Bay in the divisional round of the 1982 playoffs, when he made seven receptions for 142 yards during a 37–26 win over the Packers.

Hill helped the Cowboys overcome a 23–3 halftime deficit to Washington in the 1983 regular-season opener by collaborating with Danny White on a pair of long scoring plays in the third quarter. Hill's TD grabs, which covered 75 and 51 yards, brought the Cowboys to within six points of the Redskins in a game they eventually won 31–30.

Although the Cowboys ended up losing their 1983 wild card matchup with the Los Angeles Rams 24–17, Hill established a new franchise playoff record by making nine receptions during the contest, amassing in the process 115 receiving yards and one touchdown.

Hill again performed brilliantly in defeat on September 15, 1985, making 11 receptions for 181 yards and two touchdowns during a 26–21 loss to the Detroit Lions.

Hill had another huge game later that year, making 10 receptions for 161 yards and one touchdown during a 24–10 win over the Atlanta Falcons on October 27, 1985.

NOTABLE ACHIEVEMENTS

- Surpassed 50 receptions four times, topping 70 catches once (74 in 1985).
- Surpassed 1,000 receiving yards three times.
- Averaged more than 20 yards per reception once (20.7 in 1981).
- Finished third in NFL with 10 touchdown receptions in 1979.
- Led Cowboys in: pass receptions five times; touchdown receptions four times; and receiving yardage eight times.
- Ranks among Cowboys career leaders in: pass receptions (5th); touchdown receptions (5th); receiving yardage (3rd); total yardage (6th); yards per reception (4th); and touchdowns scored (tied-8th).
- Two-time NFC champion (1977 and 1978).
- Super Bowl XII champion.
- Three-time Pro Bowl selection (1978, 1979, and 1985).
- 1978 First-Team All-NFC selection.
- Two-time Second-Team All-NFC selection (1979 and 1985).

Waters added, "People watched Cliff Harris. The quarterback, offensive line, the offensive coordinator, they all watched Cliff Harris. If they didn't, someone might get carried off the field. One player could change an entire team's game plan."

Randy White also praised his former teammate, stating, "Cliff was a 110-percent guy. He had no regard for his body. He would knock your head off."

More than just a threat to opposing wide receivers, the 6-foot, 190-pound Harris proved to be a thorn in the side of running backs as well, playing the game much like a linebacker. One of the first defensive backs to crowd the line of scrimmage, Harris adopted a style different than the one previously employed by most safeties, who typically remained deep in the secondary in an effort to prevent long passes. Finding Tom Landry's Flex Defense very much to his liking since it challenged him both physically and intellectually, Harris later explained, "It was such an intricate, complex defense. It was for the psychologically thinking player and the physical player at the same time. In the secondary, we had double coverages and man-to-man. These were modern defenses that allowed us to confuse the quarterback. It fit my style."

After earning Pro Bowl and All-NFC honors in each of the previous two seasons, Harris made First-Team All-Pro for the first of three straight times in 1976. The following year, he recorded a career-high five interceptions for the league's number-1-ranked defense, helping to lead the Cowboys to their second Super Bowl title. Commenting on his teammate's exceptional performance, Roger Staubach stated, "You can dissect Cliff 100 different ways and he's still a fantastic football player."

Harris continued to play at an All-Pro level until 1979, when he retired to go into the oil business. Looking back at his decision, Harris recalled, "Coach Landry wanted me to play another two or three years. But I had a bad neck and compressed vertebrae. I was a hard hitter and knew how to do it innately, but when I hurt my neck I had to change my style a little. I had a great opportunity to join the oil business."

Harris left the game with 29 regular-season interceptions and another six in the playoffs. He also recovered 18 fumbles on defense, which ties him for the second-most in franchise history.

Reflecting back on Harris's playing career, *Talk of Fame Network* co-host Clark Judge suggested, "Not only was Harris one of the game's top safeties and an all-decade choice; he was an innovator—playing the position as both a safety and linebacker, much as box safeties today do. He could cover, and he was a relentless and sure tackler."

CAREER HIGHLIGHTS

Best Season

Although the fact that Harris had yet to establish much of a reputation prevented him from earning either Pro Bowl or All-Pro honors in 1971, he performed extremely well for the Cowboys in his second year in the league, recording two interceptions during the regular season, picking off another two passes in the playoffs, and finishing third in the NFL with 952 kickoff and punt return yards and an average of 28.4 yards per kickoff return. Nevertheless, Harris had his finest all-around season in 1977, when he helped the world champion Cowboys finish first in the league in total defense by recording a career-high five interceptions, en route to earning consensus First-Team All-Conference and First-Team All-NFL honors for the second straight time.

Memorable Moments / Greatest Performances

Harris, who intercepted two passes as a rookie in 1970, recorded both those interceptions in one game, picking off Fran Tarkenton twice during a 28–10 victory over the New York Giants on September 27, 1970. Harris returned one of those picks 60 yards, which ended up being the longest such return of his career.

Almost exactly one year later, during a 42–7 blowout win over the Philadelphia Eagles on September 26, 1971, Harris recorded a career-long 77-yard kickoff return.

Harris had an outstanding 1971 postseason, recording interceptions in two of the Cowboys' three victories. After picking off a Gary Cuozzo pass that he returned 30 yards during the Cowboys' 20–12 win over Minnesota in the divisional round of the playoffs, Harris intercepted a John Brodie aerial during Dallas' 14–3 victory over San Francisco in the NFC championship game.

Although the Cowboys lost their November 2, 1975, matchup with the hated Washington Redskins 30–24 in overtime, Harris scored the only touchdown of his career early in the fourth quarter, returning his second interception of the game 27 yards for a TD that put the Cowboys up 24–17.

Harris intercepted two passes in one game for the third and final time in his career in the 1977 regular-season opener, picking off Fran Tarkenton twice during the Cowboys' 16–10 overtime win over the Minnesota Vikings.

NOTABLE ACHIEVEMENTS

- Scored one defensive touchdown during career.
- Recorded five interceptions in 1977.
- Finished third in NFL with 952 kickoff and punt-return yards in 1971.
- Finished third in NFL with average of 28.4 yards per kickoff return in 1971.
- Led Cowboys in interceptions twice and tackles once.
- Missed just three games entire career, appearing in every game for the Cowboys in each of his last nine seasons.
- Ranks among Cowboys career leaders with 29 interceptions (9th) and 18 fumbles recovered on defense (tied-2nd).
- Five-time NFC champion (1970, 1971, 1974, 1977, and 1978).
- Two-time Super Bowl champion (VI and XII).
- Six-time Pro Bowl selection (1974, 1975, 1976, 1977, 1978, and 1979).
- Three-time First-Team All-Pro selection (1976, 1977, and 1978).
- Five-time First-Team All-NFC selection (1974, 1976, 1977, 1978, and 1979).
- 1975 Second-Team All-NFC selection.
- NFL 1970s All-Decade Team.
- Pro Football Hall of Fame All-1970s First Team.
- Pro Football Reference All-1970s Second Team.
- Named to Cowboys' 25th Anniversary Team in 1984.
- Named to Cowboys' 50th Anniversary Team in 2009.
- Named to *Sports Illustrated* All-Century Team in 1999.
- Inducted into Cowboys Ring of Honor in 2004.

25

TONY ROMO

O ften criticized for his postseason failures, Tony Romo rarely receives the credit he deserves for being one of the best quarterbacks of his era and, certainly, one of the finest signal-callers ever to play for the Cowboys. An extremely efficient passer, Romo threw for more than 3,000 yards seven times during his career, topping the 4,000-yard mark on four separate occasions. Romo also tossed more than 30 touchdown passes four times and completed more than 65 percent of his passes six times, en route to compiling a quarterback rating in excess of 90.0 in nine different seasons. Along the way, Romo set single-season Cowboy records for most passing yards, most touchdown passes, highest completion percentage, and highest passer rating, while also establishing himself as the franchise's career leader in each of those categories. And, even though he won just two of his six postseason starts during his time in Dallas, Romo led the Cowboys to four NFC East titles, earning in the process four Pro Bowl selections and one All-Pro nomination.

Born in San Diego, California, on April 21, 1980, while his father was serving in the US Navy, Antonio Ramiro Romo spent much of his youth traveling around the country with his parents, before they finally returned to their original home in Burlington, Wisconsin, where his father became a carpenter and construction worker and his mother took a job as a grocery-store clerk. After playing mostly baseball as a child, young Antonio began to display an affinity for football while attending Burlington High School, earning All–Racine County and Wisconsin Football Coaches Association All-State First-Team honors as a senior quarterback. An excellent all-around athlete, Romo also started for the school's basketball team and played golf and tennis.

Following his graduation from Burlington High, Romo enrolled at Eastern Illinois University in Charleston, Illinois, where he established himself as arguably the top quarterback in all of Division I-AA football. En route to earning All–Ohio Valley Conference, All-America, and Ohio Valley

presence, good mobility, and superb instincts, which he often used to elude the opposing team's pass rush and extend plays so that he might find receivers breaking into the open after altering their initial routes. Throwing the ball well on the run, Romo proved to be equally effective from inside or outside the pocket.

Yet, even as Romo rose to prominence among NFL quarterbacks, he became noted for his inability to lead the Cowboys on a deep playoff run, often failing to come up with big plays when the team needed him to do so. Romo's playoff struggles began in the wild card round of the 2006 postseason tournament, when, after guiding the Cowboys on an eight-play, 70-yard drive in the game's final minutes to set up a potential game-winning field goal against Seattle, he bobbled the snap from center. After recovering the ball, Romo attempted to run it into the end zone but was stopped short of the goal line, leaving the Cowboys with a heartbreaking 21–20 loss. Romo made another critical blunder against the Giants in their playoff matchup the following year, throwing an interception from the New York 23 yard line with only 16 seconds left in the game, resulting in a crushing 21–17 defeat for Dallas. And, after guiding the Cowboys to their first playoff win since 1996 in the opening round of the 2009 postseason tournament, Romo lost two fumbles and threw an interception during a 34–3 loss to the Minnesota Vikings the following week. Unfortunately, these crucial miscues tended to obscure from the general public the degree to which Romo excelled during the regular season.

After having his 2010 season cut short by a broken left collarbone that limited him to just six games, Romo returned to top form the following year, concluding the 2011 campaign with 4,184 yards passing, 31 touchdown passes, only 10 interceptions, a quarterback rating of 102.5, and a completion percentage of 66.3, despite playing virtually the entire season with a broken rib and a punctured lung he sustained against San Francisco in Week 2. Although Romo subsequently led all NFL quarterbacks with 19 interceptions in 2012, he also ranked among the league leaders with 4,903 yards passing, 28 TD passes, and a completion percentage of 65.6. Romo again posted excellent numbers in 2013, passing for 3,828 yards, throwing 31 touchdown passes and just 10 interceptions, completing 63.9 percent of his passes, and finishing the year with a QBR of 96.7. Yet, in spite of Romo's strong play, the Cowboys finished just 8-8 all three seasons.

Having undergone back surgery to repair a herniated disk he suffered during a come-from-behind victory over Washington in Week 15 of the 2013 campaign, Romo put together arguably his finest all-around season the following year, when, playing behind the league's best offensive line, he passed for 3,705 yards, threw 34 TD passes and only nine interceptions, and established career-high marks in completion percentage (69.9) and QBR (113.2), leading the league in each of the last two categories. Romo's outstanding play, which led the Cowboys to the NFC East title, earned him Pro Bowl and Second-Team All-Pro honors. Yet, Dallas once again faltered in the postseason, losing to Green Bay in controversial fashion in the divisional round after edging out Detroit one week earlier. Romo, though, could not be faulted in any way for the loss since he completed 15 of 19 passes and threw for a pair of touchdowns.

Romo, who performed brilliantly in 2014 despite suffering two fractures in the transverse process of his spine that forced him to miss one game, experienced further injury woes the following year, breaking his left collarbone during a Week 2 win over Philadelphia. After sitting out the next eight weeks, Romo returned to action, only to have his season come to an end two starts later when he re-injured his left shoulder after being sacked by Carolina linebacker Thomas Davis on Thanksgiving. Subsequently sidelined for most of the 2016 campaign after suffering a compression fracture to the L1 vertebra in his back during the preseason, Romo turned over the starting quarterback duties to rookie Dak Prescott, who performed better than anyone might have expected, at one point leading the team to 11 consecutive victories. With speculation abounding that Romo might reclaim the starting job once he returned to action, the veteran quarterback put that notion to rest during an emotional press conference he held after being reassigned to the active roster in Week 11. With the Cowboys' record standing at 8-1, Romo conceded his role as starting quarterback to Prescott, telling the assembled media, "He's earned the right to be our quarterback. As hard as that is for me to say, he's earned that right. . . . I think Dak knows I have his back. And I know he has mine."

Romo also called his injury a "soul-crushing moment" and stated that he felt a "tremendous amount of guilt" for letting down his teammates, the fans, and the organization. Romo added:

> If you think for a second that I don't want to be out there, then you've probably never felt the pure ecstasy of competing and winning. That hasn't left me. In fact, it may burn more now than ever. It's not always easy to watch. I think anyone who's been in this position understands that. What is clear is that I was that kid once, stepping in, having to prove yourself. I remember the feeling like it was yesterday. It really is an incredible time in your life. If I remember one thing from back then, it's the people who helped

Romo threw for more than 4,000 yards in a season four times.
Bigcats Lair/Wikipedia

me along when I was young, and, if I can be that to Dak, I've tried to be, and I will be going forward. . . . I think you all know that something magical is happening to our team. I'm not going to allow this situation to negatively affect Dak or this football team by becoming a constant distraction.

Romo then closed his address to the media by saying, "Lastly, I just want to leave you with something I've learned in this process as well. I feel like we have two battles or two enemies going on: One with the man across from you. The second with the man inside of you. I think once you control the one inside of you, the one across from you doesn't really matter. I think that's what we're all trying to do."

Romo's heartfelt statements left a lasting impression on everyone in attendance and earned him a tremendous amount of respect throughout the league. They also convinced team management that the time had come to part ways with the veteran QB and permanently turn over control of the offense to Prescott. After the Cowboys spent the next several weeks trying to decide whether they should trade Romo to another team or give him his outright release, the 37-year-old quarterback announced his retirement from the NFL on April 4, 2017. Shortly thereafter, Romo accepted a job with CBS to serve as the color commentator alongside Jim Nantz on NFL telecasts. Romo ended his playing career with 34,183 yards passing, 248 touchdown passes, 117 interceptions, five rushing touchdowns, a completion percentage of 65.3, and a quarterback rating of 97.1.

In assessing Romo's quarterback play during his time in Dallas, Hall of Famer Troy Aikman commented, "He's a special player. Unfortunately, not enough people recognize that."

CAREER HIGHLIGHTS

Best Season

Romo had several outstanding seasons for the Cowboys, any one of which could easily be identified as the finest of his career. However, while he established career-best marks in passing yardage (4,903) in 2012, touchdown passes (36) in 2007, and interception percentage (1.6) in 2009, Romo performed most efficiently in 2014, when, en route to leading the Cowboys to the NFC East title, he earned his lone All-Pro selection by passing for 3,705 yards, throwing 34 touchdown passes and only nine interceptions, and leading all NFL quarterbacks with a completion percentage of 69.9, a quarterback rating of 113.2, and five game-winning drives, establishing career-high marks in each of the last three categories.

Memorable Moments / Greatest Performances

Romo exhibited his ability to direct the Cowboys on offense in his very first start, leading the team to 25 unanswered fourth-quarter points during a 35–14 win over the Carolina Panthers on October 29, 2006. He finished

Romo nearly led the Cowboys to an improbable comeback win over the New Orleans Saints on December 23, 2012, completing a pair of TD passes in the final 3:35 of regulation to tie the score at 31–31, before Saints placekicker Garrett Hartley won the game with a 20-yard field goal 4½ minutes into the overtime session. Romo finished the afternoon with 416 yards passing and four TD passes.

Although the Cowboys ended up losing a 51–48 shootout to Peyton Manning and the Denver Broncos on October 6, 2013, Romo performed brilliantly, passing for a career-high 506 yards, while tying his career-high mark with five touchdown passes.

Finding himself engaged in another see-saw battle four weeks later, Romo led the Cowboys on a 90-yard scoring drive in the final 2:44 of the fourth quarter that culminated with a 7-yard TD pass to Dwayne Harris with only 35 ticks left on the clock. The touchdown connection, which gave the Cowboys a 27–23 victory over the Minnesota Vikings, put the finishing touches on an afternoon in which Romo tossed two touchdown passes and threw for 337 yards.

Romo provided further late-game heroics in the next-to-last game of the 2013 regular season, when he hit DeMarco Murray with a 10-yard TD pass with just 1:08 left in the fourth quarter, giving the Cowboys a dramatic 24–23 win over the Washington Redskins. However, the victory, which helped keep the Cowboys' slim playoff hopes alive, proved costly to Romo, who suffered what was later diagnosed as a season-ending herniated disk injury. Praising his quarterback for his heroic effort, Dallas head coach Jason Garrett later said, "He might have had his finest hour. . . . We talk about mental toughness, being your best, regardless of circumstances. Somehow, some way, he helped us win that ballgame."

Romo turned in another outstanding effort on November 23, 2014, when he led the Cowboys to a 31–28 win over the Giants by completing four touchdown passes, delivering the last of those to Dez Bryant from 13 yards out with only 1:01 left in the fourth quarter.

However, Romo topped that performance four weeks later, leading the Cowboys to a lopsided 42–7 victory over the Indianapolis Colts on December 21, 2014, by tossing four touchdown passes and setting a single-game franchise record by completing 90 percent of his passes, failing to connect on only two of his 20 pass attempts.

NOTABLE ACHIEVEMENTS

- Passed for more than 3,000 yards seven times, topping 4,000 yards on four occasions.
- Threw more than 30 touchdown passes four times.
- Completed more than 65 percent of his passes six times.
- Posted touchdown-to-interception ratio of better than 3–1 three times.
- Posted quarterback rating above 90.0 nine times, finishing with mark above 100.0 twice.
- Led NFL quarterbacks in: completion percentage once; quarterback rating once; game-winning drives once; and fourth-quarter comebacks once.
- Finished second in NFL in: touchdown passes once; completion percentage once; and fourth-quarter comebacks twice.
- Finished third in NFL in: passing yardage three times; completion percentage once; interception percentage once; and game-winning drives once.
- Threw five touchdown passes in one game twice.
- Holds Cowboys record for most passing yards in one game (506 vs. Denver on 10/06/13).
- Holds Cowboys single-season records for: most pass attempts (648 in 2012); most pass completions (425 in 2012); most passing yardage (4,903 in 2012); most touchdown passes (36 in 2007); highest completion percentage (69.9 in 2014); and highest passer rating (113.2 in 2014).
- Holds Cowboys career records for: most passing yardage (34,183); most touchdown passes (248); highest completion percentage (65.3); and highest quarterback rating (97.1).
- Ranks second in Cowboys history in pass completions (2,829) and pass attempts (4,335).
- Four-time division champion (2007, 2009, 2014, and 2016).
- Five-time NFC Offensive Player of the Week.
- Two-time NFC Offensive Player of the Month.
- 2011 Ed Block Courage Award winner.
- Four-time Pro Bowl selection (2006, 2007, 2009, and 2014).
- 2014 Second-Team All-Pro selection.

26

CORNELL GREEN

A gifted athlete who starred at two different positions over the course of his 13 seasons in Dallas, Cornell Green contributed significantly to the success the Cowboys experienced during that time with his tremendous versatility and outstanding cover skills. A member of Cowboy teams that won seven division championships, two NFC titles, and one Super Bowl, Green spent his first eight years in Dallas playing cornerback, before manning the strong safety position his final five seasons. Excelling at both posts, Green made All-Pro four times, earned five All-Conference selections, and appeared in five Pro Bowls while serving as a member of the Dallas secondary, with his outstanding play also eventually earning him spots on the Cowboys' 25th Anniversary Team and the Pro Football Reference All-1960s Second Team. Amazingly, Green accomplished all he did even though he never played a single down of football in college.

Born in Oklahoma City, Oklahoma, on February 10, 1940, Cornell M. Green grew up in Richmond, California, and attended nearby El Cerrito High School. Green then enrolled at Utah State University, where he established himself as one of the greatest basketball players in that school's history. En route to earning All–Skyline Conference honors three straight times and All-America honors twice as a 6'3" forward, Green set the Aggie career record for most rebounds (1,067), a mark that still stands today. He also scored a total of 1,890 points, which places him fifth in school annals.

Having played basketball exclusively while in college, Green intended to pursue a career on the hardwood when the Chicago Zephyrs selected him in the fifth round of the 1962 NBA Draft. Green's mindset remained the same when, on a tip from Utah State basketball coach LaDell Anderson, the Cowboys offered him $1,000 to attend their 1962 training camp in Marquette, Michigan. Looking back at his thought process at the time, Green stated that he viewed the Dallas offer as a $1,000 bonus, recalling, "I figured I'd go there for a week. . . . and they'd cut me."

Cornell Green spent his final five seasons in Dallas playing strong safety, after starring at cornerback his first eight years in the league.
Courtesy of Steve Liskey, Retrocards.net

But, with the Cowboys, who employed a philosophy at the time of finding the best available athletes and molding them into football players, taking note of Green's outstanding all-around athletic ability, the former Utah State basketball star made the team as an undrafted free agent, and even started three games at defensive back, en route to earning a spot on the NFL All-Rookie Team. In explaining his seamless transition to a

27

DEZ BRYANT

One of the most prolific wide receivers to ever don a Cowboys uniform, Dez Bryant has served as an integral member of the Dallas offense for the past seven seasons, making significant contributions to two division championship teams during that time. Surpassing 80 receptions and 1,200 receiving yards three times each, Bryant has proven to be a perfect complement on the outside to tight end Jason Witten and the Cowboys' powerful running game, establishing himself as one of the league's top deep threats despite drawing double-coverage from opposing defenses much of the time. The Cowboys' single-season record-holder for most touchdown receptions (16), Bryant ranks second only to Bob Hayes in team annals in career TD catches (67). He also ranks among the franchise's all-time leaders in pass receptions (sixth), receiving yards (sixth), all-purpose yards (ninth), and touchdowns scored (fourth), with his outstanding play over the course of his seven seasons in Dallas earning him three trips to the Pro Bowl and one All-Pro selection.

Born in Lufkin, Texas, on November 4, 1988, to a 15-year-old mother who eventually served time in prison for dealing crack cocaine, Desmond Demond Bryant suffered through a difficult childhood that offered him little in the way of stability. Living in eight different homes while attending Lufkin High School, Bryant nevertheless managed to establish himself as a star on the gridiron, catching 48 passes for 1,025 yards and 16 touchdowns as a junior, before making 53 receptions for 1,027 yards and 21 touchdowns in his senior year, when he earned All-State honors and All-America recognition from both *Parade* and *SuperPrep* magazines. Also excelling in track and field at Lufkin High, Bryant competed in the triple-jump, the 110- and 300-meter hurdles, and served as a member of the 4 x 100-meter and 4 x 200-meter relay squads.

Recruited by several major college programs, including Texas A&M and Texas Tech, Bryant ultimately elected to enroll at Oklahoma State University, where he spent the next two-plus years playing under head

Dez Bryant ranks second only to Bob Hayes in franchise history with 67 career touchdown catches.
Courtesy of Keith Allison

coach Mike Gundy. After a solid freshman campaign in which he caught 43 passes for 622 yards and six touchdowns, Bryant earned First-Team All–Big 12 and consensus All-America honors as a sophomore by recording 87 receptions, 1,480 receiving yards, and 19 touchdowns, two of which came on punt returns. However, Bryant subsequently found himself declared ineligible for most of his junior year for violating an NCAA regulation by failing to fully disclose his interaction with former NFL star Deion Sanders.

Choosing to forgo his final year of eligibility at Oklahoma State, Bryant entered the 2010 NFL Draft widely considered to be the most talented receiver coming out of the college ranks that year. But, with concerns over his character causing him to drop to the latter stages of the first round, Bryant ended up being selected by the Cowboys with the 24th overall pick after they moved up three places by engineering a trade with the New England Patriots.

Entering the league with a chip on his shoulder, Bryant performed well as a rookie, making 45 receptions for 561 yards and six touchdowns, scoring twice on punt returns, and amassing a total of 1,069 all-purpose yards, before having his season cut short by a fractured ankle he suffered during

Bryant made arguably his biggest reception of the year two weeks later, when his 13-yard TD grab with 1:01 left in the fourth quarter gave the Cowboys a hard-fought 31–28 win over the New York Giants during which he made seven receptions for 86 yards and two touchdowns.

Bryant tied his career high by scoring three TDs during a 38–27 victory over the Philadelphia Eagles on December 14, 2014, collaborating with Tony Romo on scoring plays that covered 4, 26, and 25 yards. He finished the game with six catches and 114 receiving yards.

Yet, Bryant experienced the most memorable moment of his career to-date on November 13, 2016, when, just one day after losing his father, he made six receptions for 116 yards and hauled in a 50-yard TD pass from Dak Prescott during a 35–30 victory over the Pittsburgh Steelers. Bryant, who dedicated his touchdown reception to his late father, subsequently received high praise from teammate Jason Witten, who stated, "I don't know that there's anybody in my career that I've been more proud of, to have the relationship that I've had. To see him as a person, as a player, and the relationship I can have as tight end-receiver—that's certainly something that I'll cherish for a long time."

NOTABLE ACHIEVEMENTS

- Has surpassed 80 receptions three times, topping 90 catches twice.
- Has surpassed 1,200 receiving yards three times, topping 900 yards another time.
- Has made more than 10 touchdown receptions three times.
- Has returned two punts for touchdowns.
- Led NFL with 16 touchdown receptions in 2014.
- Finished second in NFL with 16 touchdowns in 2014.
- Has finished third in NFL in touchdown receptions twice.
- Has led Cowboys in receptions twice and receiving yards three times.
- Holds Cowboys single-season record for most touchdown receptions (16 in 2014).
- Ranks among Cowboys career leaders with: 462 pass receptions (6th); 6,621 receiving yards (6th); 7,354 all-purpose yards (9th); 67 touchdown receptions (2nd); 69 touchdowns scored (4th); and 416 points scored (6th).
- Two-time division champion (2014 and 2016).
- Three-time Pro Bowl selection (2013, 2014, and 2016).
- 2014 First-Team All-Pro selection.

28

ERIK WILLIAMS

H is period of dominance limited to a few short seasons by a serious automobile accident that nearly ended his playing career, Erik Williams failed to maintain the level of greatness he displayed his first few years in Dallas. Yet, even though the lingering effects of the injuries he sustained during that unfortunate accident likely prevented Williams from going down as one of the best offensive linemen in NFL history, he managed to carve out quite a successful career for himself. En route to helping the Cowboys win six division titles, three NFC championships, and three Super Bowls over the course of his 10 seasons in Dallas, Williams appeared in four Pro Bowls and earned All-Pro and All-Conference honors twice each. Meanwhile, the massive right tackle's aggressiveness and nasty temperament helped him build a reputation as perhaps the only man in the league capable of completely shutting down the great Reggie White, whom he dominated both physically and mentally.

Born in Philadelphia, Pennsylvania, on September 7, 1968, Erik George Williams grew up just two miles from Veterans Stadium, in the southwest portion of the city. Too big for the weight limits of youth league football, Williams instead competed in rough-and-tumble pickup games on the local streets that started out as two-hand touch but gradually evolved into full-blown tackle. After later establishing himself as a dominant defensive lineman at John Bartram High School, Williams enrolled at tiny Central State University in Wilberforce, Ohio, when poor grades prevented him from landing a major-college scholarship. Converted into an offensive tackle at Central State, Williams ended up earning All-America honors by helping to lead the Marauders to the NAIA national championship in 1990.

With pro scouts expressing concerns over the level of competition he faced in college, Williams slipped to the third round of the 1991 NFL Draft, where the Cowboys selected him with the 70th overall pick. Serving primarily as Nate Newton's backup at right tackle his first year in the league, Williams saw very little action as a rookie, appearing in 11 games, only three of

Only a serious automobile accident likely prevented Erik Williams from going down as the greatest offensive tackle in Cowboys history.
Courtesy of AmazingHDPic.com

which he started. However, Williams's strong performance at training camp the following year convinced the Dallas coaching staff to move Newton to left guard, leaving the starting right tackle assignment to the second-year lineman. Looking back at his thought process upon learning of his promotion, Williams said, "The day in training camp they named me the starter at right tackle, my first thought was, 'I gotta get ready for Reggie [White].' We weren't playing them till October, but, even early in the season, I watched extra film of him. I was edgy. Put yourself in my shoes. I'm from Philadelphia, I watched Reggie growing up, and I wanted to be like him. Now my job is to block him for a team in the NFL. I mean, that was big, man."

After playing White to a standoff in their first meeting, a 31–7 loss to the Eagles in Philadelphia on October 5, Williams made a name for himself throughout the league by out-performing his adversary in their second encounter, holding him without a sack during a 20–10 win over the Eagles four weeks later. Williams went on to help the Cowboys capture the NFL title in both 1992 and 1993, earning Pro Bowl and consensus First-Team All-Pro honors in the second of those campaigns with his superb blocking.

Known affectionately to his teammates as "Big E," Williams rapidly emerged as the NFL's premier offensive tackle. Standing 6'6" and weighing 324 pounds, Williams made excellent use of his long arms to fend off oncoming pass-rushers attempting to pressure quarterback Troy Aikman. Meanwhile, his nasty disposition and aggressive style of play helped him dominate the opposition in the running game, putting so much fear into opposing defensive linemen that Michael Strahan singled him out for praise during his Hall of Fame induction speech. Williams also made an extremely strong impression on Reggie White, who, according to Green Bay Packer scouts, dreaded going up against him. Employing every questionable tactic at his disposal against his greatest foe, Williams put his right fist into White's throat, gouged his eyes, dove at his knees from his blind side, and leg-whipped him whenever possible. In discussing the manner in which he often extended the rules for his benefit, Williams explained, "Nothing wrong with a head slap, a head butt, or an extra hit after the play. You've got to establish yourself as the boss out there."

Unfortunately, Williams' reign as the dominant offensive tackle in the league proved to be short-lived, since he suffered several serious injuries in a one-car accident on October 24, 1994, that limited his effectiveness somewhat the remainder of his career. Suffering two torn ligaments in his right knee, a broken rib, torn ligaments in his left thumb, and facial lacerations that required plastic surgery, Williams missed the rest of the 1994 season, contributing to Dallas's loss to San Francisco in the NFC championship

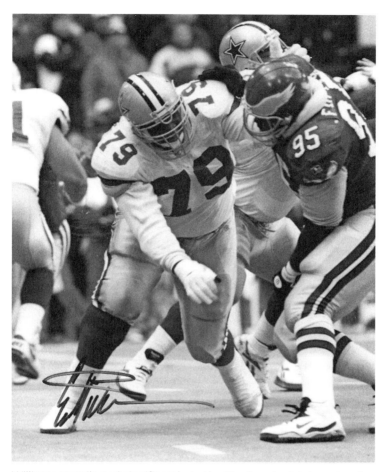

Williams contributed significantly to the Cowboys' mini dynasty of the 1990 with his superior blocking at the point of attack.
Courtesy of BucknutCollectibles.com

game. However, he returned to the Cowboys the following year, when, despite playing at less than 100 percent, he helped lead them to their third NFL championship in four years.

Although Williams never quite regained his earlier form, he remained one of the league's top offensive linemen the next few years, earning three more trips to the Pro Bowl, First-Team All-Pro honors in 1996, and Second-Team All-NFC recognition that same season. The fact that Williams accomplished all he did at less than 100 percent serves as a testament to just how dominant a player he truly was. Troy Aikman later said, "Before the car wreck, he was the best offensive lineman in the NFL. I thought he was on a path to Canton." Williams remained in Dallas until 2000, spending one final season with the Baltimore Ravens, before announcing his retirement following the conclusion of the 2001 campaign.

Hardly a choirboy during his playing days, Williams was acquitted of sexual assault in 1995. Two years later, he survived an accusation of rape when the court dismissed his case after it surfaced that the woman had made a false police report. Williams's troubles with the law continued after his playing career ended, with police arresting him in 2002 amid charges that he assaulted his wife at their home.

COWBOYS CAREER HIGHLIGHTS

Best Season

Although Williams also performed magnificently for the Cowboys the previous season, the 1993 campaign would have to be considered the finest of his career. En route to earning Pro Bowl and consensus First-Team All-Pro honors, Williams helped the Super Bowl champion Cowboys amass a total of 5,615 yards that gave them the league's second-ranked offense. Emmitt Smith proved to be the greatest beneficiary of Williams's superb blocking, gaining 1,486 yards on the ground and 1,900 yards from scrimmage.

Memorable Moments / Greatest Performances

Williams experienced one of the more memorable moments of his career in the final regular-season game of his rookie campaign, when he overcame a slow start to help Emmitt Smith capture the NFL rushing title. With the Cowboys trailing the Atlanta Falcons 27–24 late in the third quarter, Williams replaced an injured Nate Newton at right tackle. After being driven to the turf by the opposing defensive end on his first play from scrimmage, Williams buried his man on the next play, enabling Smith to score what proved to be the game-winning touchdown from 6 yards out. Turning in several other outstanding runs behind Williams during the final quarter, Smith ended up edging out Barry Sanders for the rushing title by finishing the game with 160 yards on the ground.

Williams gained national notoriety on November 1, 1992, when, during a 20–10 win over the Philadelphia Eagles, he held Reggie White to no sacks and just three tackles, earning in the process NFC Offensive Player of the Week honors.

off another two passes in the playoffs, with his fabulous play earning him NFL Defensive Player of the Year honors. However, with Sanders once again becoming a free agent at season's end, he elected to sign a seven-year deal with the Dallas Cowboys worth $35 million, making him the league's highest-paid player. Sanders later revealed in his book, *Power, Money & Sex: How Success Almost Ruined My Life*, that, even though the Oakland Raiders offered him more money than any other team, he chose to sign with the Cowboys for a number of reasons, including his desire to win back-to-back Super Bowls, his wish to garner more significant playing time on offense, and his friendship with Dallas wide receiver Michael Irvin.

Forced to undergo arthroscopic surgery on his injured ankle during the early stages of the 1995 campaign, Sanders had to wait until Week 9 to make his Cowboys debut. Performing well for the team during the second half of the season, Sanders ended up recording two interceptions and picking off another pass during the playoffs, in helping the Cowboys win their third NFL title in four years. Fully healthy and well rested the following year after electing to sit out the baseball season, Sanders earned Pro Bowl and First-Team All-Pro honors by intercepting two passes, recovering three fumbles, one of which he returned for a touchdown, and making 36 receptions for 475 yards and one touchdown on offense. Although the Cowboys failed to make the playoffs for the first time in seven years in 1997, Sanders once again earned Pro Bowl and First-Team All-Pro honors by intercepting two passes, scoring one defensive touchdown, and returning 33 punts for 407 yards and one touchdown. He accomplished all that despite going through a messy divorce that caused him to attempt to take his life by driving his car off a cliff. Sanders later wrote in his autobiography, "The car went down [some 30 or 40 feet] and hit and there wasn't a scratch on me or on the car."

The fact that Sanders recorded just six interceptions over the course of his first three seasons in Dallas can be attributed solely to the unwillingness of opposing quarterbacks to throw the ball anywhere in his vicinity. In discussing the overall impact Sanders made on the Dallas defense, Emmitt Smith noted, "You don't get to this level by not performing. A lot of guys play the game, but, when you start looking at his performance and what he's been able to accomplish in the period of time that he played, you know he shut down one side of the football field. That says a lot about an athlete and a player."

Former Cowboys safety Ray Horton offered, "I think Deion really did revolutionize the man-to-man football game of taking half the field away. What he did in essence was outrun the football. If you threw the ball his way, he would outrun the ball."

Sanders put together a tremendous all-around year for the Cowboys in 1998, once again earning Pro Bowl and First-Team All-Pro recognition by recording five interceptions, which he returned for 153 yards and one touchdown, gaining another 100 yards on seven pass receptions, and leading the league with two punt-return touchdowns and an average of 15.6 yards per return. He followed that up with another strong performance in 1999, earning the last of his eight Pro Bowl selections and All-Pro nominations by picking off three passes and returning 30 punts for 344 yards and one touchdown. Released by the Cowboys for salary-cap reasons prior to the start of the ensuing campaign, Sanders left Dallas having recorded 14 interceptions, scored a total of eight touchdowns (three on defense, one on offense, and four on punt returns), made 49 pass receptions for 624 yards, and gained another 1,320 yards on special teams, with his four punt-return touchdowns representing a franchise record.

Just three days after being released by the Cowboys, the 32-year-old Sanders signed a seven-year, $56-million contract with the Washington Redskins. However, he ended up spending just one season in Washington, recording four interceptions for the Redskins in 2000, before announcing his retirement at the end of the year. After serving as an analyst on CBS's NFL pregame show in 2002 and 2003, Sanders decided to mount a comeback, spending the next two years playing for the Baltimore Ravens, before leaving the game for good following the conclusion of the 2005 campaign. Sanders retired with career totals of 53 interceptions, 1,331 interception-return yards, 493 tackles, 10 defensive touchdowns, 60 pass receptions for 784 yards and three touchdowns, 155 kickoff returns for 3,523 yards and three touchdowns, and 212 punt returns for 2,199 yards and six touchdowns, with his 19 touchdowns scored on returns representing an NFL record. After retiring as an active player, Sanders returned to the role of analyst, spending the last several seasons working in that capacity for the NFL Network.

Leaving behind him a legacy of greatness, Sanders continues to draw praise for the way he helped the position of cornerback evolve, with fellow Hall of Famer Ronnie Lott suggesting:

Deion was one of the few guys that started playing defense but being offensive, meaning that every time there was an opportunity for him to touch the ball he could score. Very seldom do you find guys who play defense and want to be offensive. All of us want to be defensive. But very seldom do you find guys that have that ability to not only create turnovers but take it to the bank and deposit

30

DON PERKINS

The first in a long line of outstanding running backs to play for the Cowboys, Don Perkins spent his entire eight-year NFL career in Dallas, establishing himself during that time as the third-leading rusher in franchise history. En route to leading the Cowboys in rushing in seven of his eight seasons, Perkins accumulated more than 800 yards on the ground four times, setting a club record that stood for 10 years in 1962 by rushing for 945 yards. The versatile Perkins, who played both halfback and fullback during his career, also proved to be an effective receiver coming out of the backfield, enabling him to surpass 1,000 yards from scrimmage on three separate occasions. Perkins' strong running, versatility, and willingness to do whatever the team asked of him helped the Cowboys capture three division titles and two Eastern Conference championships, earning him in the process six trips to the Pro Bowl, two All-Pro selections, and eventual induction into the Cowboys Ring of Honor.

Born in Waterloo, Iowa, on March 4, 1938, Donald Anthony Perkins earned eight letters while attending local Waterloo West High School—four in football and another four in track, where he competed as a sprinter. Continuing to star on the gridiron after enrolling at the University of New Mexico, Perkins played halfback on offense and defensive back on defense, while also leading the nation in kickoff returns as a junior, with his outstanding all-around play earning him All-Skyline honors three times and recognition as the Skyline Sophomore of the Year. Perkins also received Third-Team All-America honors as a senior in 1959.

Although the Baltimore Colts selected Perkins in the ninth round of the 1960 NFL Draft, with the 106th overall pick, the expansion Cowboys, who entered the league too late to participate in that year's draft, had previously signed him to a personal-services contract for a $1,500 bonus and a $10,000 salary that made him their property if and when they received an NFL franchise. Choosing to honor the contract once Dallas officially joined the fraternity of NFL teams, the league awarded Perkins to the Cowboys

Don Perkins ranks third in franchise history with 6,217 yards rushing.
Courtesy of Steve Liskey, Retrocards.net

but made them compensate Baltimore with a ninth-round pick in the 1962 NFL Draft.

Perkins' time in Dallas began somewhat ominously when he suffered a foot injury during training camp that forced him to sit out the entire 1960 campaign. However, after laying claim to the starting halfback job the following year, Perkins ended up earning Pro Bowl and NFL Offensive Rookie of the Year honors by rushing for 815 yards, scoring five touchdowns, amassing 298 yards on 32 pass receptions, and compiling another

Perkins again starred against New York on October 11, 1964, when he carried the ball 17 times for 137 yards during a 13–13 tie with the Giants, tying his career-high mark in rushing yardage in the process.

Perkins proved to be the lone bright spot of a 13–3 loss to the Green Bay Packers on October 24, 1965, carrying the ball 22 times, for a season-high 133 yards.

Perkins helped lead the Cowboys to a 26–14 victory over the Cleveland Browns on November 24, 1966, by rushing for 111 yards and one touchdown.

Although the Cowboys lost the 1966 NFL Championship Game to the Packers 34–27, Perkins rushed for more yardage in the contest than anyone else, carrying the ball 17 times for 108 yards and one touchdown—a 23-yard scamper that tied the score at 14–14 late in the first quarter.

Perkins topped the 100-yard mark for the final time in his career on November 17, 1968, when he carried the ball 13 times for 103 yards and one touchdown during a 44–24 blowout of the Washington Redskins, with his 28-yard TD run early in the fourth quarter giving the Cowboys a comfortable 20-point lead.

NOTABLE ACHIEVEMENTS

- Rushed for more than 800 yards four times, surpassing 900 yards once (945 in 1962).
- Surpassed 1,000 yards from scrimmage three times.
- Finished second in NFL in rushing touchdowns once and all-purpose yards once.
- Led Cowboys in rushing yardage seven times.
- Ranks among Cowboys career leaders in: rushing yardage (3rd); rushing touchdowns (4th); and rushing attempts (3rd).
- Two-time NFL Eastern Conference champion (1966 and 1967).
- 1961 NFL Offensive Rookie of the Year.
- Six-time Pro Bowl selection (1961, 1962, 1963, 1966, 1967, and 1968).
- 1962 First-Team All-Pro selection.
- 1967 Second-Team All-Pro selection.
- Pro Football Reference All-1960s Second Team.
- Named to Cowboys' 25th Anniversary Team in 1984.
- Named to Cowboys' 50th Anniversary Team in 2009.
- Inducted into Cowboys Ring of Honor in 1976.

31

NATE NEWTON

One of the NFL's top offensive lineman for nearly a decade, Nate Newton spent 13 seasons in Dallas, during which time he helped the Cowboys win six division titles, three NFC championships, and three Super Bowls. Excelling at both left guard and right tackle, Newton made six trips to the Pro Bowl, earned All-Pro honors twice, and made All-Conference five straight times, while helping to pave the way for Emmitt Smith to establish himself as the league's all-time leading rusher. Yet, in spite of his many accomplishments, Newton began his pro career in ignominious fashion, going undrafted by all 28 NFL teams, before nearly being waived by the Cowboys due to weight and conditioning problems.

Born in Orlando, Florida, on December 20, 1961, Nathaniel Newton Jr. attended Jones High School, where he played football and basketball, wrestled, and participated in the shotput in track and field. Manning the fullback position on the gridiron until his junior year, Newton moved to the defensive line following a growth spurt that left him better suited to compete in the trenches.

Despite being recruited by several Division I colleges, Newton chose to remain close to home and enrolled at Florida A&M University. Continuing to pursue football as a career path while at Florida A&M, Newton played on both sides of the ball as a sophomore, before concentrating exclusively on offense his final two seasons. Yet, even though Newton earned All-MEAC honors as a right tackle his senior year, all 28 NFL teams bypassed him in the 1983 Draft amid concerns over his small-college background, prompting him to sign with the Washington Redskins as an undrafted free agent.

Cut by the Redskins during training camp, Newton suffered serious injuries in a car accident that very same evening, causing him to sit out the entire 1983 season. However, he returned to the football field the following year, spending the next two seasons playing for the United States Football League's Tampa Bay Bandits, who claimed his services in 1983 with a "territorial" draft pick. Newton remained in Tampa Bay until the USFL folded

Before emerging as a star in Dallas, Nate Newton went undrafted by all 28 NFL teams.
Courtesy of MearsOnlineAuctions.com

following the conclusion of the 1985 campaign, after which he signed with the Cowboys as a free agent.

Finally arriving in the NFL at nearly 25 years of age, Newton spent his first season in Dallas serving as a backup offensive lineman, during which time he acquired the nickname "The Kitchen" since his huge frame made him appear even bigger than Chicago's William "The Refrigerator" Perry. Although promoted to starting left guard the following season, Newton continued to struggle with his weight for another two years, until Jimmy Johnson assumed control of the team in 1989. Challenged to a foot race by Johnson, who nearly cut him from the squad, Newton lost to his 46-year-old head coach, convincing him that he needed to work harder on his physical conditioning.

After getting into the best shape of his young career, the 6'3", 320-pound Newton began to realize his full potential under Johnson, who moved him to right tackle prior to the start of the 1990 campaign. However, even though Newton performed well at his new position, the coaching staff shifted him back to left guard following the arrival of Erik Williams in 1992. Better suited to play along the interior of the offensive line, Newton thrived as never before, earning Pro Bowl and All-NFC honors five straight times from 1992 to 1996, while also earning First-Team All-Pro recognition in both 1994 and 1995. Meanwhile, with the Dallas offensive line functioning as a well-oiled machine, the Cowboys won five straight division titles and three Super Bowls over the course of those five seasons.

An extremely powerful man, Newton excelled as both a pass-protector and a run-blocker, becoming known at the height of his career for holding his own against some of the league's greatest defensive linemen, including Green Bay's Reggie White, who often lined up at tackle in the Packer defense. And, despite manning an unglamorous position, Newton developed a reputation as one of the Cowboys' more colorful players, drawing attention to himself with his outgoing personality, gregarious manner, and braggadocio ways.

After failing to earn any postseason honors in 1997, Newton made the Pro Bowl for the sixth and final time in 1998, tying him with Rayfield Wright and John Niland for the second-most Pro Bowl appearances of any offensive lineman in franchise history, with only Larry Allen (10) having more. However, the 1998 season proved to be Newton's last in Dallas, since the Cowboys released him as part of a youth movement following the conclusion of the campaign. The 37-year-old veteran subsequently signed with the Carolina Panthers, with whom he spent his final NFL season serving as a backup, before announcing his retirement at the end of 1999. In addition to his numerous Pro Bowl and All-Conference selections, Newton's outstanding play earned him a spot on the Pro Football Reference All-1990s Second Team.

Although Newton had a childlike demeanor that endeared him to teammates and fans alike, he proved to be far from innocent off the playing

Newton earned six Pro Bowl selections as a member of the Cowboys.
Courtesy of MearsOnlineAuctions.com

field. Arrested twice within a span of five weeks late in 2001 for possessing huge quantities of marijuana, Newton ended up serving 30 months in federal prison for drug trafficking. He also had other issues, with the most serious of those being domestic abuse, which his wife of eight years later detailed in her 2015 memoir entitled *Silent Cry: The True Story of Abuse and Betrayal of an NFL Wife*. Discussing openly during an interview with *Sports*

Illustrated how her former husband changed shortly after they married, Dorothy Newton revealed:

> The first violence was after the first Super Bowl win. During my time with Nate, there were three Super Bowl wins and, in fact, we married in January, 1992. By the fall season, it had all started. I think that was the first time he physically abused me, although I could see signs, as the verbal abuse began.
>
> I do believe there is a root cause to the violence and the things that he placed upon me; I believe the success and the community and the sports bubble; I'm not making excuses. There are a lot of pressures involved. It happened quite often.

Although Ms. Newton went on to say that her former husband found religion while in prison and has since turned his life around, speaking to children involved in athletics about his past and serving as a member of the North Dallas Community of God, she added that he has never apologized to her for his abusive behavior.

COWBOYS CAREER HIGHLIGHTS

Best Season

Newton played his best ball for the Cowboys in 1994 and 1995, earning consensus First-Team All-Pro honors both years. The Cowboys featured the NFL's fifth best rushing offense in the first of those campaigns, gaining a total of 1,953 yards on the ground, while averaging 3.6 yards per carry. They followed that up by finishing second in the league with 2,201 yards rushing in 1995, while averaging 4.4 yards per carry. Newton's play at the left guard position, at least to some degree, contributed to that discrepancy. Furthermore, after failing to repeat as NFL champions the previous year, the Cowboys ended up winning the Super Bowl in 1995. All things considered, Newton had the most successful season of his career in 1995.

Memorable Moments / Greatest Performances

Although the Cowboys lost the final game of the 1988 regular season to Philadelphia 23–7, Newton experienced one of his more memorable moments during the contest when he recorded the only pass reception of his career, collaborating with quarterback Steve Pelluer on a 2-yard completion.

However, as an offensive lineman, Newton usually found himself living vicariously through the success of others. That being the case, he experienced one of his greatest thrills on October 31, 1993, when the Cowboys rushed for 271 yards during a 23–10 victory over the Philadelphia Eagles.

Newton had another big game on November 7, 1994, when he helped pave the way for Cowboy running backs to gain 209 yards on the ground during a 38–10 mauling of the Giants.

Newton helped lead another assault on the Giants' defense in the 1995 regular-season opener, providing much of the blocking up front for Dallas backs who rushed for 232 yards and four touchdowns during a 35–0 whitewashing of New York.

NOTABLE ACHIEVEMENTS

- Three-time NFC champion (1992, 1993, and 1995).
- Three-time Super Bowl champion (XXVII, XXVIII, and XXX).
- Six-time Pro Bowl selection (1992, 1993, 1994, 1995, 1996, and 1998).
- Two-time First-Team All-Pro selection (1994 and 1995).
- Four-time First-Team All-NFC selection (1992, 1993, 1994, and 1995).
- 1996 Second-Team All-NFC selection.
- Pro Football Reference All-1990s Second Team.

32

GEORGE ANDRIE

An outstanding pass-rusher and excellent run-stuffer, George Andrie spent virtually his entire 11-year NFL career playing alongside Bob Lilly on the right side of the Dallas Cowboys' Doomsday Defense, making significant contributions to teams that won six division titles, two conference championships, and one Super Bowl. One of the NFL's top pass-rushers for much of the 1960s, Andrie led the Cowboys in sacks four straight times at one point, en route to compiling the fifth-highest sack total in franchise history. Displaying a nose for the football as well over the course of his career, the big defensive end scored two regular-season touchdowns and another two playoff TDs during his time in Dallas, with his fumble return against Green Bay in the Ice Bowl proving to be a pivotal play in one of the most memorable games in team annals. Andrie's stellar all-around play ended up earning him five Pro Bowl selections, one First-Team All-Pro nomination, and three Second-Team selections before he left the game in 1972.

Born in Grand Rapids, Michigan, on April 20, 1940, George Joseph Andrie attended local Catholic Central High School, from which he graduated in 1958. After also being wooed by Michigan State University, Andrie ultimately chose to accept a scholarship offer to play football at Wisconsin's Marquette University, where he spent his sophomore and junior years starring as a slot-back on offense and a defensive lineman on defense. However, after the school posted a record of just 3-6 in 1960, it elected to drop its football program, citing financial issues as the cause. Left without a team, Andrie briefly transferred to Tulsa, before returning to Marquette later in 1961. Uncertain of his ability to succeed at the pro level, Andrie spent his senior year at Marquette focusing on his studies and working on his physical conditioning.

Having spent an entire year away from the game, Andrie drew little interest from most NFL teams following his graduation in 1962. Nevertheless, the Cowboys, whose player personnel director, Gil Brandt, had

One of the NFL's top pass-rushers during the 1960, George Andrie led the Cowboys in sacks four straight times.
Courtesy of Steve Liskey, Retrocards.net

graduated from the University of Wisconsin nearly a decade earlier, elected to take a chance on Andrie, selecting him in the sixth round of that year's NFL Draft, with the 82nd overall pick.

Given little chance of making the Cowboys' roster when he arrived at his first training camp in 1962, the 6'6", 245-pound Andrie impressed everyone with his intelligence and outstanding all-around ability, with Bob Lilly recalling years later, "He didn't play his senior year, and he was a little bit rusty. But he was a big guy and he had a great attitude, and he was very intense when he got his uniform on. . . . Coach Landry was installing the Flex-defense about the time George came along, and nobody could learn it in one year, but George probably learned more of it in one year than any of us."

Replacing Nate Borden at starting right defensive end, Andrie performed so well in his first year in the league that he ended up earning a spot on the NFL All-Rookie team. After a solid 1963 campaign, Andrie spent one year at left end, before moving back to the right side of the line, where he spent the remainder of his career.

Playing alongside Lilly, who opposing teams often double- and triple-teamed, certainly helped Andrie emerge as a defensive force. But Andrie also possessed exceptional ability himself, with his size and strength enabling him to hold his ground against the run, and his quickness and agility allowing him to develop into an elite pass-rusher who led the team in sacks each year from 1964 to 1967, with his personal high coming in 1966, when he brought down opposing quarterbacks behind the line of scrimmage 18½ times. Over the course of his career, the big defensive end, who eventually added another 10 pounds to his frame, recorded a total of 97 unofficial sacks, placing him fifth in that category in franchise history. Andrie's long arms also made him extremely proficient at batting down passes if he found himself unable to get to the quarterback.

More than just a pass-rusher, Andrie helped anchor the league's stingiest run defense—one that surrendered a total of only five rushing touchdowns from 1968 to 1969. The Cowboy defense also held opposing ball carriers to an average of just 3.3 yards per carry over the course of those two seasons. Andrie's overall contributions to the unit earned him All-Pro honors four straight times, from 1966 to 1969, with his lone First-Team selection coming in the last of those campaigns.

In addition to his outstanding on-field performance, Andrie proved to be one of the league's most durable players, missing only two games his entire career (with a dislocated elbow in 1963), and starting 136 out of a possible 140 contests from 1962 to 1971. Commenting on his longtime teammate's ability to play through injuries, Bob Lilly stated, "George was a stalwart. Never missed a game. I don't think he ever missed a game. Played with bad knees, bad elbows, cuts, bruises, all the things, in today's world, a lot of guys wouldn't play with."

An exceptional big-game player as well, Andrie recorded 6½ sacks, recovered a fumble, intercepted a pass, and scored two touchdowns in 13

Andrie ranks fifth in Cowboys history with 97 unofficial sacks.
Courtesy of PristineAuction.com

career playoff games, with Dallas perennial Pro Bowl offensive lineman John Niland commenting, "You could count on him—especially in a big game. He always had his head in the big game and played very well."

Andrie continued to excel at right defensive end for the Cowboys until 1972, when he announced his retirement following a season in which he appeared in only three games due to back problems. In addition to earning four All-Pro selections, Andrie made five consecutive trips to the Pro Bowl, appearing in the annual All-Star tilt each year from 1965 to 1969. Following his retirement, Andrie worked with Bob Lilly in a beer distribution business in Waco, Texas, before founding a promotional products company in 1979. He eventually returned to his hometown of Grand Rapids, Michigan, where he currently resides.

Looking back at Andrie's playing career, Gil Brandt suggested, "George's career was way above expectations. I think anytime that you're picked in the 5th or 6th round and haven't played football the previous year, and he came in and did what he did, I think that speaks for itself."

Bob Lilly added, "He was very underrated. He stayed very low to be as big as he was. He made some great plays. He had the most quarterback sacks [in one season] before Harvey Martin beat his record [20 in 1977]. I don't think he got any recognition, really. He would be a very, very good football player today, as I think Jethro [Pugh] would be."

CAREER HIGHLIGHTS

Best Season

Andrie earned his lone First-Team All-Pro selection in 1969, when he helped lead the Cowboys to a record of 11-2-1 and their fourth straight division title. Nevertheless, he had his finest season in 1966, when, en route to earning one of his three Second-Team All-Pro nominations, he recorded a career-high 18½ sacks, which remained a single-season franchise record until Harvey Martin broke it 11 years later. During the latter stages of the campaign, Andrie began a string of eight straight games in which he sacked the opposing quarterback. The streak, which extended into the 1967 season, remains the fourth longest in club history.

Memorable Moments / Greatest Performances

Andrie scored two regular-season touchdowns over the course of his career, with the first of those coming on November 7, 1965, when, during a 39–31 victory over the San Francisco 49ers at the Cotton Bowl, he recovered a fumble in the end zone.

Andrie again lit the scoreboard in the final game of the 1966 season, when, during the first quarter of a 17–7 win over the Giants at Yankee Stadium on December 18, he picked off a Gary Wood pass and returned it 6 yards for a TD.

Andrie also recorded a safety against the Giants on October 27, 1969, tackling New York quarterback Fran Tarkenton in the end zone in the fourth quarter of a Monday night game Dallas won by the lopsided score of 25–3. Andrie's sack of Tarkenton punctuated an extraordinary effort by the Doomsday Defense, which surrendered just 40 yards rushing and brought down Tarkenton behind the line of scrimmage a total of 10 times.

An outstanding big-game player, Andrie performed particularly well against the Packers in the 1966 and 1967 NFL championship games. After sacking Green Bay quarterback Bart Starr twice in the first of those contests, Andrie recorded 2½ of the Cowboys' eight sacks of Starr in the 1967 title game, otherwise known as the Ice Bowl. He also scored the Cowboys' first touchdown in that game, scooping up a Starr fumble and returning it 7 yards, to bring Dallas to within a touchdown of Green Bay midway through the second quarter. The Cowboys subsequently scored another 10 unanswered points, to take a 17–14 fourth-quarter lead, before Starr successfully negotiated a quarterback sneak in the closing moments, to give the Packers a 21–17 victory.

Andrie later teamed up with Jethro Pugh to record a safety during the Cowboys' 5–0 win over Detroit in the opening round of the 1970 playoffs, helping his linemate bring down Lions quarterback Greg Landry in the end zone during the latter stages of the contest.

Although the Cowboys ended up losing Super Bowl V to the Baltimore Colts 16–13 on a last-second field goal by Jim O'Brien, Andrie perhaps delivered the most memorable blow of the contest, knocking out starting Colts quarterback Johnny Unitas midway through the second quarter with a vicious shoulder tackle.

Andrie made another pivotal play in the 1971 NFC championship game, intercepting a second-quarter John Brodie pass deep in San Francisco territory and returning it to the 49ers' 2 yard line, to help set up a 1-yard touchdown plunge by Calvin Hill in a contest the Cowboys went on to win 14–3.

NOTABLE ACHIEVEMENTS

- Scored two career touchdowns (1 fumble return and 1 interception return).
- Recorded double-digit sacks four times.
- Led Cowboys in sacks four straight seasons (1964, 1965, 1966, and 1967).
- Ranks fifth in Cowboys history with 97 unofficial sacks.
- Missed only two games entire career, playing in every game from 1964 to 1971.
- Two-time NFL Eastern Conference champion (1966 and 1967).
- Two-time NFC champion (1970 and 1971).
- Super Bowl VI champion.
- Member of 1962 NFL All-Rookie Team.
- Five-time Pro Bowl selection (1965, 1966, 1967, 1968, and 1969).
- 1969 First-Team All-Pro selection.
- Three-time Second-Team All-Pro selection (1966, 1967, and 1968).

33
MARK STEPNOSKI

One of the finest centers of his era, Mark Stepnoski helped the Cowboys win three division titles and two Super Bowls between 1991 and 1994. Spending nine of his 13 NFL seasons in Dallas, Stepnoski did two tours of duty with the club, centering the Cowboys' offensive line from 1989 to 1994 and, then again, from 1999 to 2001. Proving to be an exceptional blocker at the point of attack during that time, Stepnoski helped the Cowboys advance to the playoffs on five separate occasions, earning in the process three trips to the Pro Bowl, two All-Pro selections, and a spot on the Cowboys' 50th Anniversary Team in 2009.

Born in Erie, Pennsylvania, on January 20, 1967, Mark Matthew Stepnoski attended local Cathedral Preparatory School, where he earned All-State and *Parade* High School All-America honors as an offensive tackle. Recruited by several major colleges as he neared graduation, Stepnoski ultimately elected to enroll at the University of Pittsburgh, where he spent the next four years starting at guard, helping to clear the way for Craig Heyward and Curvin Richards to become two of the nation's leading rushers. After being named a Third-Team All-American as a sophomore, Stepnoski earned First-Team recognition in each of the next two seasons, performing so well as a senior that he ended up being one of the three finalists for that year's Outland Trophy, presented annually to the best interior lineman in college football.

Considered by most pro scouts to be too small to succeed in the NFL, Stepnoski slipped to the third round of the 1989 NFL Draft, where the Cowboys selected him with the 57th overall pick. Switched to center upon his arrival in Dallas, Stepnoski spent his first year in the league being tutored by veteran center Tom Rafferty, before assuming the starting role during the latter stages of the campaign. Stepnoski continued to function in that capacity the next five seasons, starting 75 out of a possible 80 games during that time, as the Cowboys gradually built themselves into an NFL powerhouse. Combining with Erik Williams, Mark Tuinei, Nate Newton, and Kevin Gogan from 1992 to 1994 to form what became known as "The

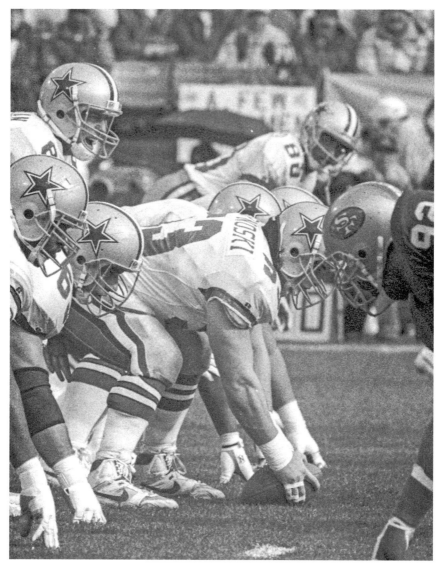

Mark Stepnoski helped the Cowboys advance to the playoffs five straight times during the 1990s.
Courtesy of George A. Kitrinos

Great Wall of Dallas," Stepnoski went on to establish himself as the leader of one of the greatest offensive lines in NFL history, providing ample protection for quarterback Troy Aikman in the passing game, while opening up huge holes for Emmitt Smith in the running game.

Although somewhat undersized at 6'2" and 269 pounds, Stepnoski used his athletic ability, leverage, and balance to outmaneuver bigger defensive linemen, becoming in the process one of the league's top centers. In discussing the attitude he applied to his craft, Stepnoski explained, "If you're just out there doing what you're supposed to be doing and doing it well, it doesn't matter how big you are."

Considered to be one of the league's strongest players by Troy Aikman, Stepnoski drew praise from his quarterback, who noted, "He works exceptionally hard at it [his strength], and I think that's what's made him the player he is. I think his work ethic is unmatched for guys up front in the offensive line, and he's got tremendous leverage. Because he's not as big as guys he goes up against, leverage is extremely important for him."

After earning the first of his three straight trips to the Pro Bowl and Second-Team All-Pro recognition in 1992 by anchoring the offensive line of the Super Bowl champions, Stepnoski made First-Team All-NFC for the second of three straight times when Dallas repeated as league champions the following year. Although the Cowboys failed to capture their third consecutive NFL championship in 1994, Stepnoski earned All-Pro honors for the second and final time as a member of the team.

A free agent following the conclusion of the 1994 campaign, Stepnoski elected to sign with the Houston Oilers, for whom he spent the next four seasons starting at center, earning two more trips to the Pro Bowl and one more All-Pro selection during that time. Although the Cowboys ended up winning the Super Bowl once in Stepnoski's absence, Troy Aikman suggested during a 1997 interview that the team had yet to find a suitable replacement for him, stating, "He's a guy who we hated to see leave, quite honestly. He and I came in together here in Dallas back in '89. . . . I think we've been trying to look for someone to fill that spot ever since."

Meanwhile, Stepnoski made an extremely favorable impression on his new teammates in Houston, with Oilers quarterback Steve McNair saying, "He's always there in the right place using the right technique, and he's got quick feet, and he gets good position on the guards. That's what gets him to the Pro Bowl every year."

Houston guard Kevin Donnalley, who lined up immediately to Stepnoski's right, praised his teammate for his strength and balance, commenting, "That's how he's able to neutralize and play at 260 pounds. You rarely see him out of position when blocking somebody. If he does, he usually gets washed up in some of the bulk out there. But usually he's ready for stuff and just paves things and really studies film. That's why he's one of the best, and will be for some time."

Stepnoski remained with the Oilers when they moved to Tennessee in 1997. However, after becoming a free agent once again, he rejoined the Cowboys in 1999, spending three more solid years in Dallas, before announcing his retirement following the conclusion of the 2001 campaign. He ended his career having earned five trips to the Pro Bowl, three All-Pro selections, and four All-Conference nominations.

An advocate for the legalization of marijuana, Stepnoski found his stance to be in direct opposition to that of his alma mater, Cathedral Preparatory School, which rescinded his nomination to the institution's Athletic Hall of Fame. For that same reason, Stepnoski ended up immigrating to Canada following the conclusion of his playing career.

COWBOYS CAREER HIGHLIGHTS

Best Season

Stepnoski earned Second-Team All-Pro honors in both 1992 and 1994, helping the Cowboys rank among the NFL's top offenses both years. However, while only the UPI accorded Stepnoski First-Team All-NFC honors in 1994, he received consensus First-Team All-Conference recognition two years earlier, while also being named First-Team All-Pro by the Newspaper Enterprise Association. Factoring everything into the equation, 1992 would have to be considered the finest season of Stepnoski's career.

Memorable Moments / Greatest Performances

With Stepnoski serving as the quarterback of the offensive line, the success the Cowboys experienced in the running game often hinged on his personal performance. That being the case, Stepnoski turned in one of his finest efforts in the opening round of the 1990 playoffs, when the Cowboys rushed for 188 yards during their 41–10 victory over the Phoenix Cardinals.

Stepnoski and the rest of the Dallas offensive line turned in another dominant performance against Phoenix on September 22, 1991, when the Cowboys gained 181 yards on the ground during a 17–9 win over the Cardinals.

Stepnoski helped pave the way for Dallas running backs to rush for 196 yards during a 41–17 blowout of the Atlanta Falcons on December 21, 1992.

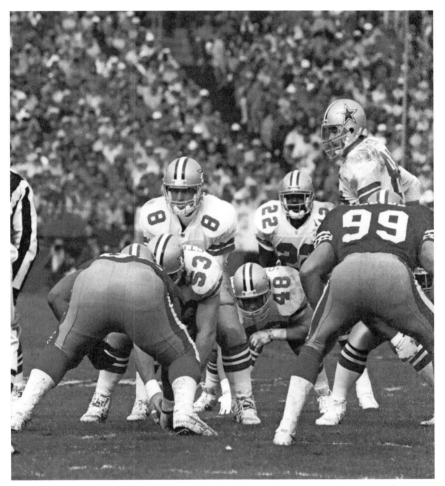

Seen here preparing to snap the ball to quarterback Troy Aikman, Mark
Stepnoski (#53) established himself as the leader of "The Great Wall of Dallas"
during his time with the Cowboys.
Courtesy of George A. Kitrinos

Stepnoski also performed exceptionally well during the Cowboys'
34–10 victory over Philadelphia in the opening round of the 1992 postseason tournament, anchoring an offensive line that helped Dallas running
backs gain 160 yards on the ground.

NOTABLE ACHIEVEMENTS

- Two-time NFC champion (1992 and 1993).
- Two-time Super Bowl champion (XXVII and XXVIII).
- Three-time Pro Bowl selection (1992, 1993, and 1994).
- Two-time Second-Team All-Pro selection (1992 and 1994).
- Three-time First-Team All-NFC selection (1992, 1993, and 1994).
- NFL 1990s All-Decade Team.
- Pro Football Hall of Fame All-1990s Second Team.
- Pro Football Reference All-1990s Second Team.
- Named to Cowboys' 50th Anniversary Team in 2009.

34

JIM JEFFCOAT

Often overlooked and underappreciated, Jim Jeffcoat spent 12 years in Dallas, but rarely received the credit he deserved for being one of the top defensive ends in franchise history. Experiencing numerous highs and lows in his years with the Cowboys, Jeffcoat spent the early part of his career playing for winning teams, before persevering through five straight losing seasons and, finally, sharing in the glory days of the early 1990s. Through it all, Jeffcoat continued to perform at a high level, annually ranking among the team leaders in sacks and tackles, while also appearing in 188 consecutive non-strike games. An excellent pass-rusher, Jeffcoat posted double-digit sacks five times for the Cowboys, en route to amassing a total of 94½ sacks that places him seventh in team annals. Strong against the run as well, Jeffcoat recorded more than 70 tackles in five different seasons. Although Jeffcoat never earned All-Pro or Pro Bowl honors, he proved to be a huge contributor to Cowboys teams that won four division titles, two conference championships, and two Super Bowls.

Born in Cliffwood, New Jersey, on April 1, 1961, James Wilson Jeffcoat Jr. grew up in nearby Matawan, where he earned All-America honors in football and lettered in wrestling while attending Matawan Regional High School. Jeffcoat then enrolled at Arizona State University and spent three years starting at defensive end. Playing his best ball for the Sun Devils as a senior in 1982, Jeffcoat earned All–Pac-10 honors and Honorable Mention to the All-America Associated Press and *Sporting News* teams.

Subsequently selected by the Cowboys in the first round of the 1983 NFL Draft, with the 23rd overall pick, Jeffcoat joined a team in Dallas that had appeared in each of the last three NFC championship games. Although the Cowboys failed to advance beyond the first round of the postseason tournament in Jeffcoat's first year in the league, they remained a very strong team with an imposing defensive line that featured starters Randy White, Harvey Martin, Ed "Too Tall" Jones, and John Dutton. As a result, Jeffcoat spent most of his rookie campaign serving on special teams,

Jim Jeffcoat ranks among the Cowboys' career leaders in both sacks and tackles.
Courtesy of ICollector.com

recording just two quarterback sacks. However, after Martin announced his retirement at season's end, Jeffcoat took over at starting right defensive end the following year. Acquitting himself extremely well in his first year as a starter, the 6'5", 274-pound Jeffcoat finished second on the team with 11½ sacks, recorded 82 tackles, and scored the first of his four career touchdowns after recovering a fumble. Continuing to improve his play by studying films of former Cowboy standouts Bob Lilly and George Andrie, Jeffcoat had another excellent year in 1985, recording 12 sacks and 77 tackles, recovering two fumbles, and scoring another touchdown, this time on a career-long 65-yard interception return against the New York Giants.

With much of the team's veteran nucleus having retired by 1986, the Cowboys subsequently entered into a period of mediocrity Dallas fans had not witnessed since the franchise's earliest days in the league. Yet, Jeffcoat continued to perform well, having arguably his two finest seasons in 1986 and 1989. After recording a team-leading 14 sacks in the first of those campaigns, he registered 11½ sacks and a career-high 100 tackles in the second.

In addition to his outstanding play on the field, Jeffcoat gradually emerged as a leader in the clubhouse, endearing himself to his teammates and coaches with his quiet demeanor and strong work ethic. Shunning the spotlight, Jeffcoat spoke to the media only when necessary, perhaps contributing to his lack of notoriety throughout the league. Yet, the veteran defensive end proved to be a major factor in the resurgence the Cowboys experienced during the early part of the 1990s, providing guidance and leadership to his younger teammates.

After spending the previous eight seasons starting at right defensive end, Jeffcoat assumed more of a complementary role in 1992, when the presence of Tony Tolbert and Charles Haley prompted head coach Jimmy Johnson to turn him into a situational pass-rusher. Excelling in his new role, Jeffcoat helped lead the Cowboys to their third NFL title by making 10½ sacks during the regular season, before recording another two sacks in the playoffs. Although somewhat less productive the following year, Jeffcoat still managed to finish second on the team with six sacks, helping the Cowboys capture their second straight world championship in the process. Jeffcoat remained in Dallas one more year, recording eight sacks in 1994, before signing a lucrative free-agent contract with the Buffalo Bills at season's end. He left the Cowboys with career totals of 94½ sacks, 689 tackles, and 149 quarterback pressures, placing him among the franchise's all-time leaders in each of the first two categories.

Jeffcoat ended up spending three years in Buffalo, recording just eight sacks during that time, before announcing his retirement following the conclusion of the 1997 campaign. He ended his career with 102½ sacks, 745 tackles, 194 quarterback pressures, two interceptions, 11 fumble recoveries, 18 forced fumbles, and four touchdowns, compiling the vast majority of those numbers while playing for the Cowboys.

Following his playing days, Jeffcoat returned to Dallas, where he spent seven seasons serving on the Cowboys' coaching staff, mostly as defensive ends coach. Under Jeffcoat's tutelage, linemen Greg Ellis and Ebenezer Ekuban overcame adversity and developed into solid players. After leaving the Cowboys in 2005, Jeffcoat spent two years working in the private business sector, before joining Kevin Sumlin's staff at the University of Houston as defensive line coach in 2008. He has since assumed a similar role on the coaching staffs of San Jose State and the University of Colorado.

COWBOYS CAREER HIGHLIGHTS

Best Season

Jeffcoat had a big year for the Cowboys in 1986, when he recorded a career-high 14 sacks, which placed him seventh in the league rankings. Nevertheless, he had his finest all-around season in 1989, when, playing for a Cowboys team that compiled a regular-season record of just 1-15, he made 11½ sacks, recorded a career-high 100 tackles and 42 quarterback pressures, and recovered three fumbles, which he returned for a total of 77 yards and one touchdown.

Memorable Moments / Greatest Performances

Jeffcoat, who recorded just two sacks as a rookie in 1983, got both of those in one game, bringing down Kansas City quarterbacks twice during a 41–21 victory over the Chiefs on November 20.

Jeffcoat, who displayed a propensity for making big plays during his time in Dallas, recorded the first of his four career touchdowns on October 21, 1984, when he recovered a fumble in the end zone during the latter stages of the fourth quarter, thereby tying the score with New Orleans at 27–27. Rafael Septien subsequently kicked a 41-yard field goal during the overtime session, giving the Cowboys a thrilling 30–27 come-from-behind victory in a game they earlier trailed by 21 points heading into the fourth quarter.

Jeffcoat crossed the opponent's goal line for the second time in his career on December 15, 1985, when, during a crucial game against the New York Giants that had huge playoff implications, he completely shifted the momentum of the contest by intercepting a deflected Phil Simms pass and returning it 65 yards for a TD that knotted the score at 14–14 midway through the second quarter. Jeffcoat, who also recorded two sacks during the 28–21 Cowboys win, earned NFC Defensive Player of the Week honors for his strong performance.

Jeffcoat again proved to be a thorn in the side of Simms and the Giants on November 2, 1987, when he picked off a Simms pass and returned it 26 yards for a touchdown during a 33–24 Dallas win over New York.

Although the Cowboys suffered a humiliating 30–7 defeat at the hands of the arch-rival Washington Redskins on September 24, 1989, Jeffcoat scored the last of his four career touchdowns during the game, rumbling 77 yards for the Cowboys' only points of the contest after recovering a fumble midway through the first quarter.

Jeffcoat had a big game against Philadelphia on October 19, 1986, recording 3½ of the 10 sacks the Cowboys registered during a 17–14 win over the Eagles.

Jeffcoat began his final season in Dallas in grand fashion, sacking Pittsburgh quarterback Neil O'Donnell three times during a 26–9 victory over the Steelers in the 1994 regular-season opener.

However, Jeffcoat turned in the most memorable performance of his career on November 10, 1985, when, during a 13–7 win over the Redskins, he sacked Joe Theismann a club record five times and recorded 11 tackles, en route to earning NFC Defensive Player of the Week honors.

NOTABLE ACHIEVEMENTS

- Scored four career touchdowns (two interception returns and two fumble returns).
- Finished in double digits in sacks five times.
- Amassed more than 80 tackles three times, recording 100 tackles in 1989.
- Led Cowboys in sacks three times and tackles once.
- Appeared in 188 consecutive non-strike games.
- Ranks among Cowboys career leaders with: 94½ sacks (7th); 689 tackles (10th); and four touchdowns scored on defense (3rd).
- Two-time NFC champion (1992 and 1993).
- Two-time Super Bowl champion (XXVII and XXVIII).
- Two-time NFC Defensive Player of the Week.

35

JETHRO PUGH

His career spanning two distinct eras of Cowboys football, Jethro Pugh spent his 14 years in Dallas playing alongside legendary defensive linemen such as Bob Lilly, Randy White, Harvey Martin, and Ed "Too Tall" Jones. As a result, Pugh never received the acclaim he so richly deserved, failing to earn Pro Bowl honors at any time during his career, and making Second-Team All-Pro just once. Nevertheless, the massive defensive tackle, whom sportswriter Jim Murray once called "the greatest defensive lineman in the NFL never selected to the Pro Bowl," served the Cowboys well over the course of his career, helping them win 10 division titles, five conference championships, and two Super Bowls. And, even though Pugh spent his first 10 seasons playing in the shadow of the great Bob Lilly, he amassed more sacks than his longtime teammate, leading the Cowboys in that category five straight times at one point, en route to compiling the sixth-highest total in franchise history.

Born in Windsor, North Carolina, on July 3, 1944, Jethro Pugh Jr. attended local W. S. Etheridge High School, before enrolling at nearby Elizabeth City State College at the tender age of 16 following his graduation. A two-way player for the Elizabeth City State football team, Pugh twice earned All-CIAA honors while playing defensive end for the Vikings.

Scouted by Cowboys player personnel director Gil Brandt while in college, the 6'6", 260-pound Pugh arrived in Dallas shortly after Brandt tabbed him in the 11th round of the 1965 NFL Draft, with the 145th overall pick. Looking back years later at the qualities that prompted him to select Pugh, who the AFL's Oakland Raiders also sought to sign, Brandt recalled, "He was a pup when we got him. He was just 20 years old. He had never been on a weight program. But the guy was a tremendous athlete. He had speed. He had long arms. He could do anything. . . . He would have been a top-10 type player in the draft today."

After serving as a backup defensive end to starters George Andrie and Willie Townes his first two years with the Cowboys, Pugh moved to the

Despite never earning Pro Bowl honors, Jethro Pugh proved to be a huge
contributor to Cowboys teams that won 10 division titles, five conference
championships, and two Super Bowls.
Courtesy of Dallas Cowboys

interior of the Dallas defense in 1967, replacing Jim Colvin as the starting
left tackle—a position he manned for the remainder of his career. Excelling
at his new post, Pugh quickly developed into one of the league's top tackles,
even though the presence of Lilly and Andrie to his right often prevented
him from receiving his just due. After recording a safety and leading the
NFL with four fumble recoveries in 1967, Pugh emerged as the Cowboys'
best pass-rusher the following year, leading the team in sacks in each of the

next five seasons. Tackling opposing quarterbacks behind the line of scrimmage an average of 12½ times per year from 1968 to 1972, Pugh recorded a
career-high 15½ sacks in the first of those campaigns, earning in the process
his lone Second-Team All-Pro selection.

Even though the contributions Pugh made to the success the Cowboys
experienced during that time went largely unnoticed by outsiders, those
within the organization knew how much he meant to the team. Gil Brandt
suggested, "He was a terribly unsung person among that bunch of great players." Linemate Bob Lilly added, "He was very smart, and he had some real
smooth moves to get around his blockers. For a guy as big and tall as he was,
he stayed real low. He had good balance, was pretty quick and very agile."

A consummate team player, Pugh chose not to let the lack of recognition he received bother him, learning from coach Tom Landry that awards
do not define a man. In discussing his former coach, Pugh later revealed,
"Coach Landry was so fair and honest. He put my mind at rest. He was a
powerful guy."

In addition to doing an outstanding job of rushing the passer, Pugh
excelled against the run, using his size and athleticism to his advantage. He
also proved to be extremely durable, never missing more than two games
in any single season, and starting 120 out of a possible 126 contests from
1966 to 1974. In fact, Pugh started 12 games in 1971 even though he spent
much of the season suffering from appendicitis. Opting to delay his surgery
until the offseason, Pugh made it through the campaign by taking shots of
penicillin.

A stabilizing force on the interior of the Dallas Doomsday Defense
throughout the first half of his career, Pugh assumed a similar role as the
faces along the Cowboys' defensive front changed. After spending his first
several seasons being overshadowed by Lilly and Andrie, Pugh once again
put his ego aside when Harvey Martin and Ed "Too Tall" Jones joined him
on the d-line during the mid-1970s. Yet, through it all, Pugh remained one
of the team's unsung heroes, helping the Cowboys win five NFC titles and
two Super Bowls. And, by the time Pugh announced his retirement following the conclusion of the 1978 campaign, he had helped the Cowboys
advance to the playoffs 12 times and recorded a total of 95½ unofficial
sacks—a figure that places him sixth in franchise history.

Following his retirement, Pugh opened a number of western-themed
gift shops at Dallas–Fort Worth International Airport in Texas. He later
expanded his business and partnered with The Paradise Shops, which are
present at 64 airports across the United States and Canada. Pugh also continued to host an annual Jethro Pugh Celebrity Golf Tournament in Dallas

Pugh led the Cowboys in sacks five straight times from 1968 to 1972.
Courtesy of Steve Liskey, Retrocards.net

to raise funds for the United Negro College Fund until he died of natural causes at the age of 70, on January 7, 2015.

Upon learning of Pugh's passing, Cowboys owner Jerry Jones stated, "He was loved and appreciated by his teammates and Cowboys fans for decades, and his spirit will be felt when our team travels to Green Bay this weekend."

Gil Brandt expressed similar sentiments, saying, "He had the respect of everybody. He was a tremendous person. The guy will be missed."

Roger Staubach added, "Jethro was not only a great player, but he was one of the nicest, most generous and humble human beings you ever want to meet."

CAREER HIGHLIGHTS

Best Season

Although Pugh recorded double-digit sacks in each of the next three seasons as well, he had his best year for the Cowboys in 1968, when, en route to earning All-Pro honors for the only time, he led the team with a career-high 15½ sacks and helped anchor a defense that allowed the opposition just two rushing touchdowns all year.

Memorable Moments / Greatest Performances

Although there is no official record of how many sacks Pugh himself recorded during the contest, the Dallas left tackle led an assault on quarterbacks Dick Shiner and Kent Nix during a 28–7 victory over the Steelers on December 8, 1968, that resulted in the two Pittsburgh signal-callers being sacked a total of eight times.

Pugh, who also recorded two regular-season safeties during his career, made his biggest end-zone stop in the opening round of the 1970 playoffs, when he combined with linemate George Andrie to bring down Detroit quarterback Greg Landry for two points during the Cowboys' 5–0 win over the Lions.

Pugh recorded the only pass interception of his career on September 20, 1970, when he picked off a Norm Snead pass during the Cowboys' 17–7 victory over the Philadelphia Eagles in the opening game of the regular season.

An outstanding postseason performer, Pugh recorded 4½ sacks during the 1967 playoffs, with three of those coming against Green Bay quarterback Bart Starr in the NFL championship game. Pugh made one of the game's key plays midway through the second quarter, when he jarred the ball loose from Starr, enabling George Andrie to scoop up the pigskin deep in Green Bay territory and lumber into the end zone for the Cowboys' first points of the contest.

Nevertheless, there is little doubt that the play for which Pugh is remembered most is one that Cowboy fans would like to forget. With the Cowboys clinging to a slim 17–14 lead in the closing moments of that same 1967 NFL championship game and a berth in Super Bowl II at stake, Green Bay tried unsuccessfully to run the ball into the Dallas end zone from the 1 yard line on consecutive plays. After calling their final timeout with just 16 seconds left in the contest, the Packers turned to Bart Starr, who, behind a double-team block on Pugh by right guard Jerry Kramer and center Ken Bowman, snuck the ball into the end zone for the game-winning score. Discussing the play in his classic football book, *Instant Replay*, Kramer wrote:

> Bart called the "hut" signal. Jethro was on my inside shoulder, my left shoulder. I came off the ball as fast as I ever have in my life. I slammed into Jethro hard. All he had time to do was raise his left arm. He didn't even get it up all the way, and I charged into him. His body was a little high, the way we'd noticed in the movies, and, with Bowman's help, I moved him outside. Willie Townes, next to Jethro, was down low, very low. He was supposed to come in low and close to the middle. He was low, but he didn't close. He might have filled the hole, but he didn't, and Bart churned into the opening and stretched and fell and landed over the goal line.

The play, which subsequently became known simply as "The Block" in Green Bay, forced Pugh to unjustly spend the rest of his life receiving much of the blame for the Cowboy loss. Yet, even though Pugh found himself being pushed into the end zone by a pair of blockers while standing on a sheet of ice, Dallas tight end Pettis Norman revealed that his teammate learned to accept the unfair criticism directed at him, stating, "He dealt with it, became reconciled to it." However, Bob Lilly came to Pugh's defense, suggesting, "He [Pugh] actually held his place very well. I know if they had run on me with two men blocking in those conditions, I would have slid back like Jethro. As it was, they didn't move him far."

NOTABLE ACHIEVEMENTS

- Recorded two safeties during career.
- Recorded double-digit sacks five times.

- Led NFL with four fumble recoveries in 1967.
- Led Cowboys in sacks five straight seasons (1968, 1969, 1970, 1971, and 1972).
- Ranks sixth in Cowboys history with 95½ unofficial sacks.
- Tied for fourth all-time on Cowboys with 14 seasons played.
- Two-time NFL Eastern Conference champion (1966 and 1967).
- Five-time NFC champion (1970, 1971, 1975, 1977, and 1978).
- Two-time Super Bowl champion (VI and XII).
- 1968 Second-Team All-Pro selection.

36

CHARLIE WATERS

The other half of the Cowboys' brilliant safety tandem of the 1970s, Charlie Waters spent much of his career starting alongside Cliff Harris in the back end of Dallas's defensive secondary after earlier failing to distinguish himself as a cornerback. Playing for the Cowboys a total of 11 seasons, Waters used his athleticism and exceptional ball-hawking ability to record 41 interceptions, which ranks as the third-highest total in franchise history. At his best when it mattered most, Waters also recorded an NFL-record nine interceptions in postseason play. Excelling on special teams as well, Waters established a league mark by blocking four punts over the course of two games in 1977, turning one of those blocked kicks into a touchdown. Waters's stellar all-around play helped lead the Cowboys to seven division titles, five conference championships, and two Super Bowl victories, earning him in the process three trips to the Pro Bowl, two All-Pro selections, two All-NFC nominations, and a spot on the Cowboys' 25th Anniversary Team.

Born in Miami, Florida, on September 10, 1948, Charles Tutan Waters moved with his family to South Carolina, where he starred in football and baseball while attending North Augusta High School. Proving to be particularly proficient on the gridiron as a quarterback and wide receiver, Waters accepted a football scholarship from Clemson University following his graduation from North Augusta, after which he went on to win the starting quarterback job as a junior. Reflecting back on his decision to enroll at Clemson, Waters recalled:

> I remember Coach Frank Howard and Coach Art Baker recruited me when I was at North Augusta High School. Alabama, Georgia and Tennessee were also looking at me with a few other schools. Many of the schools I heard from wanted me to play defensive back and wide receiver, but I had my heart set on playing quarterback. I chose Clemson since they wanted me to play quarterback

and I loved the idea of playing in-state. Plus, my brother, Keith, was already at Clemson playing on the baseball team.

Although Waters did a solid job behind center for the Tigers in his junior year, he moved to wide receiver the following season after Billy Ammons reclaimed his starting quarterback job once he returned to the team from injury. Performing extremely well at the split end position as a senior, Waters caught 44 passes for 738 yards, en route to earning All-ACC honors.

After being selected by the Cowboys in the third round of the 1970 NFL Draft, with the 66th overall pick, Waters failed to make much of an impression as a wide receiver at his first training camp, prompting some members of the coaching staff to call for his release. But, even though Waters lacked elite speed, his quickness, athleticism, soft hands, and intelligence intrigued Tom Landry, who decided to convert him into a defensive back. Making the Cowboys' roster as a backup to starting free safety Cliff Harris, Waters went on to start six games and record five interceptions his first year in the league, en route to earning a spot on the NFL All-Rookie Team.

With Harris and Cornell Green firmly entrenched at the two safety positions, Landry elected to move Waters to cornerback in 1971. Unable to succeed at his new post, Waters struggled in a part-time role the next four seasons, often getting burned deep by the league's faster receivers, although he managed to record a team-leading six interceptions in 1972. In assessing his performance one day, Waters commented, "If you learn by mistakes, I ought to be a genius."

However, Waters eventually found his niche, taking over for Green at strong safety after the latter announced his retirement prior to the start of the 1975 campaign. Emerging as one of the league's best players at the position, Waters used his athleticism, superb instincts, and high football IQ to become one of the team's leaders on defense. No longer forced to cover receivers one-on-one, Waters focused primarily on playing his zone and making tackles. In explaining the success he experienced at strong safety, Waters stated, "I utilized the knowledge I had on offense. I loved to study the game. I wasn't fast or mean or anything special. I was just an athlete who utilized brainpower. That's the way Coach Landry played, and I think he was partial to me because of that."

Combining with Cliff Harris to give the Cowboys arguably the best pair of safeties in the league, Waters developed a symbiotic relationship with his defensive mate, with Harris recalling, "Charlie and I had a unique bond. Though we were very competitive with each other, we worked together very

Charlie Waters combined with Cliff Harris to give the Cowboys arguably the NFL's best safety tandem during the 1970s.
Courtesy of Steve Liskey, Retrocards.net

well, like no tandem on the Cowboys ever has. I truly felt that Charlie, at times, knew what I was thinking."

In discussing the two men who played alongside him in the Dallas secondary for eight years, Mel Renfro offered, "Charlie was more of the captain and the leader. Charlie was the one you turned to for leadership. Cliff, we called him 'kamikaze,' he would hit anything. He would hurt teammates in practice."

Waters recorded an NFL-record nine career interceptions in postseason play.
Courtesy of Dallas Cowboys

After performing well his first year at strong safety, Waters made the Pro Bowl for the first of three straight times in 1976. He also earned Second-Team All-NFC and Second-Team All-Pro honors in 1977, before being named First-Team All-Conference and Second-Team All-Pro again the following year.

Waters's string of Pro Bowl appearances ended in 1979, when he suffered a torn anterior cruciate ligament in his right knee during a preseason game that forced him to sit out the entire year. Although Waters recorded five interceptions when he returned to the team the following year, he no longer possessed the same quickness and agility he had prior to the injury. Waters spent one more year in Dallas, serving the Cowboys as a player-coach in 1981, during which time he helped develop the cover skills of rookie defensive backs Everson Walls and Michael Downs. Choosing to announce his retirement following the conclusion of the campaign, Waters ended his career with 41 interceptions and 584 interception-return yards.

Following his playing days, Waters decided to pursue a career in coaching, eventually spending two seasons serving as the defensive coordinator for the Denver Broncos and one year fulfilling that same role at the University of Oregon, before entering the private business sector. Waters has spent most of the past two decades working with his longtime friend and former teammate, Cliff Harris, at a gas marketing company. He also spent one season working alongside Brad Sham as the color commentator for the Cowboys Radio Network.

CAREER HIGHLIGHTS

Best Season

Waters played his best ball for the Cowboys in 1977 and 1978, earning Pro Bowl, All-Conference, and All-NFL honors both years. In addition to intercepting three passes and scoring a touchdown on a blocked punt in the first of those campaigns, Waters picked off another three passes during the Cowboys' successful playoff run to the NFL title. He followed that up by recording four interceptions and a safety during the 1978 regular season, before picking off two passes and recovering a fumble during the postseason. It's an extremely close call, but, since Waters earned his lone First-Team All-NFC selection in 1978, I opted to identify that as his finest season.

Memorable Moments / Greatest Performances

Waters recorded the first interception of his career during a 21–17 win over the Philadelphia Eagles on November 1, 1970, picking off a Norm Snead pass and returning the ball 20 yards.

Waters intercepted two passes in one game for the first time in his career in the 1970 regular-season finale, picking off Houston quarterbacks twice during a 52–10 thrashing of the Oilers.

Waters proved to be a significant contributor to the Dallas cause the following week, recovering two fumbles during the Cowboys' 5–0 win over Detroit in the opening round of the playoffs.

Waters scored the first of his three career touchdowns on November 12, 1972, returning one of his two interceptions on the day 28 yards for a TD during a 33–24 victory over the St. Louis Cardinals.

Waters had a huge game against San Francisco in the divisional round of the 1972 postseason tournament, helping the Cowboys record a 30–28 win over the 49ers by intercepting John Brodie twice.

Waters helped lead the Cowboys to a 23–10 victory over the Giants on November 11, 1973, by picking off New York quarterback Randy Johnson twice.

Waters scored the second touchdown of his career on December 13, 1975, when he put the finishing touches on a 31–10 win over the Redskins by returning an interception 20 yards for a TD during the latter stages of the contest.

Waters, who set an NFL record by blocking four punts over the course of two consecutive games in 1977, scored the last of his three touchdowns during a 16–10 win over the Eagles on October 23, 1977, when he returned one of those blocked kicks 17 yards for a TD.

Waters experienced his finest moment when he intercepted Chicago quarterback Bob Avellini three times during the Cowboys' lopsided 37–7 victory over the Bears in their 1977 divisional playoff matchup.

Waters also turned in a tremendous performance against Los Angeles in the 1978 NFC championship game, recording a pair of interceptions, a fumble recovery, and half-a-sack during the Cowboys' 28–0 shutout win over the Rams.

NOTABLE ACHIEVEMENTS

- Scored three touchdowns during career (two on interception returns and one on a blocked punt).
- Recorded at least five interceptions in a season four times.
- Amassed more than 100 interception-return yards in a season twice.
- Led Cowboys in interceptions three times.

- Ranks among Cowboys career leaders with 41 interceptions (3rd) and 584 interception-return yards (2nd).
- Holds NFL record for most career postseason interceptions (nine).
- Holds NFL record for most punts blocked in two consecutive games (four).
- Five-time NFC champion (1970, 1971, 1974, 1977, and 1978).
- Two-time Super Bowl champion (VI and XII).
- Named to 1970 NFL All-Rookie Team.
- Three-time Pro Bowl selection (1976, 1977, and 1978).
- Two-time Second-Team All-Pro selection (1977 and 1978).
- 1978 First-Team All-NFC selection.
- 1977 Second-Team All-NFC selection.
- Named to Cowboys' 25th Anniversary Team in 1984.

37

JAY NOVACEK

Signed by the Cowboys as a Plan B free agent in 1990 after accomplishing very little his first few years in the league with the St. Louis/Phoenix Cardinals, Jay Novacek went on to establish himself as the best tight end to play for Dallas prior to the arrival of Jason Witten. Nearly the equal of Witten as a pass receiver, Novacek made at least 59 receptions and accumulated more than 600 receiving yards for the Cowboys four times each, en route to earning five consecutive trips to the Pro Bowl, five All-Conference selections, and two All-Pro nominations. A solid blocker as well, Novacek also proved to be an asset to the Dallas running game, with his excellent all-around play helping Dallas win four division titles, three NFC championships, and three Super Bowls. And, even though Witten eventually surpassed him as the greatest tight end in franchise history, Novacek continues to hold the distinction of being the finest athlete ever to man the position for the Cowboys.

Born in Martin, South Dakota, on October 24, 1962, Jay McKinley Novacek grew up in the state of Nebraska, where he attended Gothenburg High School. A three-sport star at Gothenburg, Novacek earned All-State honors as a quarterback in football and a forward in basketball, while also excelling in track and field, winning state titles in the hurdles and pole vault as a senior.

After accepting a football scholarship from the University of Wyoming, Novacek began his college career on the gridiron as a wide receiver, before eventually moving to tight end. Although Wyoming's run-oriented Wishbone offense afforded Novacek few opportunities to display his skills as a pass receiver, he still managed to make 83 receptions for 1,536 yards and 10 touchdowns in college, earning honorable-mention All-America and Western Athletic Conference First-Team honors as a senior by setting an NCAA single-season record for the highest yards-per-reception average (22.6) ever posted by a tight end. Meanwhile, Novacek continued to star in track and field, winning the WAC decathlon championship and placing fourth in the

Jay Novacek ranks ninth in Cowboys history with 339 career receptions.
Courtesy of George A. Kitrinos

NCAA championships as a senior by setting school records for most decathlon points (7,615) and highest pole vault jump (16 feet, 4 inches), before going on to compete in the 1984 Olympic Trials as a decathlete.

Selected by the St. Louis Cardinals in the sixth round of the 1985 NFL Draft, with the 158th overall pick, Novacek spent three injury-marred, mostly unproductive seasons in St. Louis, accumulating only 22 receptions and 260 receiving yards during that time, before the team relocated to Phoenix, Arizona, in 1988. Finally establishing himself as a viable option in the passing game his fourth year in the league, Novacek made 38 receptions and finished third on the Cardinals with 569 receiving yards and four touchdown catches in 1988. However, after Novacek's production fell off to just 23 catches, 225 receiving yards, and one touchdown the following year, Phoenix chose not to protect him, leaving him eligible to sign with any team under Plan B free agency.

Subsequently signed by the Cowboys, Novacek went on to have a breakout season in 1990, finishing second on the team with 59 receptions, 657 receiving yards, and four touchdown catches, en route to earning Second-Team All-NFC honors. He followed that up with a similarly productive 1991 campaign, earning the first of his five consecutive Pro Bowl selections, First-Team All-NFC honors, and Second-Team All-Pro recognition by making 59 receptions for 664 yards and four touchdowns. Novacek then emerged as the league's top tight end in 1992, when, despite breaking his finger early in the season, he recorded 68 receptions, 630 receiving yards, and six touchdown catches for the Super Bowl champion Cowboys, earning in the process his lone First-Team All-Pro nomination. Choosing not to disclose his injury to the media until the end of the regular season, Novacek later said, "Injuries are like pressure. They are both just excuses."

Gradually developing into Troy Aikman's security blanket over the course of his first few seasons in Dallas, Novacek became a perfect fit for Norv Turner's offense, doing a particularly outstanding job of finding the soft spot in the defense on third-down situations. Although more of a pass-receiving tight end, the 6'4", 234-pound Novacek proved to be a deceptive blocker as well, doing a solid job of locking up his defender at the line of scrimmage.

Continuing to perform well in each of the next two seasons, Novacek amassed a total of 91 receptions, 920 receiving yards, and three touchdown catches in 1993 and 1994, with the Cowboys repeating as NFL champions in the first of those campaigns. Excelling in particular during the playoffs, Novacek made 15 receptions for 142 yards and two touchdowns in the Cowboys' three postseason contests in 1993, before catching 16 passes for

Novacek earned five trips to the Pro Bowl, five All-NFC selections, and two All-Pro nominations during his time in Dallas.
Courtesy of George A. Kitrinos

176 yards in only two games the following year. In discussing his ability to produce in the clutch, Novacek said, "What is pressure? You can't touch pressure or feel pressure. It doesn't exist. The way I figure it, either you do it or you don't. You catch it or you don't."

Cowboys offensive lineman John Gesek expressed his confidence in Novacek's ability to make the big catch when he stated, "He is our go-to-guy. When we need him, he always finds a way to get open, a way to make the play. . . . He catches balls nobody else can catch, and gets first downs that nobody else would get."

High praise for someone who shared the playing field with Michael Irvin, who earned the nickname "The Playmaker" during his time in Dallas.

But, while Irvin drew attention to himself with his constant banter and post-catch histrionics, Novacek did his job without much fanfare, choosing not to engage his opponent in trash-talk and calmly handing the ball to the referee after he scored a touchdown.

Novacek continued to conduct himself in an extremely professional manner in 1995, when he earned First-Team All-NFC and Pro Bowl honors for the final time by making 62 receptions for 705 yards and five touchdowns during the regular season, before catching another 13 passes for 133 yards and one touchdown during the Cowboys' successful playoff run to the NFL title. However, after scoring the first touchdown of Super Bowl XXX by hauling in a 3-yard TD pass from Troy Aikman, Novacek suffered a back injury that eventually led to his premature retirement. Plagued by a degenerative disk in his back that forced him to sit out the entire 1996 season, Novacek officially announced his retirement on July 15, 1997, ending his career with 442 receptions, 4,630 receiving yards, and 30 touchdown catches. Over the course of his six seasons in Dallas, Novacek made 339 receptions for 3,576 yards and 22 touchdowns. Meanwhile, his 62 receptions, 645 receiving yards and six touchdown catches in postseason play all rank third in franchise history.

Following his playing days, Novacek served as a spokesperson for the Alltel Wireless "Yards 4 Youth Football" program in West Texas and also became involved in the National Dairy Council's NFL School Program *Fuel Up to Play 60* campaign. In addition, Novacek has conducted a youth football camp at the University of North Texas, in Denton, Texas, every summer for the last 20 years.

COWBOYS CAREER HIGHLIGHTS

Best Season

Novacek compiled nearly identical numbers his first two seasons in Dallas, making 59 receptions and four touchdown catches in both 1990 and 1991, while amassing 657 yards through the air in the first of those campaigns and 664 yards in the second. He posted similarly impressive numbers in his last NFL season, finishing 1995 with 62 receptions, five touchdown catches, and a career-high 705 receiving yards, earning in the process First-Team All-NFC honors and the last of his five straight Pro Bowl selections. However, Novacek earned First-Team All-Pro honors for the only time in 1992, when he accumulated 630 receiving yards and established career-high marks in receptions (68) and touchdown catches (six) for the NFL champion Cowboys, making that his finest all-around season.

Memorable Moments / Greatest Performances

Although the Cowboys lost their September 30, 1990, meeting with the Giants 31–17, Novacek caught his first touchdown pass as a member of the Cowboys during the contest, closing out the scoring with a 7-yard TD reception late in the fourth quarter. He finished the game with nine receptions for 85 yards.

Novacek surpassed 100 receiving yards in a game for the first time in his career one month later, making seven receptions for 105 yards and one touchdown during a 21–10 loss to the Philadelphia Eagles on October 28.

Novacek helped lead the Cowboys to a 20–17 win over the Green Bay Packers on October 6, 1991, by hauling in a 13-yard TD pass from Troy Aikman and making 11 receptions for 121 yards.

Although the Cowboys suffered a 34–10 defeat at the hands of the Detroit Lions three weeks later, Novacek made a career-long 49-yard pass reception during the contest, finishing the day with 10 catches for 131 yards.

Novacek came up big for the Cowboys during the latter stages of their 31–27 victory over the Denver Broncos on December 6, 1992, catching 50 yards worth of passes during their 78-yard game-winning drive in the game's final minutes. He finished the afternoon with seven receptions for 87 yards and one touchdown.

Novacek scored the Cowboys' first points of Super Bowl XXVII, tying the game with Buffalo at 7–7 in the first quarter by collaborating with Troy Aikman on a 23-yard scoring play. He finished the contest with seven receptions for 72 yards.

Novacek again performed extremely well in the opening round of the 1994 postseason tournament, helping to lead the Cowboys to a 35–9 rout of the Packers by making 11 receptions for 104 yards.

NOTABLE ACHIEVEMENTS

- Surpassed 50 receptions four times, topping 60 catches twice.
- Topped 600 receiving yards four times.
- Ranks ninth in Cowboys history with 339 career receptions.

- Three-time NFC champion (1992, 1993, and 1995).
- Three-time Super Bowl champion (XXVII, XXVIII, and XXX).
- Five-time Pro Bowl selection (1991, 1992, 1993, 1994, and 1995).
- 1992 First-Team All-Pro selection.
- 1991 Second-Team All-Pro selection.
- Three-time First-Team All-NFC selection (1991, 1992, and 1995).
- Two-time Second-Team All-NFC selection (1990 and 1994).

38

EUGENE LOCKHART

A victim of bad timing, Eugene Lockhart arrived in Dallas in 1984, one year after the Cowboys made the last of nine consecutive playoff appearances. Claiming the team's starting middle linebacker job as a rookie, Lockhart continued to function in that role until 1990, one year before the Cowboys began another lengthy string of playoff appearances that resulted in three NFL championships. But, even though Lockhart played for teams that posted a winning record in just two of his seven seasons in Dallas, he gained respect throughout the league for his consistently outstanding play that made him one of the NFL's top linebackers. A fierce hitter whose jarring tackles earned him the nickname "Mean Gene, the hitting machine," Lockhart led the Cowboys in tackles six times, establishing single-season franchise records for most tackles and most solo tackles along the way. Bringing down opposing ball carriers more than 100 times in six of his seven seasons in Dallas, Lockhart annually ranked among the league leaders in that category, earning in the process one All-Pro selection and one All-Conference nomination, in spite of his team's poor play, which likely prevented him from receiving numerous other postseason honors.

Born in Crockett, Texas, on March 8, 1961, Eugene Lockhart Jr. attended David Crockett High School, where he starred on the gridiron, prompting the University of Houston to offer him a full football scholarship. Spending his final two seasons at Houston starting at middle linebacker for the Cougars, Lockhart led the team with 134 tackles as a senior, earning him Second-Team All–Southwest Conference honors.

Selected by the Cowboys in the sixth round of the 1984 NFL Draft, Lockhart began his first year in the league backing up veteran middle linebacker Bob Breunig. However, Lockhart assumed the starting role midway through the campaign after Breunig suffered a back injury that forced him to retire at the end of the year. Performing extremely well over the season's final eight games, Lockhart finished the year with 2½ sacks, one

Eugene Lockhart established a single-season franchise record when he recorded a league-leading 222 tackles in 1989.
Courtesy of Steve Liskey, Retrocards.net

interception, and a team-leading 86 tackles (49 solo), earning him a spot on the NFL All-Rookie Team.

Continuing his outstanding play in 1985, Lockhart recorded 3½ sacks and led the Cowboys with 128 tackles, four fumble recoveries, and three forced fumbles, helping them compile a record of 10-6 that landed them in the playoffs for the only time during his tenure with the club. He followed that up with another exceptional performance in 1986, finishing the season with a team-leading 121 tackles (77 solo) and a career-high five sacks. Although a players' strike and a fractured right fibula limited Lockhart to just nine games in the ensuing campaign, he still managed to finish third on the team with 80 tackles (52 solo).

An extremely intense player who led by example, Lockhart became known as a workingman's middle linebacker during his time in Dallas. Although the 6'2", 235-pound Lockhart lacked exceptional foot speed, he possessed good quickness, superb instincts, a nose for the football, and did an excellent job of shedding blocks, contributing to his ability to record huge numbers of tackles. Meanwhile, Lockhart's punishing hits, which earned him the aforementioned nickname, made him one of the league's most feared defensive players.

Unfortunately, the Cowboys failed to surround Lockhart with similarly talented players much of the time, particularly in 1988 and 1989, when they posted a composite record of 4-28. Yet, in spite of the team's poor play, Lockhart continued to perform at an elite level, making 121 tackles (72 solo) and recovering two fumbles in the first of those campaigns, before earning his lone All-Pro selection the following year by recording a league-leading and franchise-record 222 tackles (154 solo).

Lockhart had another outstanding season in 1990, leading the 7-9 Cowboys with 139 tackles (72 solo), en route to earning Second-Team All-NFC honors. But, with new head coach Jimmy Johnson employing a defensive system that placed a heavy emphasis on speed, the 30-year-old Lockhart became expendable, leading to the Cowboys including him in a trade they completed with the New England Patriots just prior to the 1991 NFL Draft that sent Lockhart, two other players, and a pair of early-round draft picks to New England for the first overall pick of the draft, which the Cowboys subsequently used to select Russell Maryland. Lockhart, who gave so much of himself to the Cowboys during his time in Dallas, expressed his feelings about leaving the team while cleaning out his locker, commenting, "It's a cold business—a cold, cold business. And it's even colder in New England." Lockhart left Dallas having amassed a total of 897 tackles (557 solo) that continues to place him among the franchise's all-time leaders. He also recorded 16 sacks, intercepted six passes, recovered 10 fumbles, and scored two touchdowns.

Lockhart ended up spending two seasons in New England, recording a total of 134 tackles for the Patriots in 1991 and 1992, before being waived by the team prior to the start of the 1993 campaign. He subsequently announced his retirement, ending his career with more than 1,000 tackles and those 16 sacks, six interceptions, and two touchdowns.

Some 16 years after Lockhart left the game, he ran afoul of the law, being indicted with eight others on federal charges of organizing a $20 million mortgage fraud scheme in the Dallas area. Convicted of the crime in late 2012, Lockhart spent three years of his 54-month sentence in prison, before being released on probation, which he has yet to complete as of this writing. Seeing the error of his ways during his period of incarceration, Lockhart has since developed a sense of spirituality and a connection with God he previously lacked, revealing that he learned a lot about himself during the three days he spent in solitary confinement when he first arrived in prison. Reflecting back on the emotions he experienced at the time, Lockhart said:

> The people that I had hurt and all the things I felt I was getting away with, He showed it to me. Detail by detail, person by person, whatever I'd done, He showed it to me, and that's when that hurt, hurt so much—to the point I was in a fetal position and God was just pouring it on me, pouring it on me and I couldn't do nothin' but cry. I cried because I hurt people. I'd done wrong and I wasn't raised like that . . . at that time, it sounded like a great opportunity for me to still be able to live the lifestyle that I was accustomed to while playing football.

Lockhart continued, "I think that besides my relationship with Jesus Christ and my relationship with my wife and family, going to prison was perhaps one of the best things that ever happened to me because I got that chance to find out exactly who I am, what my purpose in life is. My purpose is to serve. . . . I've been broken, but God has put me back together again. I have a purpose to live and I'm gonna live within my purpose."

COWBOYS CAREER HIGHLIGHTS

Best Season

Lockhart performed extremely well for the Cowboys in his first full season as a starter, concluding the 1985 campaign with a team-leading 128 tackles, three forced fumbles, and four fumble recoveries, while also recording 3½ sacks and one of his two career touchdowns. Nevertheless, there is little doubt that he had his finest season in 1989, when he earned his lone All-Pro nomination by leading the NFL with a franchise-record 222 tackles and 154 solo tackles. Lockhart also intercepted two passes, deflected eight others, recovered two fumbles, and recorded two sacks.

Memorable Moments / Greatest Performances

Lockhart recorded the first of his six career interceptions during a 14–3 loss to the Bills on November 18, 1984, subsequently returning the ball 32 yards into Buffalo territory.

Although the Cowboys lost their December 9, 1984, meeting with the Redskins 30–28, Lockhart recorded two sacks in one game for the only time in his career, getting to Washington quarterback Joe Theismann twice during the contest.

Lockhart scored the first of his two career touchdowns on October 13, 1985, when he picked off a David Woodley pass and returned it 19 yards for a TD during a 27–13 victory over Pittsburgh.

Although the Cowboys suffered a heartbreaking 44–38 overtime loss to the Minnesota Vikings on Thanksgiving Day in 1987, Lockhart performed admirably during the contest, intercepting a pass and recording a sack of Vikings quarterback Tommy Kramer.

Lockhart crossed the opponent's goal line for the second and final time in his career on October 8, 1989, when he recovered a fumble and returned the ball 40 yards for a touchdown during a 31–13 loss to the Green Bay Packers.

Lockhart again performed valiantly in defeat the following week, recording an interception and a sack during a 31–14 loss to the San Francisco 49ers.

Once again excelling in defeat later that same season, Lockhart recorded a career-high 16 solo tackles during a 19–10 loss to the Phoenix Cardinals on October 29, 1989.

NOTABLE ACHIEVEMENTS

- Scored two career touchdowns (one interception return and one fumble return).
- Recorded five sacks in 1986.

- Recorded more than 100 tackles five times, surpassing the 200-mark once (222 in 1989).
- Led NFL with 222 tackles in 1989.
- Led Cowboys in tackles six times (1984, 1985, 1986, 1988, 1989, and 1990).
- Holds Cowboys single-season records for most tackles (222) and most solo tackles (154), both in 1989.
- Ranks seventh in Cowboys history with 897 tackles and 557 solo tackles.
- Named to 1984 NFL All-Rookie Team.
- 1989 Second-Team All-Pro selection.
- 1990 Second-Team All-NFC selection.

39

CALVIN HILL

The first Cowboys player to rush for more than 1,000 yards in a season, Calvin Hill accomplished the feat twice en route to gaining more yardage on the ground than all but three running backs in franchise history. Amassing more than 800 yards rushing in four of his six seasons in Dallas, Hill helped the Cowboys win four division titles, two NFC championships, and one Super Bowl. Along the way, the Yale University graduate established himself as one of the finest all-around backs in team history, excelling as a runner, pass receiver, blocker, and even, upon occasion, as a passer. Hill's outstanding play earned him four trips to the Pro Bowl, two All-Pro selections, and two All-Conference nominations. Yet, had Hill not been plagued with injuries much of his time in Dallas, he likely would have accomplished considerably more.

Born in Baltimore, Maryland, on January 2, 1947, Calvin G. Hill grew up in the Bronx, New York, where he attended Riverdale Country High School on a scholarship. Starring in multiple sports while at Riverdale, Hill excelled in baseball, basketball, track and field, and football, often leading his teams to victory over other Ivy Preparatory School League opponents in the metropolitan New York City area. After guiding the Riverdale football squad to three straight undefeated seasons as its T-formation quarterback, Hill elected to enroll at Yale, where he hoped to become the first black signal-caller in that school's history. However, Hill's aspirations ended shortly after he arrived at his first practice, when the coaching staff moved him to halfback, where he remained for the rest of his football career. An outstanding all-around athlete, Hill played tight end and linebacker in some games as well, while also distinguishing himself as a sprinter and jumper for the school's track team, winning the 1967 and 1968 long jump and triple jump at the Ivy League Heptagonal Outdoor Track and Field Championship.

Hill's athleticism and versatility convinced the Cowboys to select him with the 24th overall pick of the 1969 NFL Draft, making him the first player from an Ivy League school ever to be drafted in the first round. After

Calvin Hill earned NFL Offensive Rookie of the Year honors in 1969, when he gained 942 yards on the ground and 1,174 yards from scrimmage.
Courtesy of Dallas Cowboys

initially being tried at linebacker and tight end upon his arrival at training camp, Hill settled in at halfback, where he replaced Dan Reeves as the starter. Making an early impression on 49ers announcer Hugh McElhenny during a preseason contest against San Francisco, Hill drew praise from the Hall of Fame running back, who gushed, "You [Cowboys fans] have something to be excited about. This guy has to be a starter for you. He has natural ability to start with. A natural, built-in change of pace. Because of his long strides, he appears to be coasting. He looks slow, then wow, he puts it on the floorboard."

Quickly establishing himself as one of the league's elite running backs, Hill gained 805 yards on the ground through the first nine games of the season, prompting Tom Landry to say, "He might be the best ball-carrier I've seen in 20 years of pro football. . . . He knows how to set up a block, where to go inside, when to go outside. You think he's stopped and he stretches out for three or four more yards."

But, then, in his typically restrained fashion, Landry added, "We've never had a rookie step in and play the way he has. He's amazing to watch. But you're not sure what you have until the defense starts keying on you. The whole team keys on [Gale] Sayers, but he still makes his 1,000 yards. Don't get the idea I want to discourage the prospects of this young fellow. He has the runner's instinct. We saw it several times during the rookie camp. You can't teach a runner how to run. He has to know."

However, while rushing for a then-team record 150 yards during a 41–28 victory over the Washington Redskins in Week 9, Hill fractured his toe, forcing him to sit out the next two games and play the remainder of the year in so much pain that he required an injection before each game. Far less effective when he returned to the lineup in Week 12, Hill rushed for only 137 yards in the final three games of the regular season, leaving him with a first-year total of 942 yards that placed him second in the NFL to Gale Sayers. He also ranked among the league leaders with eight rushing touchdowns, 1,174 yards from scrimmage, 1,299 all-purpose yards, and an average of 4.6 yards per carry, earning in the process NFL Offensive Rookie of the Year honors, the first of his four Pro Bowl selections, and his lone First-Team All-Pro nomination.

Still bothered by his ailing toe the following year, Hill suffered through an injury-marred 1970 campaign during which he also missed playing time due to complications from an infected blister in the same foot and a back injury he sustained in Week 9. Appearing in 12 games, Hill rushed for only 577 yards and four touchdowns, later explaining his poor performance by saying, "My foot hurt a little in 1970, and I couldn't do certain things. I couldn't push off on it hard. I couldn't make hard cuts."

Once again plagued by injuries in 1971, Hill missed nearly half the season after suffering a torn anterior cruciate ligament in his right knee during a 20–13 victory over the New York Giants. Nevertheless, he ended up scoring 11 touchdowns in only eight games, while also rushing for 468 yards and averaging 4.4 yards per carry.

Hill rushed for more than 1,000 yards twice, becoming in 1972 the first
player in franchise history to accomplish the feat.
Courtesy of RMYAuctions.com

Fully healthy in 1972, Hill became the first running back in franchise
history to surpass the 1,000-yard mark, earning his second Pro Bowl selection by rushing for 1,036 yards and six touchdowns, making a career-high
43 receptions for 364 yards and another three touchdowns, and averaging
4.2 yards per carry. He followed that up by gaining 1,142 yards on the
ground, scoring six touchdowns, averaging 4.2 yards per carry, and catching
32 passes for 290 yards in 1973, en route to earning First-Team All-NFC,
Second-Team All-NFL, and Pro Bowl honors. Despite missing two games
due to injury in 1974, Hill earned Second-Team All-Conference honors
and his final Pro Bowl nomination by rushing for 844 yards, scoring seven
touchdowns, and tying his career high by averaging 4.6 yards per carry.

The 1974 campaign ended up being Hill's final season in Dallas. After
signing with Hawaii of the World Football League, he appeared in three
WFL games in 1975, before suffering a torn medial collateral ligament in

his right knee that sidelined him for the remainder of the year. When the league folded at season's end, Hill returned to the NFL as a member of the Washington Redskins, with whom he spent the next two years serving as a backup. He then spent four seasons in Cleveland, serving the Browns primarily as a third-down back during that time, before announcing his retirement following the conclusion of the 1981 campaign. Hill ended his career with 6,083 yards rushing, 271 pass receptions for 2,861 yards, 65 touchdowns, and an average of 4.2 yards per carry. Over the course of his six seasons in Dallas, Hill rushed for 5,009 yards, made 139 receptions for 1,359 yards, scored 45 touchdowns, and averaged 4.3 yards per carry. In addition to ranking fourth all-time in franchise history in rushing yardage, Hill ranks fourth in rushing attempts (1,166) and fifth in rushing touchdowns (39).

Following his retirement, Hill began a career in consulting, eventually serving as a board member of several different organizations. He also works as a corporate motivational speaker, serves as a consultant to the Cleveland Browns and Alexander & Associates, Inc., a Washington, DC, corporate consulting firm, and works for the Dallas Cowboys as a consultant who specializes in providing assistance to troubled players.

COWBOYS CAREER HIGHLIGHTS

Best Season

Hill likely would have posted the best numbers of his career as a rookie in 1969 had he not broken his toe in Week 9. As it is, he finished the year with 942 yards rushing, eight touchdowns, 1,174 yards from scrimmage, 1,299 all-purpose yards, and a career-high average of 4.6 yards per carry, placing among the league leaders in each category. He also completed three passes, for 137 yards and two touchdowns. However, with Hill's injured toe adversely affecting his performance the final few weeks of the season, he ended up compiling more impressive numbers in both 1972 and 1973. In addition to rushing for 1,036 yards and scoring nine touchdowns in the first of those campaigns, Hill averaged 4.2 yards per carry and established career-high marks in pass receptions (43) and receiving yardage (364), giving him a total of 1,400 yards from scrimmage that placed him fourth in the NFL. He followed that up by rushing for 1,142 yards, scoring six touchdowns, once again averaging 4.2 yards per carry, and amassing a career-best 1,432 yards from scrimmage in 1973, en route to earning First-Team All-NFC and Second-Team All-Pro honors. It's an extremely close call, but, since Hill finished third in the league in rushing and second in yards from scrimmage in 1973 (he ranked seventh and fourth, respectively, in 1972), the 1973 campaign would have to be considered his finest all-around season.

Memorable Moments / Greatest Performances

Hill exhibited his wide array of skills in his first game as a rookie, rushing for 70 yards and completing a 53-yard touchdown pass to wide receiver Lance Rentzel during a 24–3 victory over the St. Louis Cardinals in the 1969 regular-season opener.

Hill followed that up by scoring two touchdowns and setting a new franchise record by rushing for 138 yards, in leading the Cowboys to a 21–17 win over the New Orleans Saints in Week 2.

Hill continued his outstanding play in Week 3, carrying the ball 10 times for 91 yards, gaining another 71 yards on three pass receptions, and completing a 44-yard pass to Lance Rentzel during a 38–7 rout of the Philadelphia Eagles on October 5, 1969. Hill, who gave the Cowboys a 14–7 lead early in the second quarter by scampering 53 yards for a touchdown, accounted for 206 yards of total offense on the day.

Hill again displayed his versatility on October 27, 1969, leading the Cowboys to a lopsided 25–3 victory over the Giants by rushing for 84 yards and completing a 40-yard TD pass to Bob Hayes.

Although Hill fractured his toe during the latter stages of the contest, he turned in arguably the finest all-around performance of his rookie campaign against Washington on November 16, 1969, breaking his own franchise record by rushing for 150 yards, making two receptions for 35 yards, returning three kickoffs for 100 yards, and scoring a pair of touchdowns during a 41–28 win over the Redskins.

Hill provided most of the offensive firepower during a 13–0 win over Atlanta on October 11, 1970, rushing for a season-high 117 yards and completing a 12-yard pass to tight end Mike Ditka.

Hill helped lead the Cowboys to a 49–37 victory over the Buffalo Bills in the 1971 regular-season opener by rushing for 84 yards, making four receptions for another 43 yards, and scoring a career-high four touchdowns.

Hill had a similarly productive afternoon against the Jets on December 4, 1971, leading the Cowboys to a convincing 52–10 win by rushing for 62 yards, gaining another 80 yards on four pass receptions, and scoring three touchdowns, two of which came on 27-yard hookups with Roger Staubach.

Hill helped the Cowboys mount a memorable comeback against San Francisco in their 1972 divisional playoff matchup, rushing for 125 yards during the 30–28 win over the 49ers.

Hill got off to a fast start in 1973, rushing for a season-high 130 yards during a hard-fought 20–17 victory over the Chicago Bears in the regular-season opener.

Hill had a huge game against Philadelphia on October 20, 1974, leading the Cowboys to a 31–24 victory over the Eagles by rushing for 140 yards and three touchdowns.

However, he topped that performance three weeks later, rushing for a pair of touchdowns and a career-high 153 yards during a 20–14 win over the 49ers on November 10, 1974.

NOTABLE ACHIEVEMENTS

- Rushed for more than 1,000 yards twice, topping the 800-yard mark two other times.
- Surpassed 1,000 yards from scrimmage three times.
- Scored more than 10 touchdowns once (11 in 1971).
- Averaged more than 4.5 yards per carry twice.
- Caught more than 40 passes once (43 in 1972).
- Threw three touchdown passes.
- Finished second in NFL in: rushing attempts once; rushing yardage once; and yards from scrimmage once.
- Finished third in NFL in: rushing attempts once; rushing yardage once; yards from scrimmage once; touchdowns once; and rushing average once.
- Led Cowboys in rushing yardage four times.
- Ranks among Cowboys career leaders in: rushing yardage (4th); rushing touchdowns (5th); and rushing attempts (4th).
- Two-time NFC champion (1970 and 1971).
- Super Bowl VI champion.
- 1969 Associated Press NFL Offensive Rookie of the Year.
- Four-time Pro Bowl selection (1969, 1972, 1973, and 1974).
- 1969 First-Team All-Pro selection.
- 1973 Second-Team All-Pro selection.
- Two-time Second-Team All-NFC selection (1973 and 1974).

40

DON MEREDITH

Often referred to as "the original Dallas Cowboy" because he signed with the team before it adopted a nickname, hired a head coach, or participated in the 1960 NFL Expansion Draft, Don Meredith joined the Cowboys prior to their inaugural season of 1960 and spent his entire nine-year career in Dallas, leading the franchise to its first three division titles and first two championship game appearances. After sharing playing time with veteran signal-caller Eddie LeBaron his first few years in the league, Meredith emerged as the Cowboys' full-time starting quarterback in 1963, continuing to function in that role until he announced his retirement following the conclusion of the 1968 campaign. Establishing himself as the team's unquestioned leader on offense during his six seasons behind center, Meredith served as one of the driving forces behind the Cowboys' rise to prominence, making huge contributions to the team both on and off the field. In addition to his three Pro Bowl selections, Meredith earned one All-Pro nomination and recognition in 1966 as the NFL's Player of the Year. And, nearly half a century after he threw his last pass for the Cowboys, "Dandy Don," as he came to be known, remains one of the most iconic figures in franchise history, known as much for his post–playing career success as for his accomplishments on the gridiron.

Born in Mount Vernon, Texas, on April 10, 1938, Joseph Donald Meredith attended local Mount Vernon High School, where he starred in football and basketball. After turning down an offer to play for head coach Bear Bryant at Texas A&M University, Meredith elected to enroll at Southern Methodist University, where he spent three years starting at quarterback, earning All-America honors in both 1958 and 1959.

After Meredith graduated from SMU, the Cowboys, who entered the league too late to participate in the 1960 NFL Draft, attempted to reserve his rights by signing him to a personal services contract they hoped the league would honor once they officially received an NFL franchise. Although the Chicago Bears subsequently selected Meredith in the third

Don Meredith led the Cowboys to their first three division titles and first two championship game appearances.
Courtesy of RMYAuctions.com

round of that year's draft, they ultimately sent him to the Cowboys in a swap of draft picks.

Following his arrival in Dallas, Meredith spent his first two years in the league serving the Cowboys almost exclusively as a backup to veteran QB Eddie LeBaron, compiling a record of 2-2-1 as a starter during that time, while tossing 11 touchdown passes and 16 interceptions. Although the Cowboys finished just 2-5-1 with Meredith behind center in 1962, the third-year quarterback posted somewhat better overall numbers as he began to garner more playing time, throwing 15 TD passes and only eight interceptions. Anointed the team's full-time starting quarterback in 1963, Meredith experienced only a moderate amount of success for a squad that concluded the campaign with a record of 4-10, completing just under 54 percent of his passes for 2,381 yards, while also throwing 17 touchdown passes and 18 interceptions. He followed that up with another mediocre performance in 1964, completing 48.9 percent of his passes for 2,143 yards, tossing nine touchdown passes, and placing near the top of the league rankings with 16 interceptions. Nevertheless, the Cowboys, who finished the year with a record of just 5-8-1, responded well to Meredith's leadership, posting a mark of 5-4-1 in the 10 games he started.

Over the course of his first few seasons in Dallas, Meredith developed a reputation as a risk-taker who liked to throw the ball deep and often set himself up as a target by running with the ball. He also became known for his grittiness and toughness, enduring in one season alone fractured ribs, a broken nose, a twisted knee, and a bout of pneumonia. Playing at a time when officials offered very little in the way of protection to quarterbacks, Meredith earned the respect of his teammates with his courage and determination, with former Cowboys receiver Pete Gent suggesting, "He [Meredith] was greatly respected by his teammates for his great skills and his nerve on the field during a period of time in the NFL when knocking out the quarterback was a tactic for winning. He would take awful physical beatings and somehow keep getting up and taking the team to wins. . . . He was one tough SOB."

Tom Landry, who objected to the manner in which the fun-loving Meredith often whistled and sang during huddles, once called his quarterback "the toughest player I ever coached."

Lee Roy Jordan concurred with the sentiments of both men, stating, "He was one tough individual. He played with many an ailment and injury, and was very, very competitive. He and Bob Hayes really set the standard for the wide-open offense, the motion guys and big plays."

The arrival of Hayes in 1965 helped open up the Dallas offense, enabling Meredith to establish new career-high marks in passing yardage (2,415) and touchdown passes (22), although he completed only 46.2 percent of his passes. Meredith also displayed his ability to perform well under pressure by leading a Cowboys team that finished 7-7 on three game-winning touchdown drives. With the infusion of more young talent in 1966, the Cowboys emerged as a championship contender, compiling a record of 10-3-1 during the regular season, before losing to the Packers 34–27 in the NFL title game. For his part, Meredith completed 51.5 percent of his passes, threw 12 interceptions, and ranked among the league leaders with 2,805 passing yards, 24 touchdown passes, and a passer rating of 87.7, en route to earning Pro Bowl honors for the first time, his lone Second-Team All-Pro selection, and recognition as the NFL Player of the Year. Yet, perhaps the most vivid memory of Meredith that Cowboys fans have from that season is the image of him being engulfed by Green Bay linebacker Dave Robinson as he desperately flung the ball into the end zone for what proved to be a game-ending interception on the final play of the NFL title tilt. Although Meredith posted relatively modest numbers the following year, concluding the 1967 campaign with 1,834 yards passing, 16 touchdown passes, 16 interceptions, a 50.2 completion percentage, and a passer rating of just 68.7, he led the Cowboys to a return trip to the NFL championship game, which they once again lost to the Packers in the closing moments, this time by a score of 21–17.

The two defeats Meredith and the Cowboys suffered at the hands of Green Bay very much came to symbolize his career. Despite performing well on the field and proving to be an outstanding leader, Meredith received much of the blame for the team's inability to "win the big one," with Dallas fans failing to accord him the proper amount of respect. Although the outgoing and free-spirited Meredith remained one of the Cowboys' most recognizable stars, he shared a love-hate relationship with the hometown fans, many of whom came to view his lasting legacy as that of a loser. However, longtime friend and broadcast partner Frank Gifford considered that assessment of Meredith to be an unfair one, saying, "He was a heck of a player. [The Cowboys] won maybe one game his first year, then he helped turn them around and they wound up in the 'Ice Bowl' against Green Bay in 1967. He was such a good athlete. A lot of people don't know that he also set a state high school scoring record in basketball."

Meredith had a very solid year for the Cowboys in 1968, leading them to their third consecutive division title by passing for 2,500 yards and 21 touchdowns, while establishing career-high marks in completion percentage (55.3) and passer rating (88.4). Nevertheless, his dissatisfaction with the treatment he received from Cowboys fans and his unhappiness over being replaced by Craig Morton during the early stages of Dallas's 31–20 loss to Cleveland in their 1968 playoff matchup prompted him to announce his retirement prior to the start of the ensuing campaign. In explaining his decision, the 31-year-old Meredith stated that he no longer felt excitement when he ran onto the field. Cowboys head coach Tom Landry, who often butted heads with his charismatic quarterback, later said, "I tried to talk him out of it. But, when you lose your desire in this game, that's it." Meredith retired with career totals of 17,199 passing yards, 135 touchdown passes, and 111 interceptions, a completion percentage of 50.7, and a passer rating of 74.8.

Soon after he retired as an active player, Meredith joined the newly formed ABC *Monday Night Football* broadcasting crew, where he did two tours of duty, serving alongside Howard Cosell and Frank Gifford from

Meredith received the Bert Bell Award in 1966 as NFL Player of the Year.
Public Domain/Wikipedia

1970 to 1973, and, then again, from 1977 to 1984 (although Keith Jackson spent one year in the booth before Gifford replaced him in 1971). During that time, the laid-back Meredith proved to be the perfect foil to Cosell, entertaining fans with his irreverent sense of humor and frequently questioning the knowledge of his pompous broadcast partner. Meredith also became known for serenading his audience when the game's result no longer appeared to be in doubt, breaking out into a rendition of Willie Nelson's "The Party's Over" by singing, "Turn out the lights, the party's over, they say all good things must end. Call it tonight, the party's over, and tomorrow starts the same old thing again."

Sadly, Meredith, who spent the previous few years being treated for emphysema, fell silent on December 5, 2010, when he died after suffering a brain hemorrhage and lapsing into a coma at 72 years of age. Following his passing, NFL commissioner Roger Goodell said in a prepared statement, "Don Meredith was one of the most colorful characters in NFL history. He was a star on the field that became an even bigger star on television. He brought joy to football fans."

Meanwhile, NFL.com paid tribute to Meredith by calling him "the original unappreciated great quarterback," and suggesting that he "might have been the most criticized player—not just quarterback—in Cowboys history, enough to make the game no fun anymore."

CAREER HIGHLIGHTS

Best Season

Meredith had a big year for the Cowboys in 1968, helping them score a league-leading 431 points by tossing 21 touchdown passes, throwing for 2,500 yards, and establishing career-high marks in completion percentage (55.3) and passer rating (88.4). Nevertheless, the 1966 campaign would have to be considered his finest season. En route to leading the Cowboys to a record of 10-3-1 and the first of their six consecutive division titles, Meredith ranked among the league leaders with 2,805 passing yards, 24 touchdown passes, and a passer rating of 87.7, establishing career-best marks in each of the first two categories. Meredith's outstanding play earned him a trip to the Pro Bowl, Second-Team All-Pro honors, and recognition as the NFL Player of the Year.

Memorable Moments / Greatest Performances

Although the Cowboys lost to the Steelers 27–21 on October 27, 1963, Meredith had the first big game of his career, completing 18 of 29 passes and throwing for 290 yards and three touchdowns during the contest.

Just one week after tossing four TD passes during a 35–20 win over the Redskins, Meredith became the first Cowboys quarterback to pass for 400 yards in a game when he threw for 460 yards and three touchdowns during a 31–24 loss to the 49ers on November 10, 1963.

Meredith followed that up with another strong performance, leading the Cowboys to a 27–20 victory over Philadelphia on November 17, 1963, by completing 25 of 33 pass attempts and throwing for 302 yards and two touchdowns.

Meredith turned in his finest effort of the 1965 campaign on December 11, when he passed for 326 yards and three touchdowns during a 27–13 win over the St. Louis Cardinals, with his longest pass completion of the day being a 46-yard scoring strike to Bob Hayes early in the second quarter.

Meredith torched the secondary of the New York Giants in the 1966 regular-season opener, throwing for 358 yards and five touchdowns during a 52–7 blowout of the Giants. Hooking up twice with Bob Hayes on long scoring plays, Meredith hit the speedster with TD passes that covered 74 and 39 yards.

Meredith led the Cowboys to another lopsided victory three weeks later, when he passed for 394 yards and tossed another five touchdown passes during a 56–7 mauling of the Philadelphia Eagles on October 9, 1966. Meredith opened the scoring by hitting Dan Reeves with a 51-yard scoring strike, before collaborating with Frank Clarke on a 23-yard scoring play and tossing TD passes of 24, 36, and 12 yards to Bob Hayes.

Meredith turned in a heroic effort five weeks later, when, despite playing with a punctured lung that made it extremely difficult for him to breathe or call signals, he led the Cowboys to a 31–30 win over the Washington Redskins on November 13, 1966, by tossing two TD passes, rushing for another score, and throwing for 406 yards. Both of Meredith's touchdown passes went to Bob Hayes, with the second of those covering 95 yards, which remains the longest pass completion in franchise history.

Meredith helped lead the Cowboys to a 38–24 victory over the Giants on September 24, 1967, by throwing four touchdown passes, with one of those being a 43-yard strike to Bob Hayes.

Meredith tied his own franchise record by throwing five touchdown passes in a game for the third and final time in his career on September 29, 1968, doing so during a convincing 45–13 victory over the Philadelphia Eagles. As one might expect, Bob Hayes recorded the longest TD reception of the day, hooking up with Meredith on a 44-yard scoring play early in the third quarter.

NOTABLE ACHIEVEMENTS

- Passed for more than 2,500 yards twice.
- Threw more than 20 touchdown passes three times.
- Completed more than 55 percent of his passes once (55.3 in 1968).
- Rushed for five touchdowns in 1966.
- Led NFL quarterbacks in yards per pass completion twice and game-winning drives once.
- Finished third in NFL in: touchdown passes three times; passer rating twice; and total offense once.
- Ranks among Cowboys career leaders in: passing yardage (5th); completions (5th); touchdown passes (5th); and pass attempts (5th).
- Holds record for longest pass completion in Cowboys history (95 yards to Bob Hayes, 11/13/66).
- Tied for first in franchise history with five TD passes in one game (accomplished three times).
- Two-time NFL Eastern Conference champion (1966 and 1967).
- Three-time Pro Bowl selection (1966, 1967, and 1968).
- 1966 Second-Team All-Pro selection.
- 1966 Bert Bell Award winner as NFL Player of the Year.
- Inducted into Cowboys Ring of Honor in 1976.

41

DEXTER COAKLEY

An outstanding athlete who fit in perfectly with a Dallas defense that stressed speed and quickness, Dexter Coakley proved to be one of the NFL's better linebackers over the course of his eight seasons with the Cowboys. An extremely consistent performer, Coakley recorded more than 100 tackles a franchise-record seven straight times, leading the team in that category on four separate occasions. Meanwhile, Coakley's ability to make big plays enabled him to intercept 10 passes as a member of the Cowboys, four of which he returned for touchdowns. Coakley's solid all-around play helped the Cowboys advance to the playoffs three times, earning him three trips to the Pro Bowl in the process.

Born in Charleston, South Carolina, on October 20, 1972, William Dexter Coakley attended local Wando High School, where he lettered in football and wrestling. Excelling on both offense and defense on the gridiron, Coakley rushed for more than 2,000 yards his final two years at Wando, while also earning All-Conference honors twice as a safety. Failing to display the same level of proficiency in the classroom, Coakley had to attend Fork Union Military Academy's post-graduate program for one year to meet academic requirements for college. He subsequently accepted a football scholarship from Appalachian State University, where he moved to linebacker after growing bigger and stronger. Excelling at his new position, Coakley became the first two-time winner of the Buck Buchanan Award, presented annually to the nation's top Division I-AA defensive player. Along the way, he set school records for most solo tackles and sacks, earning in the process All-America and Southern Conference Defensive Player of the Year honors as a sophomore, junior, and senior. Coakley also was named Southern Conference Athlete of the Year as a junior and senior, making him just the seventh player in the history of the conference to earn that distinction in consecutive years.

Still, in spite of his long list of accomplishments at the collegiate level, Coakley lasted until the third round of the 1997 NFL Draft due to

Dexter Coakley recorded more than 100 tackles in a season seven straight times, a franchise-record.
Courtesy of PristineAuction.com

concerns over his small college background and smallish, 5'10", 231-pound frame. Finally selected by the Cowboys with the 65th overall pick, Coakley quickly laid claim to the team's starting weak-side linebacker job with a strong showing during the preseason, after which he went on to dispel any notions that he lacked the ability to succeed in the NFL by earning a spot on the NFL All-Rookie Team by recording 2½ sacks, one interception, and more than 100 tackles for the first of seven consecutive times. Coakley followed that up with a similarly productive sophomore campaign, before earning the first of his three Pro Bowl selections in 1999 by making 131 tackles and a career-high four interceptions, one of which he returned 46 yards for the first pick-six of his career.

Blessed with outstanding speed and athleticism, Coakley soon emerged as a playmaker on a Dallas defense that emphasized quickness and pursuit. Noted for his tackling skills and quickness to the ball, Coakley not only annually recorded more than 100 tackles, but he also did an excellent job in pass coverage, with his 10 picks and four interception returns for touchdowns serving as a testament to his ability to stay with opposing running backs and tight ends. Furthermore, Coakley proved to be a defensive coordinator's dream, always putting forth a 100 percent effort and performing on an extremely consistent level week in and week out. A durable performer as well, Coakley failed to start just one game over the course of his eight seasons in Dallas, sitting out a 2001 contest with an injured knee.

Coakley continued his string of seven straight seasons with more than 100 tackles the next four years, earning Pro Bowl honors in both 2001 and 2003, and leading the league with two interception returns for touchdowns in the first of those campaigns. However, after signing a six-year contract extension with the Cowboys in 2001, Coakley found himself sharing playing time with second-year linebacker Brady James in 2004, limiting him to fewer than 100 tackles (91) for the first time in his career. With head coach Bill Parcells installing a new 3-4 defense, which is designed for bigger and taller linebackers, the Cowboys elected to part ways with Coakley following the conclusion of the campaign. In addition to being tied with Dennis Thurman for the most touchdown interception returns in Cowboys history (four), Coakley remains tied with Thurman for the most defensive touchdowns scored in team annals (five). He also ranks fourth in franchise history with 1,046 career tackles.

One day after being released by the Cowboys, Coakley signed a five-year contract with the St. Louis Rams for significantly more money than he earned in Dallas. However, he ended up spending just two years in St. Louis, starting the first 12 games of the 2005 campaign, before missing the final four contests with a fractured fibula and a dislocated ankle. After being reduced to a backup role in 2006, Coakley suffered the indignity of being released by the Rams prior to the start of the ensuing campaign, prompting him to announce his retirement. Coakley ended his career with 1,125 tackles, 13 interceptions, and 9½ sacks, compiling the vast majority of those numbers while playing for the Cowboys.

Following his retirement, Coakley became the linebackers coach at The Oakridge School in Arlington, Texas. He also serves as that school's softball coach and co-hosts *The Legends Show* with Mickey Spagnola, broadcasting from the Hooters in Grapevine, Texas, on the Dallas Cowboys Radio Network.

COWBOYS CAREER HIGHLIGHTS

Best Season

While Coakley proved to be a model of consistency during his time in Dallas, he had his finest all-around season for the Cowboys in 1999, when, in addition to making 131 tackles, he intercepted four passes, which he returned for 119 yards and one touchdown. Coakley's outstanding play earned him a trip to the Pro Bowl, making him the first Cowboys linebacker to be so honored since Ken Norton Jr. received an invitation in 1993.

Memorable Moments / Greatest Performances

Coakley recorded the first interception of his career in his very first game, picking off a Kordell Stewart pass during a 37–7 victory over the Pittsburgh Steelers in the 1997 regular-season opener.

Although the Cowboys lost their October 13, 1997, matchup with the Washington Redskins 21–16, Coakley scored the first of his five career touchdowns during the contest, recovering a Brian Mitchell fumble midway through the third quarter and returning the ball 16 yards for the Cowboys' first TD of the game.

Coakley contributed to a 24–7 victory over the Atlanta Falcons on September 20, 1999, by intercepting a Tony Graziani pass at the Dallas 47 yard line on Atlanta's opening drive of the game and returning the ball 43 yards to the Falcons' 10 yard line. Four plays later, Toby Gowin split the uprights from 33 yards out, giving the Cowboys an early 3–0 lead.

Coakley earned NFC Defensive Player of the Week honors later in the year, when he helped lead the Cowboys to a 20–0 win over the Miami Dolphins on Thanksgiving Day by picking off two Dan Marino passes, one of which he returned 46 yards for a touchdown.

Coakley turned in a tremendous all-around effort on October 28, 2001, leading the Cowboys to a 17–3 win over the Arizona Cardinals by returning an interception 10 yards for a touchdown, forcing a fumble, and making six tackles.

Coakley again crossed the opponent's goal line the following week, returning an interception of a Kerry Collins pass 29 yards for a score during a 27–24 overtime loss to the Giants on November 4, 2001.

Coakley scored the last of his five career touchdowns during a 21–13 victory over the Tennessee Titans on September 15, 2002, putting the Cowboys ahead to stay late in the third quarter by picking off a Steve McNair pass near midfield and returning the ball 52 yards for a TD that gave Dallas a 14–10 lead.

Coakley helped lead the Cowboys to a lopsided 38–7 victory over the Detroit Lions on October 19, 2003, by recording nine tackles and an interception, which he returned 24 yards to the Detroit 8 yard line, to set up a Quincy Carter to Terry Glenn touchdown connection on the very next play.

NOTABLE ACHIEVEMENTS

- Scored five career touchdowns (four interception returns and one fumble return).
- Recorded four interceptions and 119 interception-return yards in 1999.
- Recorded more than 100 tackles seven straight times (1997–2003).
- Led NFL with two interception-return touchdowns in 2001.
- Led Cowboys in tackles four times.
- Holds Cowboys career record for most interception-return touchdowns (four).
- Holds Cowboys career record for most defensive touchdowns scored (five).
- Ranks fourth in Cowboys history with 1,046 career tackles.
- Named to 1997 NFL All-Rookie Team.
- 1999 Week 12 NFC Defensive Player of the Week.
- Three-time Pro Bowl selection (1999, 2001, and 2003).

42

LARRY COLE

The fourth and final member of the dominant defensive line that served as the focal point of the Dallas Doomsday Defense, Larry Cole spent his entire 13-year career with the Cowboys, proving to be one of the team's most versatile and underrated players during that time. Manning all four positions along the Dallas defensive front at one time or another, Cole became best known for his outstanding work at left defensive end, where he spent most of his peak seasons playing alongside Bob Lilly and Jethro Pugh. Cole also excelled at both tackle spots, moving to the interior of the Dallas defense later in his career to accommodate standout defensive ends Harvey Martin and Ed "Too Tall" Jones. Often overlooked in favor of his more flamboyant linemates, Cole never received All-Pro honors or appeared in the Pro Bowl. Nevertheless, he used his intelligence and versatility to help the Cowboys win nine division titles, five NFC championships, and two Super Bowls.

Born in Clarkfield, Minnesota, on November 15, 1946, Lawrence Rudolph Cole attended local Granite Falls High School, before enrolling at the US Air Force Academy. After one year at Air Force, Cole transferred to the University of Hawaii, where he made a name for himself on the gridiron, before completing his college education at the University of Houston. Subsequently selected by the Cowboys in the 16th round of the 1968 NFL Draft, with the 428th overall pick, Cole later revealed that he never anticipated playing football professionally, stating, "I thought, 'Nobody's going to notice you out here [in Hawaii].'. . . Gil Brandt's computer found me."

Although Cole initially expected to compete for a job on the offensive line when he arrived at his first training camp, the Cowboys wasted little time in shifting him to the defensive side of the ball. Appearing in all 14 games as a rookie, Cole started 10 of those at left defensive end after beating out Willie Townes for the starting job. Performing extremely well his first year in the league, Cole helped solidify the left side of the Dallas defensive line, excelling against both the run and the pass, and even scoring a pair of

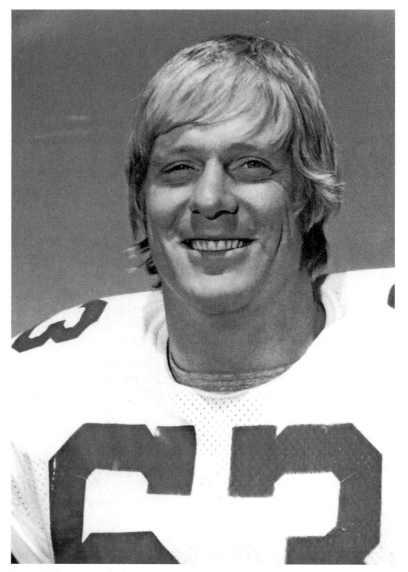

Larry Cole manned all four spots along the Dallas defensive front at different times during his 13 seasons with the Cowboys.
Courtesy of Steve Liskey, Retrocards.net

touchdowns—one on a fumble recovery and the other on an interception return. Continuing to display a penchant for making big plays the following year, Cole recorded another pick-six and recovered two more fumbles.

Although Cole lacked the natural athletic ability of some of his more talented linemates, he quickly developed a reputation for being one of the smartest players in the league, with Bob Lilly telling the *Lubbock Avalanche-Journal* in 1999, "He was a big guy and strong. He wasn't particularly fast, but he was very, very bright. We never made many mistakes. We got beat physically occasionally, but we didn't make a whole lot of mistakes. I always thought he was one of those guys that nobody thought was a great ballplayer, but I know he was."

In a moment of self-reflection, Cole suggested, "I'm the operations guy, the production guy. Give me the game plan, and I execute it. I'm not an ego guy that needs the glorification."

As a testament to his disdain for the limelight, Cole served as a founding member of the "Zero Club," joining teammates Blaine Nye and Pat Toomay in forming an exclusive unit whose members dedicated themselves to performing behind the scenes. In discussing the logic behind the creation of his club, which also listed boredom and total inactivity among its primary objectives, Cole explained, "When you're bored and inactive, time passes more slowly. So, by cultivating boredom, you can add years to your life expectancy."

Cole, who stood 6'5" and generally tipped the scales at somewhere between 250 and 255 pounds, applied a similarly analytical approach to his craft, often enabling him to out-think his opponents. Even though Cole lacked outstanding foot speed, his superb anticipation and excellent instincts usually enabled him to cover a surprising amount of territory when defending against the run. Meanwhile, his size and strength made him an effective pass-rusher.

Cole remained the Cowboys' starter at left defensive end until 1975, when he moved to right tackle after Bob Lilly retired and youngsters Harvey Martin and Ed "Too Tall" Jones joined the starting unit. Cole continued to man that post for the next two years, before splitting his final four seasons between left end and left tackle, which he considered to be his best position. Although Cole built his reputation primarily on his ability to stop the run, he ended his career in 1980 with a total of 60 unofficial quarterback sacks—a figure that currently ranks him 10th in franchise history.

In his 13 years with the Cowboys, Cole appeared in five Super Bowls and played in a total of 26 playoff games, which represented an NFL record at the time of his retirement. After spending most of his career playing in virtual anonymity, Cole found himself being praised by the local media his last few years in the league, prompting him to state during his 1980 retirement news conference, "I want to thank the media for under-publicizing

Cole is tied for second in franchise history with three interception-return touchdowns.
Courtesy of Steve Liskey, Retrocards.net

me for the first 10 years of my career and over-publicizing me for the last three years of it." Speaking at that same press conference, Dallas head coach Tom Landry commented, "We will hate to lose someone who made the contributions Larry has. But we will hate to lose Larry Cole as a person. If I had 45 guys on the team like Larry Cole, I would never retire. We're going to miss him."

Following his retirement, Cole became an extremely successful real estate developer in the Dallas–Fort Worth area, eventually starting his own business that he called Larry Cole Communities. Looking back fondly at his playing career many year later, Cole suggested, "Now is the money time, but, as far as the history of the NFL, I think I played in the most exciting period. I got a taste of the old, the Super Bowls in the middle of my career, and, when the new stadiums and TV contracts were growing, football became kind of a happening thing."

CAREER HIGHLIGHTS

Best Season

Although Cole proved to be an extremely consistent performer over the course of his career, it could be argued that he had his finest season in 1971, when, in addition to recording a team-high four fumble recoveries during the regular season, he recovered another loose ball during the Cowboys' Super Bowl win over Miami and helped anchor the league's second-stingiest run defense from his left end position. Nevertheless, Cole made his greatest overall impact in 1978, when, splitting his time between three of the four positions along the defensive line, he made significant contributions to a Dallas defense that allowed the fewest rushing yards of any team in the NFL, placed second in total yards allowed, and finished third in fewest points surrendered to the opposition. Furthermore, Cole scored one touchdown during the regular season, recorded two sacks during the playoffs, and, as one of the team's elder statesmen on defense, helped mentor younger linemates Randy White, Harvey Martin, and Ed "Too Tall" Jones.

Memorable Moments / Greatest Performances

Cole scored four defensive touchdowns during his career, with all of those ironically coming against the Redskins. Cole victimized Washington for the first time on November 17, 1968, when, during a lopsided 44–24 victory over the 'Skins, he recovered a fourth-quarter fumble and returned it 21 yards for his first career TD.

Cole again lit the scoreboard less than two weeks later, when his 5-yard touchdown interception return of a Jim Ninowski pass late in the fourth quarter cemented a 29–20 Thanksgiving Day win over the Redskins.

Cole once again helped the Cowboys defeat Washington on November 16, 1969, picking off a Sonny Jurgensen pass late in the first quarter and returning it 41 yards for a TD during a 41–28 victory over the Redskins.

Cole topped that effort, though, on November 23, 1980, when his 43-yard TD return of a 4th-quarter Mike Kruczek pass proved to be the difference in a 14–10 win over the Redskins.

However, Cole made arguably the most famous play of his career in the 1979 regular-season finale, when, with the Cowboys trailing Washington by six points late in the fourth quarter, he forced the Redskins into a punting situation by stopping John Riggins on a critical third-and-2 running play. Roger Staubach subsequently engineered what turned out to be his last game-winning TD drive, giving the Cowboys a dramatic 35–34 victory in the process.

Nevertheless, when asked to recall his favorite Cowboys moment, Cole said, "Winning the first Super Bowl. That was my fourth year. We broke our butts to finally get over the top."

NOTABLE ACHIEVEMENTS

- Scored four career touchdowns (three on interception returns and one on a fumble return).
- Recorded four career interceptions.
- Finished sixth in NFL with four fumble recoveries in 1971.
- Tied for second in Cowboys history with three interception-return touchdowns.
- Ranks 10th in Cowboys history with 60 unofficial sacks.
- Five-time NFC champion (1970, 1971, 1975, 1977, and 1978).
- Two-time Super Bowl champion (VI and XII).

43

DeMARCO MURRAY

An extremely talented player who spent his first three years in Dallas battling injuries, DeMarco Murray emerged as the NFL's top running back in 2014, when he set a Cowboys' single-season franchise record by rushing for a league-leading 1,845 yards. More than just a one-year wonder, Murray topped the 1,000-yard mark in rushing the previous season as well, while also amassing more than 1,000 yards from scrimmage on three separate occasions and scoring more than 10 touchdowns twice as a member of the team. Although Murray left "Big D" via free agency following the conclusion of the 2014 campaign, he accomplished enough over the course of his four seasons in Dallas to earn a place in these rankings, with his 4,526 yards rushing placing him sixth in team annals. Further validating Murray's credentials are his two Pro Bowl nominations, one All-Pro selection, one NFL Offensive Player of the Year nomination, and the fact that he led the Cowboys in rushing in each of his four seasons in Dallas.

Born in Las Vegas, Nevada, on February 12, 1988, DeMarco Murray attended Bishop Gorman High School, where he played football and ran track. Proving to be particularly proficient on the gridiron, Murray received All-Conference recognition three straight times and earned 2005 Sunset Region Offensive Player of the Year honors as a senior by rushing for 1,947 yards, gaining another 624 yards on 22 pass receptions, and scoring 34 touchdowns. Also excelling in track and field, Murray competed in the 100-meter dash and served as a member of the school's 4 x 100-meter relay team.

After fielding offers from several major colleges, including USC, Penn State, and Texas A&M, Murray ultimately chose to enroll at the University of Oklahoma, where he redshirted as a freshman, before establishing himself as one of the greatest players in that school's history over the course of the next four seasons. Among the many records Murray ended up setting at Oklahoma, he is the school's all-time leader in touchdowns (65), all-purpose yards (6,718), and receiving yards for a running back (1,571).

DeMarco Murray set a Cowboys single-season record in 2014, when he rushed for a league-leading 1,845 yards.
Public Domain/Wikipedia

Still, in spite of Murray's exceptional play at the collegiate level, he ended up slipping to the third round of the 2011 NFL Draft, where the Cowboys selected him with the 71st overall pick. After beginning his rookie campaign playing mostly on special teams and serving as a backup to starting running back Felix Jones, Murray assumed the starting role when Jones sprained his ankle during a Week 6 loss to the New England Patriots. Making the most out of his opportunity, Murray burst upon the NFL scene in his first start by rushing for a franchise-record 253 yards, in leading the Cowboys to a 34–7 victory over the St. Louis Rams. Murray continued to perform well over the course of the next several weeks, gaining more than 600 yards on the ground in the Cowboys' next six games, before suffering a fractured right ankle and a high ankle sprain against the Giants in Week 14. Sidelined for the final three games of the regular season, Murray ended his first year in the league with 897 yards rushing, 26 receptions for 183 yards, two touchdowns, and a stellar 5.5 yards-per-carry rushing average that placed him second in the league rankings.

Beset by injury woes once again in 2012, Murray had to sit out six games with a sprained foot, limiting him to just 161 carries, 663 yards rushing, and four touchdowns. Somewhat luckier in 2013, Murray missed only two games with a sprained MCL, enabling him to earn a trip to the Pro Bowl by rushing for 1,121 yards, gaining another 350 yards on 53 pass receptions, scoring 10 touchdowns, and finishing fourth in the league with a rushing average of 5.2 yards per carry. Appearing in all 16 games for the first time in his career the following year, Murray turned in a performance for the ages, leading the NFL with 392 carries, 1,845 yards rushing, 2,261 yards from scrimmage, and 13 rushing touchdowns, en route to earning First-Team All-Pro honors and recognition as the NFL Offensive Player of the Year. Displaying his toughness at one point during the season as well, Murray suffered a broken left hand against Philadelphia in Week 15 that forced him to undergo surgery the following day. Refusing to miss any playing time, Murray started the final two games of the regular season with his surgically repaired hand heavily bandaged, breaking Emmitt Smith's single-season franchise record for most yards rushing with a 100-yard effort against Washington in Week 17.

Certainly, running behind the league's best offensive line aided Murray immeasurably over the course of the 2014 campaign. Nevertheless, Murray's style of running suited the Dallas offense perfectly, with his straight-ahead approach helping the team establish a new identity. An excellent downfield runner, the 6-foot, 214-pound Murray possessed excellent balance and good strength, making him a perfect fit for the "smash-mouth" style of football the Cowboys employed throughout the year. Murray also did an outstanding job of using his speed and quickness to his advantage once he got into the open field, often avoiding the opposing team's linebackers and safeties once he reached the second line of defense. Extremely popular with his teammates, Murray drew praise from Jason Witten, who described him as "One of the young, bright stars, one of my favorite guys on this team. Humble, tough, loves playing ball, loves playing with his teammates. A little bit of an old-school player, but the ultimate team guy. An old-fashioned, good running back that plays the game the right way."

Yet, in spite of the tremendous performance Murray turned in for the Cowboys in 2014, the team chose not to match the five-year, $42 million contract offer the Philadelphia Eagles extended to him when he became a free agent at season's end. Convinced that much of the success Murray experienced was predicated on the effectiveness of their offensive line, the Cowboys instead elected to sign former Oakland Raiders running back Darren McFadden at a significantly lower price. With Murray headed to Philadelphia, he left the Cowboys having rushed for a total of 4,526 yards, amassed another 1,196 yards on 170 pass receptions, scored 29 touchdowns, and averaged 4.8 yards per carry.

Murray led the Cowboys in rushing in each of his four seasons in Dallas.
Courtesy of PristineAuction.com

Following his departure from Dallas, Murray ended up spending just one unsuccessful season in Philadelphia, gaining only 702 yards on the ground and averaging just 3.6 yards per carry for an offense that failed to make proper use of his abilities. Playing in a system that always ran out of the shotgun, Murray found himself being asked to run laterally much of the time, instead of north-to-south, which better suited his style of running. Growing increasingly frustrated as the season progressed, Murray finally asked out of Philadelphia—a request the Eagles granted on March 9, 2016, when they traded him to the Tennessee Titans. Finding the situation in Tennessee much more to his liking, Murray rebounded in 2016 to rank among the NFL leaders with 1,287 yards rushing, 1,664 yards from scrimmage, and nine rushing touchdowns, earning in the process his third Pro Bowl selection. Murray will enter the 2017 campaign with career totals of 6,515 yards rushing, 267 pass receptions for another 1,895 yards, and 48 touchdowns. He has averaged 4.6 yards per carry over six NFL seasons.

COWBOYS CAREER HIGHLIGHTS

Best Season

Was there ever any doubt? Murray put together one of the greatest offensive seasons in Cowboys history in 2014, when he led the NFL with 1,845 yards rushing, 2,261 yards from scrimmage, and 13 rushing touchdowns, setting single-season franchise records in each of the first two categories. Murray's brilliant performance earned him First-Team All-Pro honors and recognition as the AP NFL Offensive Player of the Year.

Memorable Moments / Greatest Performances

Murray made his breakout game as a rookie a memorable one, carrying the ball 25 times for a franchise-record 253 yards during a 34–7 victory over the St. Louis Rams on October 23, 2011. Murray's extraordinary effort, which earned him FedEx Ground NFL Player of the Week honors, included a 91-yard touchdown run on the Cowboys' opening possession that ranks as the second longest in franchise history, trailing only Tony Dorsett's 99-yard TD scamper against Minnesota in January of 1993.

Murray turned in another outstanding performance two weeks later, rushing for 139 yards and making four receptions for another 47 yards, in leading the Cowboys to a 23–13 win over the Seattle Seahawks on November 6, 2011.

Murray followed that up by rushing for 135 yards and one touchdown during a 44–7 blowout of the Buffalo Bills one week later.

Murray helped lead the Cowboys to a 24–17 victory over the New York Giants in the opening game of the 2012 regular season by rushing for 131 yards on 20 carries, which included a season-long run of 48 yards.

Murray torched the defense of the St. Louis Rams for the second time in as many meetings with them on September 22, 2013, when he rushed for 175 yards and one touchdown during a lopsided 31–7 Cowboys win.

Murray made one of his more memorable plays during his time in Dallas three months later, on December 22, 2013, when his 10-yard TD reception on fourth down with just 1:08 left in the game gave the Cowboys a come-from-behind 24–23 victory over the Washington Redskins that enabled them to remain in playoff contention. He finished the contest with 96 yards rushing and two touchdowns.

Murray turned in a number of exceptional performances over the course of the 2014 campaign, with the first of those coming on September 14, when he rushed for 167 yards and one touchdown during a 26–10 victory over the Tennessee Titans.

Two weeks later, Murray led the Cowboys to a 38–17 win over the New Orleans Saints by rushing for 149 yards and a pair of touchdowns, with his scores coming on runs of 15 and 28 yards.

However, Murray had his biggest game of the year on December 4, 2014, when he rushed for 179 yards, gained another 49 yards on nine pass receptions, and scored a touchdown during a 41–28 win over the Chicago Bears.

NOTABLE ACHIEVEMENTS

- Rushed for more than 1,000 yards twice, topping 1,800 yards once (1,845 in 2014).
- Surpassed 1,000 yards from scrimmage three times, topping 2,000 yards once (2,261 in 2014).
- Scored more than 10 touchdowns twice.
- Averaged more than 5 yards per carry twice.
- Caught more than 50 passes twice.
- Led NFL in: rushing attempts once; rushing yardage once; rushing touchdowns once; yards from scrimmage once; and all-purpose yards once.
- Led Cowboys in rushing yardage four times.
- Holds Cowboys single-game record for most yards rushing (253 vs. St. Louis on October 23, 2011).
- Holds Cowboys single-season records for most: rushing attempts (392 in 2014); rushing yardage (1,845 in 2014); and yards from scrimmage (2,261 in 2014).
- Ranks among Cowboys career leaders in: rushing yardage (6th); rushing touchdowns (tied-8th); rushing average (4th); and rushing attempts (7th).
- 2014 Division champion.
- 2011 Week 7 NFL Player of the Week.

- 2014 Associated Press NFL Offensive Player of the Year.
- Two-time Pro Bowl selection (2013 and 2014).
- 2014 First-Team All-Pro selection.

44

CHARLES HALEY

A versatile defender who excelled at both linebacker and defensive end during his NFL career, Charles Haley arrived in Dallas in 1992 as an established star, having already been named NFC Defensive Player of the Year once and earned three trips to the Pro Bowl, one All-Pro selection, and two All-NFC nominations as a member of the San Francisco 49ers. Yet, in addition to gaining widespread recognition as one of the league's best pass-rushers while helping the 49ers capture two NFL titles, Haley developed a reputation for being a malcontent whose volatile temperament and dour disposition frequently caused him to clash with teammates and coaches alike. Although the outspoken Haley hardly became a model citizen after he joined the Cowboys, he eventually created a somewhat different image of himself that caused others to view him as a solid teammate and a key contributor to three more championship teams. Earning another two Pro Bowl nominations and All-Pro selections as a member of the Cowboys, Haley also received NFC Defensive Player of the Year recognition for the second time in his career during his time in Dallas. Meanwhile, the three Super Bowl rings Haley won while playing for the Cowboys gave him a total of five, tying him with Tom Brady for the most in NFL history.

Born in Gladys, Virginia, on January 6, 1964, Charles Lewis Haley attended William Campbell High School in nearby Naruna, where he spent three years playing linebacker and tight end, earning All–Region III, All–Group AA, and Defensive Player of the Year honors as a senior by leading his team to the Seminole District championship. Failing to receive scholarship offers from any major colleges, Haley subsequently enrolled at James Madison University in Harrisonburg, Virginia, where he shuttled back and forth between linebacker and defensive end the next four seasons, earning Division I-AA All-America honors twice.

Selected by the San Francisco 49ers in the fourth round of the 1986 NFL Draft, with the 96th overall pick, Haley performed well at defensive end his first year in the league, earning a spot on the NFL All-Rookie

Charles Haley proved to be a disruptive force on defense during his time in Dallas, applying constant pressure to opposing quarterbacks.
Courtesy of George A. Kitrinos

Team by sacking opposing quarterbacks 12 times. After recording another 6½ sacks the following year, Haley moved to outside linebacker in 1988, remaining at that post for the next four seasons. Establishing himself as one of the league's elite pass-rushers during that time, the 6'5", 255-pound Haley used his strength, speed, and agility to wreak havoc on opposing offenses, amassing a total of 45 sacks from 1988 to 1991, including a career-high 16 in 1990 that earned him NFC Defensive Player of the Year honors.

Yet, even though Haley's stellar play helped the 49ers win back-to-back NFL championships in 1988 and 1989, he gradually began to wear out his welcome in San Francisco with his disruptive and antagonistic behavior that included locker room tirades and assaults, both verbal and physical, on teammates. Two incidents, in particular, changed his relationship with the team forever, with Haley claiming that the first of those occurred after he confided in a 49ers official about some personal problems, only to discover at a later date that the official subsequently disclosed the content of their conversations to several of Haley's teammates.

However, the incident that ultimately sealed Haley's fate took place in the 49ers locker room after a 1991 loss to the Raiders and Haley's close friend, Ronnie Lott. Outraged over the loss, Haley moved aggressively toward quarterback Steve Young before teammates intervened. In explaining his version of the events that transpired, Haley stated:

> It's been said that I charged at Steve Young over throwing an interception. That wasn't what happened. I was so mad. The reasons were that I wanted to beat Ronnie Lott and the Raiders so bad, and we needed the win very much to make the playoffs, which we eventually did not do. I smashed my hand through a glass door. So, I screwed up. The main thing is I'm one of the worst in the world at accepting losing.
>
> That was the situation that changed my relationship in San Francisco for good. I felt they treated me after that without any respect. The thing that got me was that different things like that happened there all the time with other players, and no one said anything. Yet, they wanted to make a spectacle of me. Sure, we had talks after that, but the whole thing was they didn't listen. They looked right past me. They looked at me like I was stupid and they thought of me as stupid. . . . It's always been negative somewhere, and I've always been a misfit. I've fought that all my life. It's been me against the world. You get tired.

Creating further animosity between himself and the organization after clashing with head coach George Seifert, Haley finally received his ticket out of town on August 26, 1992, when the 49ers traded him to the Cowboys for a 1993 second-round draft pick and a 1994 third-round selection. Upon learning of Haley's acquisition, Dallas head coach Jimmy Johnson stated, "I think everybody understands the last couple of years we have been looking for a pass rusher. We felt we had improved our defense significantly over the last couple of years, and I think this undoubtedly will make it even better. He will have an immediate impact on our pass rush."

Inserted at right defensive end upon his arrival in Dallas, Haley recorded just six sacks and 39 tackles his first year with the Cowboys. However, those numbers do not reflect the overall impact he made on the team, since, despite being double-teamed much of the time, he led the Cowboys with 42 quarterback pressures, helping them to elevate themselves from the league's 17th-ranked defense the previous season to number 1 overall in 1992. Meanwhile, Cowboys owner Jerry Jones praised Haley for the intangible qualities he brought to the team, suggesting, "He is one of the smartest players I've ever been around, and he's a guy who looks at the whole picture. He's like a coach on the field. He has been a total plus."

In discussing the manner in which he adapted to his new environment his first year in Dallas, Haley said:

> The media picked up everything from San Francisco and it followed me here. The players started reading it, and some of them started believing it. It was already judge, jury and verdict when I got here. It took 17 games for me to get to the level of where I could talk openly to some of them. The pressure of always being looked at as a troublemaker just because you're different from Joe makes it seem like there are two sets of rules, one for me and one for the team. It is constant. But I can handle this. It is a hell of a lot better than San Francisco.

After helping the Cowboys win the Super Bowl in 1992, Haley was plagued by recurring back problems throughout much of the ensuing campaign, limiting him to just four sacks and 41 tackles, although the Cowboys went on to repeat as NFL champions. Reverting back to his earlier form at one point during the season, Haley made headlines in Week 2 when he displayed his anger over the team's inability to sign holdout running back Emmitt Smith to a new deal by smashing his helmet through a wall in the locker room following a home loss to the Buffalo Bills.

Haley earned NFC Defensive Player of the Year honors in 1994, when he finished fourth in the league with 12½ sacks.
Courtesy of Dallas Cowboys

Although the Cowboys failed to capture their third consecutive NFL title in 1994, Haley put together his finest season as a member of the team after undergoing back surgery during the offseason, earning Pro Bowl, All-Pro, All-NFC, and NFC Defensive Player of the Year honors by finishing fourth in the NFL with 12½ sacks, while also recording 68 tackles, 52 quarterback pressures, and three forced fumbles. After briefly retiring following a 38–28 loss to the 49ers in the NFC championship game, Haley decided to re-sign with the Cowboys for two more years, helping them win their third NFL championship in four seasons in 1995 by recording a team-leading 10½ sacks. However, a ruptured disk suffered during a 24–17 loss to Washington in Week 14 essentially ended his season, forcing him to undergo another surgery on his back and bringing his days as a dominant pass rusher to an end. Limited to just five games the following year, Haley announced his retirement at season's end, although he later attempted a comeback with the 49ers, seeing limited duty as a backup in 1999, before leaving the game for good.

Over the course of 12 NFL seasons, Haley recorded 100½ sacks, finishing in double digits in that category six times. He also forced 26 fumbles, intercepted two passes, and scored one defensive touchdown. During his time in Dallas, Haley recorded 34 sacks, placing him 10th on the team's all-time list. Haley played for 10 division championship teams, five NFC championship teams, and five Super Bowl champions in his 12 years in the league.

Inducted into the Cowboys Ring of Honor in 2011 and the Pro Football Hall of Fame in 2015, Haley received high praise from Emmitt Smith, who stated, "Charles Haley changed the way the Cowboys played football in the 90s. And the reason why I say that is because he was such a dominant force coming off the edge, where it took two and three to block him."

Following his retirement, Haley spent two years serving the Detroit Lions as an assistant defensive coach, before becoming a special advisor for both the Cowboys and 49ers in their rookie mentoring programs. Treated with daily medication since being diagnosed with bipolar disorder, Haley now expresses mixed feelings about how he conducted himself during his playing days, saying:

> I have regrets, a whole bunch of regrets, about the way I treated my teammates, my coaches, my family, and people in general during my playing career, but, as far as winning, as far as maximizing my team's opportunity for success, I have zero. But it required a lot of sacrifice. I sacrificed my back, my knees. I've been parking in handicapped spaces for almost 10 years now. It takes me a while to get around, and I just turned 52 this past January. I'm not exactly an old man, but let me tell you, my body is old. We won Super Bowls and we made the fans happy, I mean, when it comes to playing in the NFL, that's Mount Olympus, where the football gods reside.
>
> That's why we all play, so I'm okay with how it all turned out, and I'm paying the price with my body every waking hour.

COWBOYS CAREER HIGHLIGHTS

Best Season

Haley played well for the Cowboys in 1995, earning Pro Bowl and Second-Team All-NFC honors by recording a team-leading 10½ sacks. However, he unquestionably turned in his most dominant performance as a member of the team one year earlier, when he finished fourth in the league with 12½ sacks, made 68 tackles, and recorded 52 quarterback pressures and one of his two career interceptions, earning in the process a trip to the Pro Bowl, First-Team All-Pro honors, and recognition as NFC Defensive Player of the Year.

Memorable Moments / Greatest Performances

Haley recorded his first multiple-sack game for the Cowboys on December 6, 1992, when he brought down Denver quarterbacks behind the line of scrimmage twice during a 31–27 victory over the Broncos.

Haley helped shift the momentum of Super Bowl XXVII the Cowboys' way, when, with the score tied at 7–7 late in the first quarter, he sacked Jim Kelly deep in Buffalo territory, forcing a fumble. Jimmie Jones scooped up the loose ball at the 2 yard line and ran it into the end zone, giving the Cowboys a 14–7 lead in a game they eventually won 52–17.

Haley gained a measure of revenge against his former team on October 17, 1993, when he sacked Steve Young twice during a 26–17 win over the San Francisco 49ers.

Haley earned NFC Defensive Player of the Week honors for his performance in the 1994 regular-season opener by recording four of the Cowboys' nine sacks of Pittsburgh quarterback Neil O'Donnell during a 26–9 victory over the Steelers.

Haley turned in another outstanding performance the following week, recording a sack and an interception, in helping the Cowboys defeat the Houston Oilers 20–17.

Proving to be a nuisance to Randall Cunningham throughout the contest, Haley sacked the Philadelphia QB three times during a 31–19 victory over the Eagles on December 4, 1994.

Haley earned his second NFC Defensive Player of the Week nomination as a member of the Cowboys on September 10, 1995, when he sacked John Elway twice and forced a fumble during a 31–21 win over the Denver Broncos.

NOTABLE ACHIEVEMENTS

- Finished in double digits in sacks twice.
- Finished fourth in NFL with 12½ sacks in 1994.
- Led Cowboys in sacks twice.
- Ranks 10th in Cowboys history with 34 career sacks.
- Three-time NFC champion (1992, 1993, and 1995).
- Three-time Super Bowl champion (XXVII, XXVIII, and XXX).
- Two-time NFC Defensive Player of the Week.
- 1994 NFC Defensive Player of the Year.
- Two-time Pro Bowl selection (1994 and 1995).
- 1994 First-Team All-Pro selection.
- 1994 First-Team All-NFC selection.
- 1995 Second-Team All-NFC selection.
- Inducted into Cowboys Ring of Honor in 2011.
- Elected to Pro Football Hall of Fame in 2015.

45

HERSCHEL WALKER

An extraordinary athlete who excelled in both football and track in college, Herschel Walker arrived in Dallas in 1986 amid a considerable amount of fanfare. After winning the Heisman Trophy as a junior at the University of Georgia and spending the next three years starring in the United States Football League, Walker signed a five-year, $5 million contract with the Cowboys in 1986, making him the team's highest-paid player. Although the presence of Tony Dorsett forced Walker to assume various roles in the Dallas offense over the course of the next two seasons as the two men vied for playing time and touches, the latter proved to be worth every penny the Cowboys paid him, establishing himself as one of the NFL's most potent offensive weapons. In addition to rushing for more than 1,000 yards once as a member of the Cowboys, Walker gained more than 1,500 yards from scrimmage three times, topping the magical 2,000-yard mark once. He also made more than 50 receptions and surpassed 500 receiving yards three times each, en route to earning two trips to the Pro Bowl, two All-Pro selections, and a pair of All-NFC nominations. Yet, ironically, it is for the manner in which Walker left Dallas that he is perhaps best remembered by Cowboys fans.

Born in Wrightsville, Georgia, on March 3, 1962, Herschel Junior Walker suffered through a difficult childhood, spending much of his youth being plagued by weight problems and a speech impediment. In discussing his early years, Walker revealed, "I was a little bit overweight and had a stuttering problem. I used to be afraid of the dark; I was scared to death of the dark. I remember as a little boy, I used to go outside to play real hard; my nose would bleed. I don't know what that was. And I couldn't run; I had these big old knots that swelled and stuff on my knees."

Walker continued, "I didn't love myself. I didn't love who I was, having a stuttering problem, kids picking on the way you spoke, picking on your weight."

Herschel Walker established himself as one of the NFL's most potent offensive weapons during his time in Dallas.
Courtesy of MearsOnlineAuctions.com

Walker's struggles continued until he entered the seventh grade, when he began channeling all his energy toward improving himself. Reading out loud to himself until he no longer stuttered, Walker eventually became such an outstanding student that he graduated valedictorian of his class at local Johnson County High School. Meanwhile, Walker developed a daily training regimen of 1,500 push-ups and 2,500 sit-ups that helped turn him into a finely tuned athlete who starred for the school in both football and track.

After earning 1979 National High School Scholar-Athlete of the Year honors as a senior by rushing for 3,167 yards on the gridiron and winning the shotput, 100-yard dash, and 220-yard dash events at the GHSA Class A State T&F Championships, Walker received a full football scholarship from the University of Georgia, where he continued to excel in multiple sports. Establishing himself as one of the greatest athletes in that school's history, Walker earned All-America recognition twice as a sprinter by competing in the 55- and 100-meter dashes and serving as a member of the SEC champion 4 x 100-meter relay squad in 1981. He also starred for the Bulldogs on the football field, earning All-America honors three times and winning both the Heisman Trophy and the Maxwell Award as a junior in 1982 after leading his team to the National Championship.

With Walker seeking to forgo his final year of college eligibility and the NFL not yet having lifted its ban on underclassmen, the star running back elected to join the New Jersey Generals of the newly formed United States Football League, which allowed college athletes to turn professional after their junior year and sign with their team of choice. Walker spent the next three years starring in the backfield for the Generals, accumulating a total of 5,562 yards on the ground and winning the USFL rushing title in both 1983 and 1985. Particularly dominant in the last of those campaigns, Walker rushed for 2,411 yards, establishing in the process pro football's all-time record for the most rushing yards gained in a season.

With the Cowboys expecting the USFL to last only two or three seasons, they wisely acquired Walker's NFL rights by selecting him in the fifth round of the 1985 NFL Draft, with the 114th overall pick. When the infant league subsequently folded one year later, Walker signed with the Cowboys, giving them a dynamic backfield tandem that also featured another former Heisman Trophy winner, Tony Dorsett.

Although Dorsett resented Walker's presence due to the latter's greater salary and infringement on his number of carries, the two men worked well together in 1986, with Dorsett rushing for 748 yards despite missing three games due to injury. Meanwhile, Walker gained 737 yards on the ground and led the team with 76 receptions, 837 receiving yards, 1,574 yards from scrimmage, and 14 touchdowns, finishing fourth in the league in the last category. He followed that up with a similarly productive 1987 campaign, earning Pro Bowl, First-Team All-NFC, and Second-Team All-Pro honors by rushing for 891 yards, gaining another 715 yards on 60 pass receptions, scoring eight touchdowns, and leading the league with 1,606 yards from scrimmage.

Displaying tremendous versatility his first two seasons in Dallas, Walker assumed various roles on offense, lining up at different times in the backfield, as a tight end, or as a wide receiver. Once Walker got his hands on the ball, though, he ran very much like a fullback, using his powerful 6'1", 225-pound frame to bowl over anyone who stood in his path. Yet, at the same time, Walker's world-class speed gave him the ability to run away from defenders, making him a threat to go the distance anytime he touched the ball.

With the Cowboys having traded away Dorsett prior to the start of the 1988 campaign, they decided to build their offense around Walker, who put together his finest NFL season. In addition to finishing second in the league with 1,514 yards rushing, he scored seven touchdowns and made 53 receptions for another 505 yards, giving him a total 2,019 yards from scrimmage that placed him third in the league rankings. Walker's exceptional all-around performance earned him Pro Bowl, First-Team All-NFC, and Second-Team All-Pro honors for the second straight time.

Nevertheless, with the Cowboys having compiled a record of just 3-13 in Tom Landry's last year as head coach, they completed a stunning trade with the Vikings five games into the 1989 campaign in which they sent their greatest asset to Minnesota for a host of veteran players and future draft picks. In addition to receiving running back Darrin Nelson, defensive back Isaac Holt, defensive end Alex Stewart, and linebackers Jesse Solomon and David Howard in exchange for Walker, the Cowboys acquired a 1992 first-round draft pick and six conditional draft picks, some of which they later used to select Emmitt Smith, Russell Maryland, Kevin Smith, and Darren Woodson. The deal, which has since become known as the "Herschel Walker Trade," is still considered to be one of the biggest ever made in the NFL—one that helped set up the Cowboys' next dynasty.

Reflecting back on the trade during a 2015 radio interview on *The Dan Patrick Show*, Walker said, "I think Jimmy Johnson was the reason that trade happened. I don't think it was Jerry [Jones]. If I had a team today, I'd have Jimmy Johnson as coach and I'd have Jimmy to be the one to be the general manager of that team."

Walker then added, "I'm not surprised by it. When it happened, I just went and played. When I got there to Minnesota, they didn't want me to play. The coaches didn't know the owners had traded all those players and picks. The day I showed up is the day they found out. I was in between a rock and a hard place. They didn't know what to do with me. But the notoriety of The Trade kept me able to do things later."

Unwanted by his new team's coaching staff, which failed to properly utilize his unique skill set, Walker experienced a precipitous decline in production after he joined the Vikings, gaining just 831 yards from scrimmage over the season's final 11 games, before accumulating a total of 2,114 yards from scrimmage over the course of the next two seasons. Nevertheless, Walker's 966 kickoff-return yards in 1990 enabled him to lead the NFL with 2,051 all-purpose yards. A free agent heading into the 1992 campaign, Walker signed with the Philadelphia Eagles, with whom he spent the next three years, rushing for more than 1,000 yards for the final time in his career in 1992, when he gained 1,070 yards on the ground and scored 10 touchdowns. After two more solid seasons in Philadelphia, Walker spent one year in New York returning kickoffs for the Giants, before returning to Dallas, where he assumed a similar role for the Cowboys the next two seasons. Announcing his retirement following the conclusion of the 1997 campaign, Walker ended his 12-year NFL career with 8,225 yards rushing, 512 pass receptions for another 4,859 yards, 18,168 all-purpose yards, 84 touchdowns, and an average of 4.2 yards per carry. During his time with the Cowboys, Walker rushed for 3,491 yards, caught 232 passes for another 2,556 yards, accumulated 7,993 all-purpose yards, and scored 35 touchdowns. Including his three seasons in the USFL, Walker rushed for a total of 13,787 yards, which represents the fifth-highest mark in the history of professional football. Meanwhile, Walker's 25,283 combined all-purpose yards place him first on the all-time list.

Unfortunately, Walker began to notice disturbing changes in his behavior shortly after he left the game, finding it increasingly difficult to distinguish his role in football from his role at home. Unable to rid himself of the anger and aggression he previously carried with him onto the playing field, Walker became abusive toward his wife, revealing years later, "I was out of the game. I had been out of the game for about four years and I developed this anger problem. And not that I developed it; it just manifested itself a little more severely. It totally destroyed my relationship with Cindy. I put a gun to her head; things that she said I was doing, she knew that wasn't me."

Walker's wife eventually left him, causing him to seek psychiatric help, which led to him discovering that he suffered from dissociative identity disorder—a condition in which a single person displays multiple distinct personalities known as "alters," each of which features a different type of behavior. Although Walker's symptoms surfaced much more after he ended his playing career, his condition can be traced back to his

Walker surpassed 1,500 yards from scrimmage three straight times for the Cowboys.
Courtesy of MearsOnlineAuctions.com

childhood, when he was a physically challenged first grader who stuttered when he spoke.

Walker also sought help from his pastor, Tony Evans, who later said, "While he was getting professional counseling on one side, I was providing a kind of spiritual direction on the other side. What I see is God using this episode in Herschel's life for His glory and greater witness. What it says is that Jesus Christ can heal and be the foundation of healing for the deepest kind of soul disorders."

Healed after months of prayer and drawing closer to God, Walker now says: "What I want everyone to know is that I've been blessed all my life. Jesus kept me out of prison. He kept me from harming someone. He kept me from harming myself. And I think that's the biggest thing. Because it's going to be tough. Like I said, Satan is always going to throw curve balls. But what you got to do is not be afraid to stand up at the plate and keep swinging. Because when you have God, you can't strike out. You can just swing all you want."

COWBOYS CAREER HIGHLIGHTS

Best Season

Walker performed extremely well for the Cowboys in both 1986 and 1987, ranking among the NFL leaders with 14 touchdowns, 1,574 yards from scrimmage, and an average of 4.9 yards per carry in the first of those campaigns, before leading the league with 1,606 yards from scrimmage in the second. Nevertheless, he had his finest season as a member of the Cowboys in 1988, when he became just the 10th player in NFL history to amass more than 2,000 yards from scrimmage in a season by rushing for 1,514 yards and accumulating another 505 yards on 53 pass receptions. Manning multiple positions over the course of the campaign, Walker played halfback, fullback, tight end, H-back, and wide receiver at different times, with his extraordinary all-around performance earning him Pro Bowl, First-Team All-NFC, and Second-Team All-Pro honors.

Memorable Moments / Greatest Performances

Walker made a huge impact in his very first game with the Cowboys, carrying the ball 10 times for 64 yards, gaining another 32 yards on six pass receptions, and scoring two touchdowns, including the game-winner late in the fourth quarter, in leading Dallas to a 31–28 victory over the eventual world champion New York Giants in the 1986 regular-season opener.

Walker turned in an outstanding all-around effort against another NFC East rival five weeks later, amassing 200 yards of total offense and scoring twice during a 30–6 win over the Washington Redskins on October 12. In addition to rushing for 45 yards, Walker accumulated another 155 yards on six pass receptions.

Walker rushed for more than 100 yards for the first time in his NFL career on October 26, 1986, when he carried the ball 26 times for 120 yards and two touchdowns during a convincing 37–6 victory over the St. Louis Cardinals.

Although the Cowboys lost their December 14, 1986, matchup with the Philadelphia Eagles 23–21, Walker made history during the contest by becoming the only NFL player ever to record a touchdown run of at least 84 yards and a TD reception of at least 84 yards in the same game. He finished the day with 122 yards rushing, on just six carries, and another 170 yards on nine receptions, giving him a total of 290 yards from scrimmage.

Walker again displayed his explosiveness on November 15, 1987, when he gave the Cowboys a 23–17 overtime victory over the New England Patriots by recording a 60-yard touchdown run a little over two minutes into the overtime session. He concluded the afternoon with 232 yards of total offense, gaining 173 of those on the ground and the other 59 through the air.

Walker helped the Cowboys defeat the St. Louis Cardinals 21–16 in the 1987 regular-season finale by rushing for 137 yards, gaining another 50 yards on three pass receptions, and scoring twice on a pair of 11-yard TD runs.

Walker continued to be a thorn in the side of the Cardinals after they moved to Phoenix the following year, leading the Cowboys to a 17–14 win over the newly transplanted Cards on September 12, 1988, by rushing for 149 yards and putting Dallas ahead to stay with a 3-yard TD run late in the first half.

Excelling as a kickoff returner during his second tour of duty with the Cowboys, Walker helped set up the first of Chris Boniol's four field goals by returning a kickoff 70 yards during the latter stages of the first half of a 12–6 win over the New England Patriots on December 15, 1996.

Walker proved to be one of the few bright spots during a 37–10 loss to the Washington Redskins one week later, returning a kickoff 63 yards and scoring the Cowboys' only touchdown of the game with a 39-yard run late in the fourth quarter.

Walker made his last significant contribution to the Cowboys on offense on October 19, 1997, when he collaborated with Troy Aikman on a 64-yard TD catch-and-run with just under 6½ minutes left in the game that gave the Cowboys a 26–22 victory over the Jacksonville Jaguars.

NOTABLE ACHIEVEMENTS

- Rushed for more than 1,000 yards once (1,514 in 1988).
- Surpassed 1,500 yards from scrimmage three times, topping 2,000 yards once (2,019 in 1988).
- Rushed for more than 10 touchdowns once (12 in 1986).
- Averaged more than 4.5 yards per carry once (4.9 in 1986).
- Caught more than 50 passes three times, surpassing 70 receptions once (76 in 1986).
- Surpassed 500 receiving yards three times, topping 800 yards once (837 in 1986).
- Led NFL with 1,606 yards from scrimmage in 1987.
- Finished second in NFL in: rushing yardage once; yards per rushing attempt once; and yards per kickoff return once.
- Finished third in NFL with 2,019 yards from scrimmage in 1988.
- Led Cowboys in rushing yardage twice.
- Ranks among Cowboys career leaders in: rushing yardage (9th); rushing touchdowns (10th); rushing average (10th); and rushing attempts (10th).
- 1987 Week 16 NFC Offensive Player of the Week.
- 1996 Week 8 NFC Special Teams Player of the Week.
- Two-time Pro Bowl selection (1987 and 1988).
- Two-time Second-Team All-Pro selection (1987 and 1988).
- Two-time First-Team All-NFC selection (1987 and 1988).

46

DANNY WHITE

Faced with the unenviable task of following the incomparable Roger Staubach as starting quarterback in Dallas, Danny White found himself unable to earn the favor of Cowboys fans, who often criticized him for losing three straight NFC championship games and failing to reach the same level of excellence as his predecessor. Nevertheless, White compiled an overall record of 62-30 as a starter in Dallas, earning in the process three All-NFC selections, one All-Pro nomination, and one trip to the Pro Bowl, while leading the Cowboys to five playoff appearances and a pair of division titles. And, even though White never performed at the same lofty level as Staubach, he actually completed more passes, threw more touchdown passes, and compiled a higher completion percentage, making him one of the most overlooked and under-appreciated players in franchise history.

Born in Mesa, Arizona, on February 9, 1952, Wilford Daniel White excelled in both baseball and football while attending local Mesa Westwood High School, establishing himself during that time as a top baseball prospect. After initially enrolling at Arizona State University on a baseball scholarship, White began to display more of an affinity for football after he began his college career on the gridiron as the school's punter. Earning the team's starting quarterback job midway through his sophomore campaign, White went on to lead the Sun Devils to an overall record of 33-4 over the course of the next three seasons, setting seven NCAA passing records in the process, and earning All-America honors in 1973. Concluding his college career with 6,717 passing yards, 64 touchdown passes, 42 interceptions, and an average of 41.7 yards per punt, White eventually earned the additional distinction of being named Arizona Athlete of the Century by the *Arizona Republic* in 2000.

Although the Cowboys subsequently selected White in the third round of the 1974 NFL Draft, with the 53rd overall pick, they seemed mostly interested in him as a punter since they already had Roger Staubach firmly entrenched as their starting quarterback. As a result, White instead elected

Although Danny White never took the Cowboys to the Super Bowl, he led them into the playoffs five times.
Courtesy of Steve Liskey, Retrocards.net

to sign with the World Football League's Memphis Southmen, who made him a better offer. He then spent the next two seasons starting at quarterback for the Southmen, leading them to consecutive playoff appearances, before signing with the Cowboys after the WFL folded prior to the start of the 1976 campaign.

Following his arrival in Dallas, White spent four long years serving as Staubach's backup, sitting on the sidelines as the latter directed the Cowboys to four consecutive division titles, two NFC championships, and one Super Bowl victory. Yet, even though White started just one game during that time, he absorbed a great deal of information from Staubach, who worked with him on fine-tuning his skills behind center. White also served as the Cowboys' punter those four seasons, continuing in that capacity until 1984.

Inheriting the starting quarterback job from Staubach after the latter announced his retirement following the conclusion of the 1979 campaign, the 28-year-old White did an excellent job his first year at the helm, leading a Cowboys offense that established a new franchise record by finishing first in the NFL with 454 points scored. For his part, White passed for 3,287 yards and ranked among the league leaders with 28 touchdown passes, although he also threw 25 interceptions, which represented the third-highest total in the league. Unfortunately, in what became an all-too-familiar scenario, White failed to lead the 12-4 Cowboys into the Super Bowl, guiding them to a 34–13 victory over the Rams in the first round of the playoffs and a Staubach-like 30–27 comeback win over Atlanta in the second round, before playing ineffectively during a 20–7 loss to Philadelphia in the NFC championship game. However, it should be noted that the loss to the Eagles could be attributed to a number of factors, including the exceptional all-around play of the Philadelphia defense, which shut down everything the Cowboys attempted to do on offense, and a subpar performance by the Dallas defense, which surrendered 194 yards on the ground to Wilbert Montgomery.

White put together another very solid year in 1981, leading the Cowboys to another 12-4 record during the regular season by passing for 3,098 yards and 22 touchdowns, throwing only 13 interceptions, and finishing fifth in the league with a passer rating of 87.5, en route to earning Second-Team All-NFC honors. However, the Cowboys once again came up short in the playoffs, advancing to the conference championship game for the second straight time, before suffering a heartbreaking 28–27 defeat at the hands of the San Francisco 49ers. White certainly could not be blamed for the loss, though, since he played extremely well against the 49ers, finishing the contest with 16 completions in 24 attempts, for 173 yards and two touchdowns.

White's strong play his first two seasons stemmed partly from the fact that he learned under the tutelage of Roger Staubach and proved to be a good disciple of Tom Landry's system. He also had a few other things going for him. Although White lacked Staubach's arm strength, he had just as much mobility, allowing him to throw the ball equally well out of the pocket or on the run. He also had good pocket presence, usually kept his wits about him, and possessed superior athletic ability, with Landry once stating, "Danny was the most athletic quarterback I ever coached."

White subsequently had one of his finest all-around seasons in 1982, earning Second-Team All-Pro honors and his lone Pro Bowl selection by leading the Cowboys to a record of 6-3 during the strike-shortened campaign. In addition to ranking among the league leaders with 2,079 yards passing and 16 touchdown passes, White established career-high marks in completion percentage (63.2) and passer rating (91.1). Yet, the Dallas quarterback irked many of his teammates when he publicly sided with the owners during that year's NFL players' strike. And fans of the team grew increasingly disenchanted with him after the Cowboys lost their third consecutive NFC championship game, this time to the Washington Redskins 31–17, although White missed much of the contest after suffering a concussion during the latter stages of the first half.

White remained the starter in Dallas for one more full season, leading the Cowboys to a regular-season record of 12-4 in 1983 by setting career-high marks in passing yardage (3,980) and touchdown passes (29), while also completing 62.7 percent of his passes. However, after the Cowboys lost their first-round playoff matchup with the Los Angeles Rams 24–17, with White throwing three interceptions during the game, Coach Landry elected to replace him at the helm with backup quarterback Gary Hogeboom at the start of the ensuing campaign.

The Cowboys got off to a good start in 1984 with Hogeboom calling the signals for them. But, after the fifth-year quarterback began to falter, White regained his starting job, which he retained exclusively until early in 1986, when he began splitting playing time with Steve Pelluer. After winning just three of his nine starts in 1987, White assumed a backup role the following year, sitting on the sidelines as Pelluer took over control of the team. White's days in Dallas came to an end shortly after Jerry Jones purchased the Cowboys in 1989, when the team's new owner chose not to pick up the option on his contract. White subsequently announced his retirement, ending his NFL career with 1,761 completions in 2,950 attempts, 21,959 yards passing, 155 touchdown passes, 132 interceptions, a 59.7 completion percentage, and a passer rating of 81.7. He also rushed for 482 yards and eight touchdowns, made three receptions, two of which went for touchdowns, and punted a franchise-record 610 times, for a total of 24,509 yards and an average of 40.2 yards per kick.

Following his retirement as an active player, White began a lengthy stint as head coach of the Arena League's Arizona Rattlers, whom he led to two league championships between 1992 and 2004. After leaving the

White passed for more than 3,000 yards and 20 touchdowns four times each.
Courtesy of PristineAuction.com

Rattlers, White spent three years coaching the expansion Utah Blaze, before leaving the coaching ranks at the end of 2008. Three years later, White returned to Dallas, where he has spent the past several seasons serving as the color commentator for Cowboys games on Compass Media Networks' America's Team Radio Network.

Although succeeding Roger Staubach as starting quarterback in Dallas and failing to ever reach a Super Bowl have diminished White's legacy considerably, Tom Landry held his former QB in extremely high esteem, once stating, "I don't think anybody could have followed Roger and done as well as Danny. Danny was a solid winner." Landry went on to say, "The best team I ever coached [1980] had Danny as QB."

COWBOYS CAREER HIGHLIGHTS

Best Season

White played well in leading the Cowboys to a 12-4 record in his first year as the team's starting quarterback, concluding the 1980 campaign with 3,287 yards passing, 28 touchdown passes, a completion percentage of 59.6, and a passer rating of 80.7. However, he performed far more efficiently during the strike-shortened 1982 season, earning his lone Pro Bowl and Second-Team All-Pro selections by ranking fourth in the league with 2,079 yards passing, 16 touchdown passes, a passer rating of 91.1, and a career-high completion percentage of 63.2. Furthermore, White punted the ball extremely well, averaging a career-best 41.7 yards per kick. Nevertheless, White had his most productive season in 1983, when he led the Cowboys to a record of 12-4 by establishing career-high marks in passing yardage (3,980) and touchdown passes (29), while also completing 62.7 percent of his passes, posting a passer rating of 85.6, and scoring five touchdowns, with four of those coming on the ground and the other coming on a pass reception.

Memorable Moments / Greatest Performances

White had his first big game as a starting NFL quarterback on September 21, 1980, when he led the Cowboys to a 28–17 win over the Tampa Bay Buccaneers by completing 24 of 33 passes for 244 yards and three touchdowns. White connected twice with Billy Joe DuPree on 9-yard scoring plays and also tossed a 28-yard TD pass to Butch Johnson.

White followed that up with another strong outing one week later, completing 16 of 20 passes for 217 yards and two touchdowns during a 28–7 victory over the Green Bay Packers.

White threw four touchdown passes for the first time in his career on October 12, 1980, when he led the Cowboys to a 59–14 rout of the San Francisco 49ers by collaborating with Drew Pearson three times and Billy Joe DuPree once through the air. He finished the day with 16 completions in 22 attempts, for 239 yards.

White recorded his first fourth-quarter comeback win as Cowboys quarterback three weeks later, when he gave them a 27–24 victory over the St. Louis Cardinals on November 2 by hitting Tony Hill with a 28-yard TD pass with only 45 seconds left on the clock.

White engineered another comeback against St. Louis two weeks later, when he brought the Cowboys back from a 21–10 second-quarter deficit by completing touchdown passes of 58 yards to Tony Hill and 14 yards to Drew Pearson, before Tony Dorsett put the game out of reach by scoring from 11 yards out in the fourth quarter. White finished the game with 20 completions for 296 yards and three touchdowns.

White tossed four touchdown passes for the second time in his NFL career in the 1980 regular-season finale, en route to leading the Cowboys to a 35–27 victory over the Philadelphia Eagles.

After subsequently leading the Cowboys to a 34–13 win over the Los Angeles Rams in the wild card round of the 1980 postseason tournament, White performed brilliantly under pressure against Atlanta the following week, throwing a pair of touchdown passes to Drew Pearson in the final four minutes of the contest, to give the Cowboys a heart-stopping 30–27 come-from-behind victory over the Atlanta Falcons. Dallas fans later voted the win one of the top 10 Cowboys games of all time.

White again performed heroically on October 25, 1981, when he helped the Cowboys overcome a 27–14 deficit to the Miami Dolphins midway through the fourth quarter by tossing a pair of TD passes in the game's final few minutes. After collaborating with Doug Cosbie on a 5-yard scoring play that closed the gap to 27–21, White hit Ron Springs with a 32-yard touchdown pass in the game's waning moments, to give the Cowboys a 28–27 victory. He finished the contest with 354 yards passing and three TD passes.

White passed for a career-high 377 yards in leading the Cowboys to a 27–24 overtime win over the Tampa Bay Buccaneers on October 9, 1983. Making excellent use of his running backs throughout the contest, White hit Ron Springs with an 80-yard TD pass in the first quarter, before connecting with Timmy Newsome on a 52-yard scoring play in the final period that sent the game into overtime.

White riddled New York's defense two weeks later, throwing for 304 yards and completing five touchdown passes for the only time in his career, in leading the Cowboys to a 38–20 victory over the Giants on October 30, 1983. White's biggest plays of the day proved to be a 61-yard scoring pass to tight end Doug Cosbie and a 58-yard TD strike to Tony Hill.

White followed that up with another strong outing against Philadelphia, completing 21 of 24 passes for 268 yards and two touchdowns during a 27–20 win over the Eagles.

White celebrated Thanksgiving in 1985 by throwing four touchdown passes during a 35–17 victory over the St. Louis Cardinals. In addition to connecting with Tony Hill on scoring plays that covered 16 and 53 yards, White hit Mike Renfro with an 18-yard TD pass and also hooked up with Doug Cosbie from 19 yards out.

Although the Cowboys ended up losing to the Washington Redskins 24–20 on December 13, 1987, White performed extremely well in his final game as the team's starting quarterback, passing for 359 yards and two touchdowns in defeat.

NOTABLE ACHIEVEMENTS

- Passed for more than 3,000 yards four times, topping 3,500 yards once (3,980 in 1983).
- Threw more than 20 touchdown passes four times.
- Completed more than 60 percent of his passes four times.
- Posted quarterback rating above 80.0 six times, finishing with marks higher than 90.0 twice.
- Led NFL quarterbacks with three fourth-quarter comebacks in 1987.
- Finished second in NFL in pass completions once and touchdown passes once.
- Finished third in NFL with 3,980 yards passing in 1983.
- Ranks among Cowboys career leaders in: passing yardage (4th); pass completions (3rd); touchdown passes (3rd); completion percentage (3rd); quarterback rating (3rd); and pass attempts (4th).
- Holds Cowboys career record for most punt attempts (610).
- Threw five touchdown passes vs. New York Giants on October 30, 1983.
- Two-time NFC champion (1977 and 1978).
- Super Bowl XII champion.
- 1985 Week 13 NFC Offensive Player of the Week.
- 1982 Pro Bowl selection.
- 1982 Second-Team All-Pro selection.
- Three-time Second-Team All-NFC selection (1979, 1981, and 1982).

47

BILLY JOE DuPREE

One of the best tight ends of his era, Billy Joe DuPree preceded Doug Cosbie, Jay Novacek, and Jason Witten as the first Cowboys player at the position to earn Pro Bowl and All-Conference honors on multiple occasions. Serving as an integral part of the Cowboys' passing game for most of his 11 seasons in Dallas, DuPree amassed more than 40 receptions once and 500 receiving yards twice, en route to earning a fourth-place ranking on the franchise's all-time pass reception list at the time of his retirement in 1983. Excelling as a blocker as well, DuPree helped open up holes in the running game for more highly publicized players such as Calvin Hill and Tony Dorsett, assisting the Cowboys in winning six division titles, three NFC championships, and one Super Bowl in the process. In addition to earning him three trips to the Pro Bowl, DuPree's outstanding all-around play prompted the members of the media to accord him All-NFC honors on three separate occasions.

Born in Monroe, Louisiana, on March 7, 1950, Billy Joe DuPree attended nearby Richardson High School, where he spent three years starring on the gridiron, helping his school capture the division state championship twice while serving as a co-captain his senior year. Recruited by several major colleges, DuPree ultimately accepted a scholarship offer from Michigan State University, where he went on to establish himself as arguably the greatest tight end in that school's rich history, even though the Spartans' run-oriented offense afforded him few opportunities to display his pass-receiving skills.

After earning All-America honors as a senior at Michigan State in 1972, DuPree entered the 1973 NFL Draft, where the Cowboys selected him during the latter stages of the first round, with the 20th overall pick. Adapting quickly to the pro game, DuPree had a solid rookie season, making 29 receptions for a team-leading 392 yards, while also finishing second on the club with five touchdown receptions. He followed that up with a similarly productive 1974 campaign, finishing third on the team with 29 catches

Billy Joe DuPree served as Roger Staubach's security blanket for much of the 1970s.
Courtesy of Steve Liskey, Retrocards.net

and 466 receiving yards, while also placing second with four TD grabs. After making only nine receptions for 138 yards while splitting time with Jean Fugett at the tight end position in 1975, DuPree rebounded in a big way the following year after claiming the starting job for himself, finishing second on the team to Drew Pearson with a career high 42 receptions and 680 receiving yards, en route to earning Pro Bowl and All-NFC honors for the first of three straight times.

Gaining general recognition throughout the league as one of the finest all-around players at his position, DuPree established himself as one of the circuit's better receivers even though the Cowboys relied primarily on the running game to batter their opponents into submission. Emerging as Roger Staubach's security blanket by the mid-1970s, DuPree often found himself being targeted by the Dallas quarterback in crucial situations and in those instances when the latter felt pressured by the opposing team's pass rush. However, the 6'4", 230-pound DuPree became even more well known for his punishing blocking style, which perhaps made him the NFL's most complete tight end for a period of time. Tom Landry also liked to take advantage of his speed by occasionally getting the ball into his hands on the "end-around" play.

DuPree had another solid year for the Cowboys in 1977, earning Pro Bowl and All-Conference honors for the second consecutive time by making 28 receptions for 347 yards and three touchdowns during the regular season, before catching another six passes for 110 yards and a touchdown during the Cowboys' successful run to the NFL championship. He topped that performance the following season, though, making 34 receptions for 509 yards and a career-high nine touchdowns, en route to earning the last of his three Pro Bowl and All-NFC selections.

DuPree remained with the Cowboys another five seasons, continuing to function as a starter until 1982, when he surrendered that role to Doug Cosbie. Until the very end, though, DuPree remained a pillar of strength, never missing a game his entire career, which covered a total of 181 contests, including the playoffs. DuPree also spent his final few seasons in Dallas serving as one of the team's co-captains. Announcing his retirement following the conclusion of the 1983 campaign, DuPree ended his 11-year career with 267 receptions for 3,565 yards and 41 touchdowns, with his 41 TD receptions as a tight end remaining a Cowboys record until Jason Witten surpassed it 2012. DuPree also carried the ball 26 times for 178 yards and one touchdown.

Following his playing days, DuPree spent nearly a decade working at a construction company he started shortly before he retired. More recently, he has become involved in many charities, including the Shriners and those events that provide assistance to the children of NFL Alumni. DuPree also gives his time to several inner city youth groups and serves as an active member of the Board of Trustees of Meals on Wheels of Collin County.

CAREER HIGHLIGHTS

Best Season

DuPree played his best ball for the Cowboys in 1976 and 1978, earning his only two First-Team All-NFC selections those two years. A quick look at the numbers might seem to suggest that the 1976 campaign proved to be DuPree's finest all-around season since he established career-high marks in receptions (42) and receiving yardage (680). However, he scored only two touchdowns that year. On the other hand, in addition to making 34 receptions for 509 yards in 1978, DuPree hauled in a career-best nine TD passes, which placed him fourth in the league rankings. He also had an exceptional postseason, making another 10 catches for 124 yards and two touchdowns. All things considered, the 1978 campaign ranks as the best of DuPree's career.

Memorable Moments / Greatest Performances

DuPree, who scored five touchdowns as a rookie in 1973, collected three of those in one game, crossing the opponent's goal line for the first three times in his career during a lopsided 45–10 victory over the St. Louis Cardinals on September 30, 1973. After scoring the game's first points by hauling in an 8-yard strike from Roger Staubach in the first quarter, DuPree again collaborated with Staubach on a 2-yard scoring play in the third quarter. He then closed out the scoring during the latter stages of the fourth quarter with a 1-yard TD grab on a pass thrown by Craig Morton. DuPree finished the game with a season-best six receptions and 74 receiving yards.

Although the Cowboys lost their November 17, 1974, matchup with the Washington Redskins 28–21, DuPree had a huge afternoon, making six receptions for 92 yards and two touchdowns, with his two TDs nearly enabling the Cowboys to overcome a 28–0 halftime deficit to their bitter rivals.

Less than two weeks later, DuPree made a key play during the Cowboys' memorable 24–23 comeback win over Washington on Thanksgiving

Day, when he hooked up with backup quarterback Clint Longley on a 35-yard touchdown pass midway through the third quarter that closed the gap to 16–10.

DuPree had another big game the following week, helping the Cowboys record a resounding 41–17 victory over Cleveland by making three receptions for 74 yards and one touchdown, with his 42-yard TD grab in the third quarter representing the longest reception of his career.

DuPree turned in perhaps the most memorable performance of his career on September 28, 1975, when he made six receptions for 100 yards and one touchdown against St. Louis, with his 3-yard TD grab in overtime giving the Cowboys a 37–31 win over the Cardinals.

DuPree turned in a pair of outstanding efforts during the early stages of the 1976 campaign, with the first of those coming on September 19, when he made five receptions for 108 yards during a 24–6 win over the New Orleans Saints. DuPree followed that up one week later with a five-catch, 85-yard, one-touchdown performance against Baltimore that helped lead the Cowboys to a 30–27 victory over the Colts. DuPree's 38-yard TD grab midway through the fourth quarter, which momentarily put the Cowboys up 27–24, represented one of the longest pass receptions of his career.

DuPree also came up big for the Cowboys in Super Bowl XII, making four receptions for 66 yards during their 27–10 victory over the Denver Broncos.

NOTABLE ACHIEVEMENTS

- Made more than 40 receptions once (42 in 1976).
- Amassed 680 receiving yards in 1976.
- Averaged more than 15 yards per reception four times.
- Finished fourth in NFL with nine touchdown receptions in 1978.
- Ranks eighth in Cowboys history with 41 touchdown receptions.
- Never missed a game entire career, appearing in 159 consecutive games.
- Three-time NFC champion (1975, 1977, and 1978).
- Super Bowl XII champion.
- Three-time Pro Bowl selection (1976, 1977, and 1978).
- Two-time First-Team All-NFC selection (1976 and 1978).
- 1977 Second-Team All-NFC selection.

48

BILL BATES

One of the most beloved players in Cowboys history, Bill Bates overcame the odds to carve out a successful 15-year NFL career for himself in Dallas that ties him with Ed "Too Tall" Jones and Mark Tuinei for the most seasons played as a member of the team. Contributing in numerous ways to Cowboy squads that won six division titles and three Super Bowls, Bates first established himself as a demon on special teams, before eventually earning a starting job in the secondary. Whatever role Bates assumed, though, he gave everything he had to the Cowboys, earning the respect and admiration of teammates and opponents alike with his hard work, dedication, and sense of self-sacrifice, which helped compensate for his somewhat limited athletic ability. Those same qualities endeared Bates to Cowboy fans, who came to appreciate him just as much as some of his more highly publicized teammates, many of whom frequently made headlines for their illicit actions off the playing field. In the end, Bates created a place for himself in Cowboys lore by ranking among the franchise's all-time leaders in tackles, games played, and seasons played, while also becoming the first player in NFL history to earn Pro Bowl honors primarily on the strength of his performance on special teams.

Born in Knoxville, Tennessee, on June 6, 1961, William Frederick Bates grew up a fan of the Dallas Cowboys in nearby Farragut, where he attended Farragut High School. Earning All-State honors in both football and basketball as a senior, Bates established himself as one of the state's top recruits on the gridiron by excelling on defense and special teams, recording 14 interceptions, nearly 200 tackles, and more than 1,000 return yards during his high school career. Subsequently courted by several major colleges, including Auburn, Ole Miss, Kentucky, UCLA, and Tennessee, Bates ultimately chose to remain in his home state, spending the next four years starring at safety for the Volunteers. After earning Freshman All-America honors his first year at Tennessee, Bates received All-SEC recognition as a junior and senior. Yet, in spite of his outstanding play, Bates derived little

Bill Bates played as many seasons for the Cowboys as anyone else in franchise history.
Courtesy of Dallas Cowboys

pleasure from spending his final two seasons playing under demanding head coach Johnny Majors, stating years later, "I hated it because of Johnny. Now that it's behind me, I know a lot of the things he did as a coach helped me, but I wish he would've done it in a little different way. He made me tougher. Maybe I wasn't tough enough. Maybe that's how I became tough enough to withstand almost anything."

Bypassed by all 28 teams in the 1983 NFL Draft after posting a disappointing time of 4.8 seconds in the 40-yard dash at the NFL Scouting Combine, Bates turned down an offer to play for the USFL's New Jersey Generals, who selected him in that league's draft, when his favorite team, the Cowboys, extended him an invitation to sign with them as an undrafted free agent. Despite being considered a long shot to make the team when he arrived at his first training camp, Bates ended up earning a spot on the roster as a special teams player by simply outworking his competition. Making an extremely favorable impression on everyone with his heart and hustle, Bates later drew praise from Gil Brandt, who stated, "If you didn't have scrimmages, he wouldn't have made the team because people would look at him and say he wasn't fast enough. But he worked hard and he stuck."

Serving the Cowboys primarily on special teams as a rookie, Bates contributed significantly to a Dallas team that advanced to the playoffs as a wild card by earning NFC Special Teams Player of the Year honors. At the same time, Bates did a solid job whenever he appeared as a nickel back on defense, recording four sacks, an interception, and 84 tackles over the course of the campaign. Bates followed that up with an outstanding performance in 1984, earning a trip to the Pro Bowl and First-Team All-NFC recognition by excelling on all coverage units, while also making five sacks, one interception, and 52 tackles on defense. By being named to the Pro Bowl primarily on the strength of his play on special teams, Bates became the first player to be so honored.

Displaying a tremendous amount of will and determination, Bates quickly emerged as a favorite of Cowboys head coach Tom Landry, who admired his work ethic and dedication to his profession. Although the 6'1", 204-pound Bates possessed neither outstanding size nor speed, he warded off challenges from several more talented players through the years simply by outworking them, constantly striving to improve himself in any way possible. In expressing his admiration for Bates, Landry stated on one occasion, "If we had 11 players on the field who played as hard as Bill Bates does and did their homework like he does, we'd be almost impossible to beat." Landry went on to describe Bates and Cliff Harris as "the hardest hitters I ever saw," with John Madden also praising Bates for his hitting ability by suggesting, "Every game starts with a kick. With Bill Bates on the field, every game begins with a bang!"

Meanwhile, longtime Dallas special teams coach, Joe Avezzano, commented, "You tried to replace him a lot of times with a bigger, stronger, faster player, and you just couldn't do it. At some point, you just have to acknowledge that the combination of physical and mental attributes made Bill Bates a good player."

After assuming the additional special-teams duties of holding on extra points and returning punts in 1985, Bates laid claim to the starting strong safety job in 1986. Continuing to function in that capacity the next three seasons, Bates recorded four interceptions, six sacks, and 292 tackles on defense from 1986 to 1988, making a career-high 124 stops in the last of those campaigns. Subsequently used only in the nickel defense package the Cowboys employed after Jimmy Johnson assumed control of the team in 1989, Bates spent the next several years playing middle linebacker in that particular alignment, while also leading the club in special-teams tackles three times between 1989 and 1993.

A four-time winner of the Bob Lilly Award, which annually goes to the Cowboys player who displays leadership and character on and off the field in the eyes of the fans, Bates received the additional honor of being presented with the Ed Block Courage Award by his teammates in 1993 after overcoming a knee injury that sidelined him for all but five games the previous season. Bates continued to play almost exclusively on special teams until 1997, when he announced his retirement after 15 seasons in Dallas. He ended his career with 667 tackles on defense, nearly 200 tackles on special teams, 14 interceptions, 18 sacks, and seven fumble recoveries.

Following the conclusion of his playing career, Bates remained in Dallas the next few seasons, serving the Cowboys as an assistant special teams and defensive backs coach until he elected to move on to Jacksonville, where he spent one year coaching the Jaguars' special teams. Bates has spent the last several years serving as an assistant coach at the high school level, while also running a cattle ranch in North Dallas and doing motivational speaking.

Looking back at the attitude he carried with him during his time in Dallas, Bates reveals, "It was a battle for me every day because nobody expected me to be on the team. And I just said, 'Hey, while I'm here with the Cowboys, I don't know how long it's going to be, another game, another day, whatever. I'm going to get out and see if this is as good as I can be.' I looked at every day like it might be my last."

Bates added, "So I got my head down and I'm grinding and, all of a sudden, Coach [Jimmy] Johnson comes in and we're in Super Bowls, and,

A demon on special teams, Bates led the Cowboys in special teams tackles four times.
Courtesy of MainlineAutographs.com

all of a sudden, I look up 15 years later. . . . I made it more than just one day, for sure. . . . My journey in the NFL was the culmination of hard work, not listening to the doubters, and overcoming the odds. It's all of the things people like to talk about, but don't like to write because it's not controversial."

CAREER HIGHLIGHTS

Best Season

Bates had an excellent year for the Cowboys in 1985, when, in addition to doing a superb job of covering kickoffs and punts, he made a career-high four interceptions and averaged nearly 7 yards on 22 punt returns. He also performed extremely well in 1988, when, serving as the Cowboys' starting strong safety, he made a career-high 124 tackles. Nevertheless, Bates made his greatest overall impact in 1984, becoming the first special teams player in NFL history to earn a trip to the Pro Bowl. Also doing an outstanding job in the Cowboys' nickel defense package, Bates earned First-Team All-NFC honors by recording one interception, five sacks, and 52 tackles on defense.

Memorable Moments / Greatest Performances

Bates turned in the most memorable performance of his rookie campaign on September 11, 1983, recording his first career sack and first career interception during a 34–17 victory over the St. Louis Cardinals.

Bates contributed to a 20–17 victory over the New England Patriots on November 22, 1984, by collecting two of the 10 sacks the Dallas defense recorded against Patriots quarterback Tony Eason.

Bates earned NFC Defensive Player of the Week honors in Week 2 of the 1987 season by intercepting a pair of Phil Simms passes during a 16–14 win over the New York Giants.

Bates also received recognition as the NFC Special Teams Player of the Week in Week 7 of the 1994 campaign, being accorded that honor after doing a superb job of covering punts and kickoffs during a 24–13 victory over the Philadelphia Eagles.

Bates, though, made arguably the most significant play of his career during the 1991 playoffs, when he sealed the Cowboys' 17–13 win over the Chicago Bears in the opening round of the postseason tournament by picking off a Jim Harbaugh pass during the latter stages of the contest.

NOTABLE ACHIEVEMENTS

- Recorded five sacks in 1984.
- Recorded 124 tackles in 1988.

- Led Cowboys in special teams tackles four times.
- Tied for first in Cowboys history with 15 seasons played.
- Ranks among Cowboys career leaders in tackles (8th) and games played (3rd).
- Three-time NFC champion (1992, 1993, and 1995).
- Three-time Super Bowl champion (XXVII, XXVIII, and XXX).
- 1987 Week 2 NFC Defensive Player of the Week.
- 1994 Week 7 NFC Special Teams Player of the Week.
- 1983 NFC Special Teams Player of the Year.
- 1993 Ed Block Courage Award winner.
- 1984 Pro Bowl selection.
- 1984 First-Team All-NFC selection.
- Named to Cowboys' 50th Anniversary Team in 2009 as Special Teams player.

49

FRANK CLARKE

One of 36 veteran players the Cowboys selected in the 1960 expansion draft, Frank Clarke went on to become the first true deep threat in franchise history, preceding Bob Hayes in that role. The first Cowboys receiver to amass more than 1,000 yards in a season, Clarke accomplished the feat in 1962, when he led the NFL in touchdown catches and average yards per reception. Averaging more than 20 yards per catch in consecutive seasons, Clarke led the Cowboys in receiving yardage and touchdowns four straight times, while also finishing first on the team in catches twice. Some 50 years after he played his last game for the Cowboys, Clarke continues to rank among the franchise's all-time leaders in receiving yardage, touchdown receptions, and average yards per reception. Meanwhile, Clarke's 14 TD receptions in 1962 remained a club record for 45 years, until Terrell Owens set a new mark in 2007. Although Clarke spent most of his peak seasons in Dallas playing for losing teams, he managed to establish himself as the organization's first African-American star, earning All-Pro honors once and recognition throughout the NFL as one of the league's most feared wideouts. And, after the Cowboys emerged as a championship contender, Clarke remained a clutch third-down receiver, before announcing his retirement following the conclusion of the 1967 campaign.

Born in Beloit, Wisconsin, on February 7, 1934, Frank Delano Clarke, whose parents named him after Franklin D. Roosevelt, attended Beloit Memorial High School, where he earned All-State honors in football. After continuing his success on the gridiron for two years at Trinidad State Junior College, Clarke transferred to the University of Colorado, where he joined John Wooten in becoming the first African-American varsity football player in that school's history.

Selected by the Cleveland Browns in the fifth round of the 1956 NFL Draft after earning All–Big 7 Conference honorable mention honors as a junior at Colorado, Clarke saw very little playing time over the course of the next three seasons, totaling only 10 receptions for 212 yards from 1957 to

The Cowboys' first true deep threat, Frank Clarke became the first player in franchise history to top 1,000 receiving yards in a season in 1962, when he amassed 1,043 yards through the air.
Courtesy of Steve Liskey, Retrocards.net

1959. Subsequently left unprotected by Cleveland in the 1960 NFL Expansion Draft, Clarke joined the Cowboys prior to the start of their inaugural season after they made him one of the 36 veterans they plucked off the rosters of other teams. Recalling his feelings upon learning of his selection by the Cowboys, Clarke stated, "I wasn't happy to leave Cleveland. I felt I had left a great deal unfinished. But, the more I thought, I realized that Dallas was the ideal situation where I would have more of a chance. After all, at

Cleveland they had some pretty good catchers when I was there in Preston Carpenter, Pete Brewster, and Ray Renfro."

The 6'1", 215-pound Clarke, who began his pro career as a tight end, continued to spend most of his time on the sidelines his first year in Dallas, catching just nine passes, although he scored three touchdowns and averaged 32.2 yards per reception. Previously criticized by his coaches at Colorado and Cleveland for his deficiencies as a blocker, Clarke failed to make much of an impression on the Dallas coaching staff in that area either. However, taking note of the 27-year-old Clarke's speed, soft hands, and precise route-running ability, Tom Landry decided to move him to wide receiver prior to the start of the 1961 campaign.

The change in positions ended up doing wonders for Clarke, who made 41 receptions for 919 yards and nine touchdowns his first year at wideout, while leading the NFL with an average of 22.4 yards per reception. During the latter stages of the campaign, Clarke also began a streak of seven consecutive games in which he caught at least one touchdown pass, thereby establishing a franchise record he now shares with Bob Hayes, Terrell Owens, and Dez Bryant. Carrying over his success to the 1962 season, Clarke made 47 receptions for 1,043 yards, becoming in the process the first Cowboys player to accumulate more than 1,000 yards in a season. Clarke also led the league with 14 touchdown catches and an average of 22.2 yards per reception.

In discussing the renaissance he experienced over the course of those two seasons, Clarke, who earlier received criticism for the inconsistency he displayed when trying to make shorter receptions, said in 1962, "I used to think the six-pointer was the only thing that mattered. It took me a long time to realize I was wrong. Catching the short ones ought to be easier than the long ones. It was only a question of getting more confidence in myself. I knew I had to learn to fight for the ball under pressure. . . . Eddie [LeBaron] worked with me and taught me tricks. So did Tom Landry, our coach. Now I go in there thinking I can catch them all."

After making 43 receptions for 833 yards and 10 touchdowns in 1963, Clarke earned First-Team All-Pro honors for the only time in his career the following year by catching 65 passes for 973 yards and five touchdowns. Although Clarke's offensive production fell off somewhat in 1965 after the Cowboys moved him back to his original position of tight end, he posted solid numbers, concluding the campaign with 41 receptions for 682 yards and four touchdowns. More importantly, Clarke spent a significant amount of time working with rookie wideout Bob Hayes, who later credited the veteran receiver with helping him to develop his pass-catching skills and turning him into the league's premier deep threat.

Clarke spent two more years in Dallas, during which time he made a total of 35 receptions, amassed 474 receiving yards, and scored six touchdowns while serving the Cowboys in a part-time role, before announcing his retirement after the team lost its second straight NFL championship game to the Packers in 1967. During his time in Dallas, Clarke made 281 receptions for 5,214 yards, scored 51 touchdowns, and averaged 18.6 yards per reception.

Following his playing days, Clarke became the first African-American sports anchor at a Dallas television station, anchoring sports reports for WFAA-TV on weekends when not working NFL games for CBS. He also worked at a bank and a youth council during the week. When asked years later how successful he thought he might be in today's game, Clarke responded, "I know for a fact that I would just love it. I would be something else to watch. I would have the savvy to get to the holes, and I think about how I would be quite outstanding. And, for the first time in my life, I would really enjoy me. I would love the contact with the fans."

COWBOYS CAREER HIGHLIGHTS

Best Season

Clarke earned his lone All-Pro selection in 1964, when he finished third in the NFL with 65 receptions and 973 receiving yards. He also performed extremely well in 1961, catching 41 passes for 919 yards, making nine TD receptions, and leading the league with an average of 22.4 yards per reception. Nevertheless, Clarke made his greatest overall impact the following year, concluding the 1962 campaign with 47 receptions, 1,043 receiving yards, and a league-leading 14 touchdown catches and average of 22.2 yards-per-reception. Clarke's 14 TD receptions remained a franchise record until 2007, when Terrell Owens caught 15 TD passes.

Memorable Moments / Greatest Performances

Clarke had his breakout game for the Cowboys in the 1961 regular-season opener, making six receptions for 98 yards and one touchdown during a 27–24 win over the Pittsburgh Steelers. Clarke recorded the game's first points when he hooked up with quarterback Eddie LeBaron on a 44-yard scoring play in the first quarter.

Although Clarke made only three receptions during a 28–0 victory over Minnesota three weeks later, two of those went for touchdowns. After hauling in a 23-yard TD pass from LeBaron in the third quarter, Clarke scored the game's final points in the ensuing period when he hooked up with Don Meredith on a 52-yard touchdown reception. He finished the day with 91 total receiving yards.

Even though the Cowboys suffered a 34–24 defeat at the hands of the Washington Redskins in the final game of the 1961 regular season, Clarke had a huge day, making four receptions for 159 yards and two touchdowns, which included connections of 80 and 66 yards with quarterback Eddie LeBaron.

Clarke once again torched Washington's secondary in the 1962 regular-season opener, catching 10 passes for 241 yards and three touchdowns during a 35–35 tie with the Redskins. Scoring on plays that covered 58, 11, and 55 yards, Clarke recorded the best opening day performance of any receiver during the modern era of pro football, with his 241 receiving yards representing the third-highest single-game total in franchise history.

Clarke continued his exceptional play in the weeks that followed, making at least one TD reception in each of the next five games as well. Particularly effective in Weeks 3, 5, and 6, Clarke made four receptions for 130 yards and one touchdown during the Cowboys' 27–17 victory over the Rams on September 30, 1962, scoring his TD from 66 yards out. Clarke again proved to be a huge factor during Dallas's 41–19 win over the Eagles on October 14, catching four passes for 118 yards and two touchdowns, with his scoring plays covering 8 and 57 yards. Clarke had another big day against the Steelers the following week, helping the Cowboys record a 42–27 victory over Pittsburgh by making five catches for 86 yards, including TD receptions of 45, 3, and 13 yards.

Clarke closed out the 1962 campaign by making five receptions for 114 yards and one touchdown during the Cowboys' 41–31 loss to the Giants in the regular-season finale, becoming in the process the first player in franchise history to accumulate more than 1,000 yards from scrimmage. (He finished the year with a total of 1,043 yards.)

Although the Cowboys once again lost to the Giants on October 20, 1963, this time by a score of 37–21, Clarke had another huge game, making four receptions for 168 yards and one touchdown, with his TD catch covering 75 yards.

Clarke again starred in defeat on November 10, 1963, making eight receptions for 190 yards and two touchdowns during a 31–24 loss to the San Francisco 49ers.

Clarke turned in his finest performance as a tight end on October 2, 1966, when he made seven receptions for 125 yards and one touchdown during a lopsided 47–14 victory over the Atlanta Falcons.

Clarke reached the 100-yard plateau for the last time in his career in the 1966 NFL championship game, making three receptions for 102 yards, and hooking up with Don Meredith on a 68-yard scoring play, during the Cowboys' 34–27 loss to the Packers.

Clarke recorded the only rushing touchdown of his career on November 12, 1967, when he scored on an end-around from 56 yards out during a 27–10 win over the New Orleans Saints.

Clarke also served as one of the central figures in an infamous play that took place during a 30–28 loss to the Pittsburgh Steelers on September 23, 1962, when, for the first time in an NFL game, points were awarded for a penalty. After hooking up with Eddie LeBaron on an apparent 99-yard TD catch-and-run, Clarke saw the points he scored taken off the board and replaced by two points for Pittsburgh, when officials penalized Dallas for holding in the end zone.

NOTABLE ACHIEVEMENTS

- Caught more than 40 passes five straight times, surpassing 60 receptions once (65 in 1964).
- Topped 1,000 receiving yards once (1,043 in 1962).
- Averaged more than 20 yards per reception twice.
- Scored at least 10 touchdowns twice.
- Accumulated more than 1,000 yards from scrimmage twice.
- Led NFL in touchdown receptions once and yards per reception twice.
- Finished fourth in NFL with 14 touchdowns in 1962.
- Finished third in NFL with 65 receptions and 973 receiving yards in 1964.
- Ranks among Cowboys career leaders in: pass reception yardage (7th); touchdown receptions (6th); touchdowns scored (tied-8th); and yards per reception (3rd).
- 1964 First-Team All-Pro selection.

50

TYRON SMITH

Tyron Smith has established himself as one of the NFL's most dominant offensive linemen since he arrived in Dallas. An exceptional run-blocker, Smith has spent the past few years anchoring a Dallas offensive line that has enabled Cowboy running backs to compile the second most yardage in the league in two of the last three seasons. Excelling in pass protection as well, Smith has done an outstanding job of protecting the blind side of quarterbacks Tony Romo and Dak Prescott from his left tackle position. Smith's superb play has proven to be a key factor in the Cowboys' return to prominence in the NFC East, earning him four trips to the Pro Bowl and four All-Pro selections.

Born in Inglewood, California, on December 12, 1990, Tyron Smith grew up with his mother and two sisters in Moreno Valley, California, after his father died approximately one year following his birth. A star lineman at local Rancho Verde High School, Smith excelled on both sides of the ball, earning All-America honors from Scout.com, EA Sports, and magazines such as *Parade*, *SuperPrep*, and *PrepStar*. An outstanding all-around athlete, Smith also participated in track and field at Rancho Verde, recording top throws of 14.23 meters (46 feet, 7 inches) in the shotput and 46.62 meters (152 feet, 10 inches) in the discus.

Heavily recruited by several major colleges, Smith ultimately accepted a scholarship offer from USC, where he spent his freshman year serving as a backup to starting left offensive tackle Charles Brown, before claiming the starting right offensive tackle job the following year. After being accorded All–Pac-10 and CollegeFootballNews.com Sophomore All-American honorable mention recognition his first year as a starter, Smith earned First-Team All–Pac-10 honors and won the Morris Trophy Award as the conference's top offensive lineman as a junior.

Electing to forgo his final year of college eligibility, Smith entered the 2011 NFL Draft, where the Cowboys selected him with the ninth overall pick, making him the first offensive lineman drafted in the first round by

Tyron Smith (#77) has served as the anchor of arguably the NFL's best offensive line the past few seasons, earning four Pro Bowl selections and four All-Pro nominations in the process.
Courtesy of Bruce Adler

the team since Jerry Jones assumed ownership in 1989. He also became the second-highest offensive lineman ever drafted by the Cowboys, with only John Niland, whom the team selected fifth overall in 1966, having been chosen earlier.

Immediately named the starting right tackle upon his arrival in Dallas, the 20-year-old Smith had a solid rookie season, helping to stabilize an offensive line in transition following the preseason releases of veterans Marc Columbo, Leonard Davis, Andre Gurode, and Montrae Holland. Starting every game for the Cowboys, Smith earned a spot on the NFL All-Rookie Team and First-Team All-NFL recognition from *Pro Football Focus*. He followed that up with another strong performance in 2012 after being moved to left tackle prior to the start of the campaign. It was in 2013, though, that Smith emerged as arguably the best left tackle in the league, earning Second-Team All-Pro honors and the first of his four consecutive trips to the Pro Bowl by committing just one holding penalty and allowing only one sack in his 16 starts. Smith's exceptional play so impressed former Cowboys vice president of player personnel, Gil Brandt, that the current NFL media analyst called the 23-year-old tackle a "franchise-builder," writing:

> After finding a quarterback and a pass rusher, solidifying the left tackle spot is the next most important piece of the franchise-building puzzle, and Smith is a force who's rising fast. Arm length and hand size are two key traits to consider when it comes to offensive tackles, and in those areas, Smith (36⅜-inch-long arms, 11-inch hands) is blessed. Breaking into the league as a right tackle three seasons ago, Smith shifted to the left side in 2012, going on to make the Pro Bowl this season. He's improved his footwork significantly and has a much better understanding of football, thanks to the guidance of line coach Bill Callahan. Smith is still just 23 years old, which is almost unheard of for a guy entering his fourth season in the NFL—and he can already block any defensive end in the league. Of course, when you have his size (6-foot-5, 310 pounds), you don't lose many battles.

In addition to his size, long arms, and large hands, Smith possesses excellent quickness and outstanding athleticism, posting a time of 4.95 seconds in the 40-yard dash at the 2011 NFL Scouting Combine. He also has good balance and is very strong, two qualities that give him the ability to anchor a bull rusher and recover if he gets out of position. An extremely hard worker with a mean streak, Smith has everything an offensive lineman needs to dominate the opposition, with Ross Tucker, former NFL lineman-turned-analyst, writing, "If you went into a computer lab and tried to create the perfect prototype tackle, it would be him. Smith does things to guys—toys with them, humbles them—that you honestly shouldn't be able to do to people in the NFL."

After signing an eight-year, $109 million contract extension with the Cowboys prior to the start of the 2014 season, Smith proved his worth by starting all 16 games for the NFL's second-ranked rushing offense and helping DeMarco Murray lead the league with 1,845 yards gained on the ground, earning in the process First-Team All-Pro honors. He followed that up with two more outstanding seasons, earning All-Pro honors in both 2015 and 2016, despite being plagued by several nagging injuries this past season. Still only 26 years old as of this writing, Smith figures to add significantly to his list of accomplishments over the course of the next several seasons, practically guaranteeing him a more prominent place in these rankings before his time in Dallas comes to an end.

CAREER HIGHLIGHTS

Best Season

Smith performed brilliantly for the Cowboys in 2013, earning Second-Team All-Pro honors and his first trip to the Pro Bowl by allowing just one sack and committing only one holding penalty all season long. Nevertheless, the 2014 campaign would have to be considered his finest to date. Helping the Cowboys finish second in the NFL in rushing, Smith provided much of the blocking up front for DeMarco Murray to gain a franchise-record 1,845 yards on the ground, earning in the process First-Team All-Pro honors.

Memorable Moments / Greatest Performances

Although the Cowboys ended up losing their October 2, 2011, meeting with the Detroit Lions 34–30, Smith did an outstanding job in just his fourth career start, helping Dallas accumulate a total of 434 yards on offense by holding Cliff Avril to no sacks and just two tackles.

Smith turned in another exceptional performance for the Cowboys three weeks later, opening up holes for DeMarco Murray to rush for a franchise-record 253 yards during a 34–7 win over the St. Louis Rams on October 23, 2011.

However, Smith turned in his finest effort on October 12, 2014, when he helped the Cowboys rush for 250 yards and two touchdowns during a stunning 30–23 upset win over the defending Super Bowl champion Seattle Seahawks. Once again dominating Cliff Avril, Smith held the athletic defensive end to no sacks and just one tackle, with his superb play earning him NFC Offensive Player of the Week honors, thereby making him the first offensive lineman in 10 years to gain that distinction.

NOTABLE ACHIEVEMENTS

- Two-time division champion (2014 and 2016).
- 2014 Week 6 NFC Offensive Player of the Week.
- Four-time Pro Bowl selection (2013, 2014, 2015, and 2016).
- Two-time First-Team All-Pro selection (2014 and 2016).
- Two-time Second-Team All-Pro selection (2013 and 2015).

SUMMARY

aving identified the 50 greatest players in Dallas Cowboys history, the time has come to select the best of the best. Based on the rankings contained in this book, the members of the Cowboys' all-time offensive and defensive teams are listed below. Our squads include the top player at each position, with the offense featuring the two best wide receivers, running backs, tackles, and guards. Meanwhile, the defense features two ends, two tackles, two outside linebackers, one middle linebacker, two cornerbacks, and a pair of safeties. Special teams have been accounted for as well, with a placekicker, punter, kickoff returner, punt returner, and special teams performer also being included. The placekicker was taken from the list of honorable mentions that will soon follow.

OFFENSE		DEFENSE	
Roger Staubach	QB	Ed "Too Tall" Jones	LE
Emmitt Smith	RB	Randy White	LT
Tony Dorsett	RB	Bob Lilly	RT
Jason Witten	TE	Harvey Martin	RE
Michael Irvin	WR	Chuck Howley	LOLB
Drew Pearson	WR	Lee Roy Jordan	MLB
Ralph Neely	LT	DeMarcus Ware	ROLB
John Niland	LG	Everson Walls	LCB
Mark Stepnoski	C	Darren Woodson	SS
Larry Allen	RG	Cliff Harris	FS
Rayfield Wright	RT	Mel Renfro	RCB
Dan Bailey	PK	Danny White	P
Herschel Walker	KR	Bob Hayes	PR
Bill Bates	ST		

HONORABLE MENTIONS

(THE NEXT 50)

Although I limited my earlier rankings to the top 50 players in Cowboys history, many other fine players have worn a Dallas uniform over the years, some of whom narrowly missed making the final cut. Following is a list of those players deserving of an honorable mention. These are the men I deemed worthy of being slotted into positions 51 to 100 in the overall rankings. Where applicable and available, the statistics they compiled during their time in Dallas are included, along with their most notable achievements while playing for the Cowboys.

51: BOB BREUNIG (LB; 1975–1984)

Steve Liskey, Retrocards.net

NOTABLE ACHIEVEMENTS

- Recorded nine career interceptions.
- Recorded more than 100 tackles six times, setting new franchise record (since broken) by making 167 stops in 1981.
- Led Cowboys in tackles six times.
- Ended career as second-leading tackler in franchise history.
- Recorded 18 tackles in one game vs. Philadelphia on 12/8/79.
- Five-time division champion (1976, 1977, 1978, 1979, and 1981).
- Two-time NFC champion (1975 and 1977).
- Super Bowl XII champion.
- Three-time Pro Bowl selection (1979, 1980, and 1982).
- 1980 Second-Team All-Pro selection.
- Four-time First-Team All-NFC selection (1979, 1980, 1982, and 1983).
- Named to 1999 *Sporting News* All-Time Dallas Cowboys Team.

52: FLOZELL ADAMS (OT; 1998–2009)

Big Cowboy Kev/Wikipedia

NOTABLE ACHIEVEMENTS

- Three-time division champion (1998, 2007, and 2009).
- Five-time Pro Bowl selection (2003, 2004, 2006, 2007, and 2008).
- 2007 Second-Team All-Pro selection.

53: DARYL JOHNSTON (FB; 1989–1999)

George A. Kitrinos

Cowboy Numbers: 753 Yards Rushing, 294 Receptions, 2,227 Receiving Yards, 22 Touchdowns, 3.2 Rushing Average.

NOTABLE ACHIEVEMENTS

- Made 50 receptions in 1993.
- Six-time division champion (1992–1996 and 1998).
- Three-time NFC champion (1992, 1993, and 1995).
- Three-time Super Bowl champion (XXVII, XXVIII, and XXX).
- Two-time Pro Bowl selection (1993 and 1994).

54: HERBERT SCOTT (OG; 1975–1984)

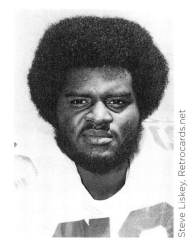

Steve Liskey, Retrocards.net

NOTABLE ACHIEVEMENTS

- Five-time division champion (1976–1979 and 1981).
- Two-time NFC champion (1975 and 1977).
- Super Bowl XII champion.
- Three-time Pro Bowl selection (1979, 1980, and 1981).
- Two-time First-Team All-Pro selection (1980 and 1981).
- Four-time First-Team All-NFC selection (1978–1981).
- 1983 Second-Team All-NFC selection.

55: MICHAEL DOWNS (DB; 1981–1988)

Dallas Cowboys

Cowboy Numbers: 34 Interceptions, 433 Int. Return Yards, 8 Sacks, 3 Touchdowns.

NOTABLE ACHIEVEMENTS

- Scored three defensive touchdowns.
- Recorded seven interceptions twice.
- Surpassed 100 interception-return yards once (126 in 1984).
- Recorded more than 100 tackles four straight times (1983–1986).
- Recorded 3½ sacks in 1984.
- Led Cowboys in interceptions twice and tackles three times.
- Ranks among Cowboys career leaders in interceptions (tied-5th) and interception-return yards (6th).
- Two-time division champion (1981 and 1985).
- Member of 1981 NFL All-Rookie Team.
- 1984 Second-Team All-Pro selection.
- Two-time First-Team All-NFC selection (1984 and 1985).

56: WALT GARRISON (FB; 1966–1974)

Steve Liskey, Retrocards.net

Cowboy Numbers: 3,886 Yards Rushing, 182 Receptions, 1,794 Receiving Yards, 39 Touchdowns, 4.3 Rushing Average.

NOTABLE ACHIEVEMENTS

- Rushed for more than 750 yards twice.
- Surpassed 1,000 yards from scrimmage once (1,174 in 1972).
- Made 40 receptions in 1971.
- Scored 10 touchdowns in 1972.
- Finished third in NFL with rushing average of 4.6 yards per carry in 1969.
- Ranks among Cowboys career leaders in: rushing yardage (8th); rushing touchdowns (7th); rushing average (8th); and rushing attempts (8th).
- Seven-time division champion (1966–1971 and 1973).
- Two-time NFC champion (1970 and 1971).
- Super Bowl VI champion.
- 1972 Pro Bowl selection.
- Named to Cowboys' 25th Anniversary Team in 1984.

57: DENNIS THURMAN (DB; 1978–1985)

Steve Liskey, Retrocards.net

Cowboy Numbers: 36 Interceptions, 562 Int. Return Yards, 5 Touchdowns.

NOTABLE ACHIEVEMENTS

- Scored five defensive touchdowns.
- Finished third in NFL with nine interceptions in 1981.
- Surpassed 100 interception-return yards twice.
- Led Cowboys in interceptions twice.
- Holds Cowboys career record for most interception-return touchdowns (four).
- Holds Cowboys career record for most defensive touchdowns (five).
- Ranks among Cowboys career leaders in interceptions (4th) and interception-return yards (3rd).
- Four-time division champion (1978, 1979, 1981, and 1985).
- 1978 NFC champion.
- 1981 Second-Team All-NFC selection.

58: DAN BAILEY (PK; 2011–PRESENT)

Keith Allison

Cowboy Numbers: 171 Field Goals Made, 191 Field Goal Attempts, 89.5 Field Goal Percentage, 763 Points Scored.

NOTABLE ACHIEVEMENTS

- Has kicked more than 30 field goals in a season twice.
- Has posted field goal percentage in excess of 90 three times.
- Has never missed an extra point attempt.
- Has led NFL in field goal percentage once and extra points made once.
- Has finished second in NFL in field goal percentage once.
- Has finished third in NFL in field goals made once.
- Holds NFL record for greatest extra point accuracy (100 percent).
- Ranks second in NFL history in career field goal percentage accuracy (89.529).
- Holds Cowboys record for most consecutive field goals made (30).
- Holds Cowboys career record for most field goals made (171).
- Ranks second in Cowboys history in field goal attempts (191).
- Ranks third in Cowboys history in points scored (763).
- Kicked six field goals in one game vs. Washington on 9/26/11.
- Three-time NFC Special Teams Player of the Week.
- Member of 2011 NFL All-Rookie Team.
- 2015 Pro Bowl selection.
- 2015 Second-Team All-Pro selection.

59: MARK TUINEI (OT; 1983–1997)

Dallas Cowboys

NOTABLE ACHIEVEMENTS

- Holds Cowboys record for most seasons played (15).
- Ranks eighth in Cowboys history in games played (195).
- Six-time division champion (1985 and 1992–1996).
- Three-time NFC champion (1992, 1993, and 1995).
- Three-time Super Bowl champion (XXVII, XXVIII, and XXX).
- Two-time Pro Bowl selection (1994 and 1995).
- Two-time Second-Team All-NFC selection (1994 and 1995).

60: DOUG COSBIE (TE; 1979–1988)

Steve Liskey, Retrocards.net

Cowboy Numbers: 300 Receptions, 3,728 Receiving Yards, 30 Touchdown Receptions.

NOTABLE ACHIEVEMENTS

- Surpassed 60 receptions twice.
- Topped 750 receiving yards twice.
- Recorded six touchdown receptions twice.
- Led Cowboys with 60 receptions in 1984.
- Three-time division champion (1979, 1981, and 1985).
- Three-time Pro Bowl selection (1983, 1984, and 1985).
- 1985 First-Team All-NFC selection.
- 1984 Second-Team All-NFC selection.

61: ROY WILLIAMS (DB; 2002–2008)

Cowboy Numbers: 19 Interceptions, 307 Int. Return Yards, 506 Tackles, 6½ Sacks, 3 Touchdowns.

NOTABLE ACHIEVEMENTS

- Returned three interceptions for touchdowns.
- Recorded five interceptions twice.
- Recorded more than 90 tackles three times.
- Led Cowboys in interceptions twice and tackles once.
- 2007 division champion.
- Member of 2002 NFL All-Rookie Team.
- Five-time Pro Bowl selection (2003, 2004, 2005, 2006, and 2007).
- 2003 First-Team All-Pro selection.
- 2003 First-Team All-NFC selection.

62: GREG ELLIS (DE/LB; 1998–2008)

Cowboy Numbers: 77 Sacks, 500 Tackles, 4 Interceptions, 97 Int. Return Yards, 20 Forced Fumbles, 2 Touchdowns.

NOTABLE ACHIEVEMENTS

- Scored two defensive touchdowns (one interception-return and one fumble-return).
- Recorded at least eight sacks five times, registering 12½ sacks in 2007.
- Led Cowboys in sacks six times.
- Ranks ninth in Cowboys history with 77 career sacks.
- Two-time division champion (1998 and 2007).
- 2007 NFL Comeback Player of the Year.
- 2007 Pro Bowl selection.

63: PAT DONOVAN (OT; 1975–1983)

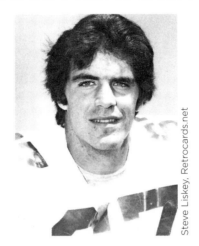

Steve Liskey, Retrocards.net

NOTABLE ACHIEVEMENTS

- Five-time division champion (1976–1979 and 1981).
- Three-time NFC champion (1975, 1977, and 1978).
- Super Bowl XII champion.
- Four-time Pro Bowl selection (1979, 1980, 1981, and 1982).
- 1981 Second-Team All-Pro selection.
- Four-time First-Team All-NFC selection (1979–1982).
- Two-time Second-Team All-NFC selection (1978 and 1983).

64: ROBERT NEWHOUSE (FB; 1972–1983)

Dallas Cowboys

Cowboy Numbers: 4,784 Yards Rushing, 120 Receptions, 956 Receiving Yards, 36 Touchdowns, 4.1 Rushing Average.

NOTABLE ACHIEVEMENTS

- Rushed for 930 yards in 1975.
- Scored 10 touchdowns in 1978.
- Threw one touchdown pass.
- Led Cowboys in rushing once.
- Ranks among Cowboys career leaders in: rushing yardage (5th); rushing touchdowns (6th); and rushing attempts (5th).
- Six-time division champion (1973, 1976–1979, and 1981).
- Three-time NFC champion (1975, 1977, and 1978).
- Super Bowl XII champion.

65: JAY RATLIFF (DT/NT: 2005–2012)

Cowboy Numbers: 27 Sacks, 227 Tackles, 4 Forced Fumbles, 13 Fumble Recoveries.

NOTABLE ACHIEVEMENTS

- Recorded 7½ sacks in 2008.
- Recorded six sacks and four fumble recoveries in 2009.
- Recorded more than 50 tackles once.
- Two-time division champion (2007 and 2009).
- 2007 Ed Block Courage Award winner.
- Four-time Pro Bowl selection (2008, 2009, 2010, and 2011).
- 2009 First-Team All-Pro selection.
- 2011 Second-Team All-Pro selection.

66: MIKE GAECHTER (DB; 1962–1969)

Steve Liskey, Retrocards.net

Cowboy Numbers: 21 Interceptions, 420 Int. Return Yards, 1 Touchdown.

NOTABLE ACHIEVEMENTS

- Scored two touchdowns during career.
- Surpassed 100 interception-return yards twice.
- Finished third in NFL with 136 interception-return yards in 1962.
- Ranks seventh in Cowboys history with 420 interception-return yards.
- Recorded second-longest interception return in franchise history on October 14, 1962, (100 yards vs. Philadelphia).
- Four-time division champion (1966, 1967, 1968, and 1969).
- Two-time Eastern Conference champion (1966 and 1967).

67: DAVE EDWARDS (LB; 1963–1975)

Steve Liskey, Retrocards.net

NOTABLE ACHIEVEMENTS

- Recorded 13 career interceptions.
- Scored one defensive touchdown.
- Recovered 17 fumbles.
- Missed only one game in 13 seasons.
- Seven-time division champion (1966–1971 and 1973).
- Two-time Eastern Conference champion (1966 and 1967).
- Three-time NFC champion (1970, 1971, and 1975).
- Super Bowl VI champion.

68: TERENCE NEWMAN (DB; 2003–2011)

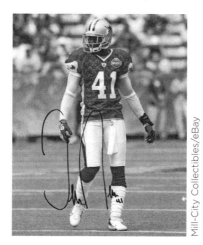

Mill-City Collectibles/eBay

Cowboy Numbers: 32 Interceptions, 345 Int. Return Yards, 542 Tackles, 2 Sacks, 4 Touchdowns.

NOTABLE ACHIEVEMENTS

- Returned three interceptions for touchdowns.
- Returned one punt for a touchdown.
- Recorded five interceptions in 2010.
- Recorded 129 interception-return yards in 2007.
- Recorded more than 75 tackles twice.
- Led Cowboys in interceptions five times.
- Intercepted three passes vs. Washington on December 14, 2003.
- Tied for seventh in Cowboys history with 32 career interceptions.
- Two-time division champion (2007 and 2009).
- 2003 Week 15 NFC Defensive Player of the Week.
- Two-time Pro Bowl selection (2007 and 2009).

69: BLAINE NYE (OG; 1968–1976)

Steve Liskey, Retrocards.net

NOTABLE ACHIEVEMENTS

- Missed only one game in nine seasons.
- Six-time division champion (1968–1971, 1973, and 1976).
- Three-time NFC champion (1970, 1971, and 1975).
- Super Bowl VI champion.
- Two-time Pro Bowl selection (1974 and 1976).
- 1976 First-Team All-NFC selection.
- 1975 Second-Team All-NFC selection.

70: TONY TOLBERT (DE; 1989–1997)

George A. Kitrinos

Cowboy Numbers: 59 Sacks, 580 Tackles, 1 Interception, 54 Int. Return Yards, 7 Forced Fumbles, 1 Touchdown.

NOTABLE ACHIEVEMENTS

- Scored one touchdown on a 54-yard interception return.
- Recorded at least seven sacks four times, registering 12 sacks in 1996.
- Surpassed 50 tackles eight times, making more than 70 stops three times.
- Led Cowboys in sacks four times.
- Led Cowboys defensive linemen in tackles seven straight times.
- Five-time division champion (1992, 1993, 1994, 1995, and 1996).
- Three-time NFC champion (1992, 1993, and 1995).
- Three-time Super Bowl champion (XXVII, XXVIII, and XXX).
- 1996 Pro Bowl selection.
- 1996 Second-Team All-Pro selection.
- 1996 First-Team All-NFC selection.

71: LANCE RENTZEL (WR; 1967–1970)

Dallas Cowboys

Cowboy Numbers: 183 Receptions, 3,521 Receiving Yards, 31 Touchdown Receptions, 32 Total Touchdowns.

NOTABLE ACHIEVEMENTS

- Surpassed 50 receptions twice.
- Topped 900 receiving yards three times, reaching 1,000-yard mark once (1,009 in 1968).
- Returned one kickoff for a touchdown.
- Led NFL with 12 touchdown catches, 13 touchdowns, and average of 22.3 yards per reception in 1969.
- Finished third in NFL with 54 receptions in 1968.
- Finished in top five in NFL in receiving yards twice.
- Led Cowboys in receptions three times and receiving yards twice.
- Ranks third in Cowboys history with average of 19.24 yards per catch.
- Four-time division champion (1967, 1968, 1969, and 1970).
- 1967 Eastern Conference champion.
- 1970 NFC champion.
- 1969 Second-Team All-Pro selection.
- 1968 First-Team All-Conference selection.

72: DAN REEVES (RB; 1965–1972)

Cowboy Numbers: 1,990 Yards Rushing, 129 Receptions, 1,693 Receiving Yards, 42 Touchdowns, 3.7 Rushing Average.

NOTABLE ACHIEVEMENTS

- Rushed for 757 yards in 1966.
- Made 41 receptions in 1966.
- Accumulated 557 receiving yards in 1966.
- Surpassed 1,000 yards from scrimmage twice.
- Scored more than 10 touchdowns twice.
- Threw two touchdown passes.
- Led NFL with 16 touchdowns in 1966.
- Finished second in NFL with eight rushing touchdowns in 1966.
- Led Cowboys in rushing once.
- Six-time division champion (1966–1971).
- Two-time Eastern Conference champion (1966 and 1967).
- Two-time NFC champion (1970 and 1971).
- Super Bowl VI champion.
- 1966 Second-Team All-Pro selection.
- 1966 First-Team All-Conference selection.

73: RON SPRINGS (RB; 1979–1984)

Cowboy Numbers: 2,180 Yards Rushing, 222 Receptions, 2,028 Receiving Yards, 38 Touchdowns, 3.6 Rushing Average.

NOTABLE ACHIEVEMENTS

- Rushed for more than 500 yards twice.
- Surpassed 40 receptions three times, making 73 catches in 1983.
- Accumulated 589 receiving yards in 1983.
- Accumulated 1,130 yards from scrimmage in 1983.
- Scored 12 touchdowns in 1981.
- Threw two touchdown passes during career.
- Tied for eighth in Cowboys history with 28 rushing touchdowns.
- Holds Cowboys single-season records for most pass receptions (73 in 1983) and receiving yards (589 in 1983) by a running back.
- Two-time division champion (1979 and 1981).

74: RAFAEL SEPTIEN (PK: 1978–1986)

Steve Liskey, Retrocards.net

Cowboy Numbers: 162 Field Goals Made, 226 Field Goal Attempts, 71.7 Field Goal Percentage, 874 Points Scored.

NOTABLE ACHIEVEMENTS

- Posted field goal percentage in excess of 80 once (81.5 in 1983).
- Scored more than 100 points three times.
- Led NFL with 27 field goals and 121 points scored in 1981.
- Holds Cowboys career record for most field goal attempts (226).
- Ranks second in Cowboys history in field goals made (162) and points scored (874).
- 1981 Pro Bowl selection.
- 1981 First-Team All-Pro selection.
- 1981 First-Team All-NFC selection.
- Named to Cowboys' 40th Anniversary Team in 2000.

75: SEAN LEE (LB; 2010–PRESENT)

Keith Allison

Cowboy Numbers: 557 Tackles, 12 Interceptions, 305 Int. Return Yards, 2½ Sacks, 2 Touchdowns.

NOTABLE ACHIEVEMENTS

- Has scored two defensive touchdowns.
- Has recorded more than 100 tackles three times.
- Intercepted four passes in 2013.
- Led NFL with 174 interception-return yards in 2013.
- Finished second in NFL with 145 tackles in 2016.
- Has led Cowboys in tackles three times and interceptions once.
- Recorded 18 tackles vs. San Diego on September 29, 2013.
- Two-time division champion (2014 and 2016).
- Three-time NFC Defensive Player of the Week.
- Two-time NFC Defensive Player of the Month.
- Two-time Pro Bowl selection (2015 and 2016).
- 2016 First-Team All-Pro selection.

76: LEON LETT (DT; 1991–2000)

George A. Kitrinos

Cowboy Numbers: 22½ Sacks and 257 Tackles.

NOTABLE ACHIEVEMENTS

- Recorded more than 50 tackles twice.
- Six-time division champion (1992–1996 and 1998).
- Three-time NFC champion (1992, 1993, and 1995).
- Three-time Super Bowl champion (XXVII, XXVIII, and XXX).
- 1996 Week 5 NFC Defensive Player of the Week.
- Two-time Pro Bowl selection (1994 and 1998).
- 1994 First-Team All-NFC selection.

77: LA'ROI GLOVER (DT; 2002–2005)

Cowboy Numbers: 21½ Sacks, 166 Tackles, 1 Interception.

NOTABLE ACHIEVEMENTS

- Recorded seven sacks in 2004.
- Recorded more than 50 tackles twice.
- Recorded one safety.
- Four-time Pro Bowl selection (2002–2005).
- Two-time Second-Team All-Pro selection (2002 and 2003).
- Two-time First-Team All-NFC selection (2002 and 2003).
- NFL 2000s All-Decade Team.
- Pro Football Hall of Fame All-2000s Second Team.
- Pro Football Reference All-2000s First Team.

78: TERRELL OWENS (WR; 2006–2008)

Cowboy Numbers: 235 Receptions, 3,587 Receiving Yards, 38 Touchdown Receptions.

NOTABLE ACHIEVEMENTS

- Surpassed 80 receptions twice.
- Topped 1,000 receiving yards three times.
- Surpassed 10 touchdown receptions three times.
- Led NFL with 13 touchdown receptions in 2006.
- Finished third in NFL with 15 touchdown receptions in 2007.
- Finished fifth in NFL with 1,355 receiving yards in 2007.
- Led Cowboys in receptions once and receiving yards three times.
- Ranks among Cowboys career leaders in: pass receiving yardage (9th); touchdown receptions (9th); and yards per reception (7th).
- Made four touchdown receptions vs. Washington on 11/18/07.
- 2007 division champion.
- 2007 Week 11 NFC Offensive Player of the Week.
- 2007 Pro Bowl selection.
- 2007 First-Team All-Pro selection.
- Pro Football Hall of Fame All-2000s Second Team.
- Pro Football Reference All-2000s First Team.

79: BRADIE JAMES (LB; 2003–2011)

Dallas Cowboys

Cowboy Numbers: 1,009 Tackles, 15½ Sacks, 2 Interceptions, 26 Int. Return Yards, 10 Forced Fumbles, 1 Touchdown.

NOTABLE ACHIEVEMENTS

- Scored one defensive touchdown.
- Recorded more than 100 tackles six straight times, registering 202 stops in 2008.
- Recorded eight sacks in 2008.
- Led Cowboys in tackles six times.
- Ranks sixth in Cowboys history with 1,009 career tackles.
- Missed only two games in nine seasons.
- Two-time division champion (2007 and 2009).

80: KEN NORTON (LB; 1988–1993)

Cowboy Numbers: 579 Tackles, 1 Interception, 25 Int. Return Yards, 7 Sacks.

NOTABLE ACHIEVEMENTS

- Recorded more than 100 tackles four times.
- Led Cowboys in tackles three times.
- Two-time division champion (1992 and 1993).
- Two-time NFC champion (1992 and 1993).
- Two-time Super Bowl champion (XXVII and XXVIII).
- 1991 Ed Block Courage Award winner.
- 1993 Pro Bowl selection.
- 1993 Second-Team All-Pro selection.

81: ZACK MARTIN (OG; 2014–PRESENT)

Keith Allison

NOTABLE ACHIEVEMENTS

- Two-time division champion (2014 and 2016).
- Member of 2014 NFL All-Rookie Team.
- Three-time Pro Bowl selection (2014, 2015, and 2016).
- Two-time First-Team All-Pro selection (2014 and 2016).
- 2015 Second-Team All-Pro selection.

82: MAT MCBRIAR (P; 2004–2011)

Dallas Cowboys

Cowboy Numbers: Averaged 45.3 yards per punt; Career long: 75 yards.

NOTABLE ACHIEVEMENTS

- Averaged better than 42 yards per punt eight straight seasons, posting average in excess of 47 yards four times.
- Recorded longest punt in NFL in 2006 (75 yards).
- Led NFL in punting average twice.
- Finished second in NFL in punting average once.
- Holds Cowboys single-season record for highest punting average (48.2 yards per punt in 2006).
- Two-time division champion (2007 and 2009).
- 2006 Week 11 NFC Special Teams Player of the Week.
- Two-time Pro Bowl selection (2006 and 2010).
- Two-time Second-Team All-Pro selection (2006 and 2010).

83: TOM RAFFERTY (C/G; 1976–1989)

Dallas Cowboys

NOTABLE ACHIEVEMENTS

- Played nine straight seasons without missing a game, appearing in 167 consecutive games at one point.
- Ranks fifth in Cowboys history in games played (203).
- Six-time division champion (1976–1979, 1981, and 1985).
- Three-time NFC champion (1975, 1977, and 1978).
- Super Bowl XII champion.

84: MILES AUSTIN (WR/KR; 2006–2013)

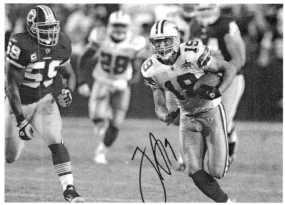

Cowboy Numbers: 301 Receptions, 4,481 Receiving Yards, 34 Touchdown Receptions, 2,146 Kickoff Return Yards, 24.1 Kickoff Return Average, 94 Rushing Yards, 1 Rushing Touchdown, 6,721 All-Purpose Yards.

NOTABLE ACHIEVEMENTS

- Surpassed 80 receptions once (81 in 2009).
- Topped 1,000 receiving yards twice.
- Finished third in NFL with 1,320 receiving yards in 2009.
- Finished fourth in NFL with 11 touchdown receptions in 2009.
- Led Cowboys in receiving yards twice.
- Ranks among Cowboys career leaders in: pass receptions (10th); pass receiving yardage (8th); and touchdown receptions (10th).
- Holds Cowboys single-game record for most pass-receiving yards (250 vs. Kansas City on October 11, 2009).
- Recorded 93-yard kickoff return for touchdown vs. Seattle in 2006 playoffs.
- Scored three touchdowns vs. San Francisco on 9/18/11.
- Two-time division champion (2007 and 2009).
- 2009 Week 5 NFC Offensive Player of the Week.
- Two-time Pro Bowl selection (2009 and 2010).

85: MARION BARBER (RB; 2005–2010)

Public Domain/Wikipedia

Cowboy Numbers: 4,358 Yards Rushing, 174 Receptions, 1,280 Receiving Yards, 53 Touchdowns, 4.2 Rushing Average.

NOTABLE ACHIEVEMENTS

- Rushed for more than 900 yards twice.
- Surpassed 50 receptions once (52 in 2008).
- Scored more than 10 touchdowns twice.
- Surpassed 1,000 yards from scrimmage three times.
- Averaged 4.8 yards per carry twice.
- Finished third in NFL with 14 rushing touchdowns and 16 total touchdowns in 2006.
- Led Cowboys in rushing three times.
- Ranks among Cowboys career leaders in: rushing yardage (7th); rushing touchdowns (3rd); rushing attempts (6th); and touchdowns scored (7th).
- Two-time division champion (2007 and 2009).
- 2007 Pro Bowl selection.

86: DAVE MANDERS
(C; 1964–1966 and 1968–1974)

Steve Liskey, Retrocards.net

NOTABLE ACHIEVEMENTS

- Six-time division champion (1966, 1968–1971, and 1973).
- 1966 Eastern Conference champion.
- Two-time NFC champion (1970 and 1971).
- Super Bowl VI champion.
- 1966 Pro Bowl selection.

87: MIKE HEGMAN (LB; 1976–1987)

Cowboy Numbers: 15½ Official Sacks, 7 Interceptions, 2 Touchdowns.

NOTABLE ACHIEVEMENTS

- Returned two fumbles for touchdowns.
- Recorded 5½ sacks in 1985.
- Scored touchdown vs. Pittsburgh in Super Bowl XIII.
- Six-time division champion (1976–1979, 1981, and 1985).
- Two-time NFC champion (1977 and 1978).
- Super Bowl XII champion.

88: THOMAS "HOLLYWOOD" HENDERSON
(LB; 1975–1979)

Steve Liskey, Retrocards.net

Cowboy Numbers: 3 Interceptions, 79 Int. Return Yards, 2 Touchdowns, 1 Safety.

NOTABLE ACHIEVEMENTS

- Returned one interception 79 yards for a touchdown.
- Returned one kickoff 97 yards for a touchdown.
- Returned interception 68 yards for TD vs. Los Angeles Rams in 1978 NFC championship game.
- Four-time division champion (1976, 1977, 1978, and 1979).
- Two-time NFC champion (1977 and 1978).
- Super Bowl XII champion.

89: DON BISHOP (DB; 1960–1965)

Steve Liskey, Retrocards.net

Cowboy Numbers: 22 Interceptions, 364 Int. Return Yards, 1 Touchdown.

NOTABLE ACHIEVEMENTS

- Scored one defensive touchdown on an 84-yard fumble return.
- Recorded at least five interceptions three times.
- Surpassed 100 interception-return yards twice.
- Finished second in NFL with eight interceptions and 172 interception-return yards in 1961.
- Finished second in NFL with 84 fumble-return yards in 1962.
- Led Cowboys in interceptions three times.
- Holds Cowboys record for most consecutive games with an interception (five in 1961).
- 1962 Pro Bowl selection.
- 1961 *Sporting News* First-Team All-NFL selection.
- 1961 First-Team All-Conference selection.

90: TRAVIS FREDERICK (C; 2013–PRESENT)

Keith Allison

NOTABLE ACHIEVEMENTS

- Has never missed a game in his four seasons with Cowboys.
- Two-time division champion (2014 and 2016).
- Member of 2013 NFL All-Rookie Team.
- Three-time Pro Bowl selection (2014, 2015, and 2016).
- 2016 First-Team All-Pro selection.
- Two-time Second-Team All-Pro selection (2014 and 2015).

91: PRESTON PEARSON (RB; 1975–1980)

Steve Liskey, Retrocards.net

Cowboy Numbers: 1,207 Yards Rushing, 189 Receptions, 2,274 Receiving Yards, 16 Touchdowns, 4.1 Rushing Average.

NOTABLE ACHIEVEMENTS

- Rushed for 509 yards in 1975.
- Surpassed 40 receptions twice.
- Topped 500 receiving yards twice.
- Accumulated 1,251 all-purpose yards in 1975.
- Led Cowboys with 47 receptions in 1978.
- Scored three touchdowns vs. Los Angeles Rams in 1975 NFC championship game.
- Four-time division champion (1976–1979).
- Three-time NFC champion (1975, 1977, and 1978).
- Super Bowl XII champion.

92: JERRY TUBBS (LB; 1960–1967)

Steve Liskey, Retrocards.net

Cowboy Numbers: 15 Interceptions, 176 Interception-Return Yards.

NOTABLE ACHIEVEMENTS

- Recorded four interceptions in 1962.
- Recorded more than 100 tackles three times.
- Led Cowboys in tackles four times.
- Two-time division champion (1966 and 1967).
- Two-time Eastern Conference champion (1966 and 1967).
- 1962 Pro Bowl selection.
- 1962 First-Team All-Conference selection.

93: RUSSELL MARYLAND (DT; 1991–1995)

Dallas Cowboys

Cowboy Numbers: 14½ Sacks, 199 Tackles, 7 Forced Fumbles, 1 Touchdown.

NOTABLE ACHIEVEMENTS

- Scored one defensive touchdown on a fumble return.
- Recorded more than 50 tackles twice.
- Four-time division champion (1992, 1993, 1994, and 1995).
- Three-time NFC champion (1992, 1993, and 1995).
- Three-time Super Bowl champion (XXVII, XXVIII, and XXX).
- 1993 Pro Bowl selection.

94: ANDRE GURODE (C/G; 2002–2010)

Mil-City Collectibles

NOTABLE ACHIEVEMENTS

- Two-time division champion (2007 and 2009).
- Five-time Pro Bowl selection (2006, 2007, 2008, 2009, and 2010).
- 2009 Second-Team All-Pro selection.

95: JOHN DUTTON (DT/DE; 1979–1987)

Dallas Cowboys

Cowboy Numbers: 18 Official Sacks, 2 Safeties, 1 Interception, 38 Int. Return Yards, 1 Touchdown.

NOTABLE ACHIEVEMENTS

- Scored one touchdown on a 38-yard interception return.
- Recorded two safeties.
- Three-time division champion (1979, 1981, and 1985).

96: ALVIN HARPER (WR; 1991–1994, 1999)

Cowboy Numbers: 124 Receptions, 2,486 Receiving Yards, 18 Touchdown Receptions, 20.0 Yards-Per-Reception Average.

NOTABLE ACHIEVEMENTS

- Surpassed 750 receiving yards twice.
- Averaged more than 20 yards per reception twice.
- Made eight touchdown receptions in 1994.
- Led NFL with average of 24.9 yards per reception in 1994.
- Finished second in NFL with average of 21.6 yards per reception in 1993.
- Recorded second-longest pass reception in NFL postseason history (94 yards) vs. Packers in 1994 playoffs.
- Tied with Bob Hayes for highest career average per reception (20.0 yards) in Cowboys history.
- Three-time division champion (1992, 1993, and 1994).
- Two-time Super Bowl champion (XXVII and XXVIII).
- 1994 Week 9 NFC Offensive Player of the Week.

97: DAT NGUYEN (LB; 1999–2005)

Defend the Star/eBay

Cowboy Numbers: 516 Tackles, 6 Sacks, 7 Interceptions, 63 Int. Return Yards, 4 Forced Fumbles.

NOTABLE ACHIEVEMENTS

- Recorded more than 100 tackles three times.
- Led Cowboys in tackles three times.
- Member of 1999 NFL All-Rookie Team.
- 2003 Second-Team All-Pro selection.
- 2003 First-Team All-NFC selection.

98: KEVIN SMITH (DB; 1992–1999)

Cowboy Numbers: 19 Interceptions, 190 Int. Return Yards, 361 Tackles, 1 Touchdown.

NOTABLE ACHIEVEMENTS

- Scored one defensive touchdown on an interception return.
- Recorded at least five interceptions twice.
- Recorded more than 100 tackles once.
- Led Cowboys in interceptions twice and passes defensed five times.
- Six-time division champion (1992–1996 and 1998).
- Three-time NFC champion (1992, 1993, and 1995).
- Three-time Super Bowl champion (XXVII, XXVIII, and XXX).
- 1993 Week 16 NFC Defensive Player of the Week.
- 1996 Second-Team All-NFC selection.

99: JULIUS JONES (RB; 2004–2007)

Cowboy Numbers: 3,484 Yards Rushing, 84 Receptions, 672 Receiving Yards, 18 Touchdowns, 3.9 Rushing Average.

NOTABLE ACHIEVEMENTS

- Rushed for more than 1,000 yards once, gaining 993 yards on the ground another time.
- Surpassed 1,200 yards from scrimmage twice.
- Scored seven touchdowns in 2004.
- Led Cowboys in rushing three times.
- Ranks 10th in Cowboys history with 3,484 yards rushing.
- 2007 division champion.
- Member of 2004 NFL All-Rookie Team.

100: DUANE THOMAS (RB; 1970–1971)

Steve Liskey, Retrocards.net

Cowboy Numbers: 1,596 Yards Rushing, 23 Receptions, 226 Receiving Yards, 18 Touchdowns, 4.9 Rushing Average.

NOTABLE ACHIEVEMENTS

- Surpassed 750 yards rushing twice.
- Led NFL with rushing average of 5.3 yards per carry in 1970.
- Led NFL with 11 rushing touchdowns and 13 total touchdowns in 1971.
- Led Cowboys in rushing twice.
- Ranks third in Cowboys history with rushing average of 4.9 yards per carry.
- Scored four touchdowns vs. St. Louis Cardinals on 12/18/71.
- Two-time division champion (1970 and 1971).
- Two-time NFC champion (1970 and 1971).
- Super Bowl VI champion.

GLOSSARY

C: Center.

COMP PCT.: Completion percentage. The number of successfully completed passes divided by the number of passes attempted.

FS: Free safety.

INTS: Interceptions. Passes thrown by the quarterback that are caught by a member of the opposing team's defense.

KR: Kickoff returner.

LCB: Left cornerback.

LE: Left end.

LG: Left guard.

LOLB: Left outside linebacker.

LT: Left tackle.

MLB: Middle linebacker.

NT: Nose tackle.

P: Punter.

PK: Placekicker.

PR: Punt returner.

QB: Quarterback.

QBR: Quarterback rating.

RB: Running back.

RCB: Right cornerback.

RE: Right end.

RG: Right guard.

ROLB: Right outside linebacker.

RT: Right tackle.

SS: Strong safety.

ST: Special teams.

TD PASSES: Touchdown passes.

TD RECS: Touchdown receptions.

TDS: Touchdowns.

TE: Tight end.

WR: Wide receiver.

SELECTED BIBLIOGRAPHY

BOOKS

Jensen, Brian. *Where Have All Our Cowboys Gone?* Lanham, MD: Taylor Trade Publishing, 2001.

Jones, Danny. *More Distant Memories: Pro Football's Best Ever Players of the 50's, 60's, and 70's*. Bloomington, IN: AuthorHouse, 2006.

Taylor, Jean-Jacques. *Game of My Life, Dallas Cowboys: Memorable Stories of Cowboys Football*. Champaign, IL: Sports Publishing, 2006.

VIDEOS

Greatest Ever: NFL Dream Team. Polygram Video, 1996.

WEBSITES

Biographies, online at Hickoksports.com
(hickoksports.com/hickoksports/biograph)

Biography from Answers.com
(answers.com)

Biography from Jockbio.com
(jockbio.com)

CapitalNewYork.com
(capitalnewyork.com)

CBSNews.com
(cbsnews.com)

DallasCowboys.com
(dallascowboys.com)

ESPN.com
(sports.espn.go.com)

Hall of Famers, online at profootballhof.com
(profootballhof.com/hof/member)

Inductees from LASportsHall.com
(lasportshall.com)

LATimes.com
(articles.latimes.com)

Newsday.com
(newsday.com)

NYDailyNews.com
(nydailynews.com/new-york)

NYTimes.com
(nytimes.com)

Pro Football Talk from nbcsports.com
(profootballtalk.nbcsports.com)

SpTimes.com
(sptimes.com)

StarLedger.com
(starledger.com)

SunSentinel.com
(articles.sun-sentinel.com)

The Players, online at Profootballreference.com
(pro-football-reference.com/players)

YouTube.com
(youtube.com)